AF601569

INTERNATIONAL SERIES OF
MONOGRAPHS ON COMPUTER SCIENCE

General Editors

DOV M. GABBAY JOHN E. HOPCROFT
GORDON D. PLOTKIN JACOB T. SCHWARTZ
DANA S. SCOTT JEAN VUILLEMIN
ZVI GALIL

THE INTERNATIONAL SERIES OF MONOGRAPHS ON COMPUTER SCIENCE

1. *The design and analysis of coalesced hashing* Jeffrey S. Vitter and Wen-chin Chen
2. *Initial computability, algebraic specifications, and partial algebras* Horst Reichel
3. *Art gallery theorems and algorithms* Joseph O'Rourke
4. *The combinatorics of network reliability* Charles J. Colbourn
5. *Discrete relaxation techniques* T. Henderson
6. *Computable set theory* D. Cantone, A. Ferro, and E. Omodeo
7. *Programming in Martin-Löf's type theory: an introduction* Bengt Nordström, Kent Petersson, and Jan M. Smith
8. *Nonlinear optimization: complexity issues* Stephen A. Vavasis
9. *Derivation and validation of software metrics* Martin Shepperd and Darrel Ince
10. *Automated deduction in multiple-valued logics* Reiner Hähnle
11. *Computation and reasoning: a type theory for computer science* Zhaohui Luo

Computation and Reasoning

A Type Theory for Computer Science

ZHAOHUI LUO
University of Edinburgh

CLARENDON PRESS • OXFORD
1994

This book has been printed digitally in order to ensure its continuing availability

OXFORD
UNIVERSITY PRESS

Great Clarendon Street, Oxford OX2 6DP

Oxford University Press is a department of the University of Oxford.
It furthers the University's objective of excellence in research, scholarship,
and education by publishing worldwide in

Oxford New York

Auckland Bangkok Buenos Aires Cape Town Chennai
Dar es Salaam Delhi Hong Kong Istanbul Karachi Kolkata
Kuala Lumpur Madrid Melbourne Mexico City Mumbai Nairobi
São Paulo Shanghai Singapore Taipei Tokyo Toronto

with an associated company in Berlin

Oxford is a registered trade mark of Oxford University Press
in the UK and in certain other countries

Published in the United States by Oxford University Press Inc., New York

© Zhaohui Luo, 1994

The moral rights of the author have been asserted
Database right Oxford University Press (maker)

Reprinted 2002

All rights reserved. No part of this publication may be reproduced,
stored in a retrieval system, or transmitted, in any form or by any means,
without the prior permission in writing of Oxford University Press,
or as expressly permitted by law, or under terms agreed with the appropriate
reprographics rights organization. Enquiries concerning reproduction
outside the scope of the above should be sent to the Rights Department,
Oxford University Press, at the address above

You must not circulate this book in any other binding or cover
and you must impose this same condition on any acquirer

A catalogue record for this book is available from the British Library

Library of Congress Cataloging in Publication Data

(Data available)

ISBN 0 19 853835 9

To Dejuan

Preface

This monograph studies a type theory and its applications to computer science. When its publication was considered three years ago, it was meant to be a simple and straightforward modification of my PhD thesis on the Extended Calculus of Constructions. However, it turns out to be a much more extensive task than I expected. Reviewing many of the ideas dealt with in the original thesis, I have found them calling for more extensive treatment and explanations, which have led me to more research in order to obtain a better understanding. The result is a further development of the type theory; many chapters are rewritten and several new chapters are added. It is my hope that the basic ideas in the development of the type theory are explained more clearly and its potential in applications is better demonstrated.

I would like to thank many people who have helped me in the course of this work. First of all, I would like to express my gratitude to Rod Burstall, my PhD supervisor, who has provided not only many interesting ideas and helpful advice, but encouragement at the right time and friendship along the way. I am greatly indebted to Thierry Coquand, Susumu Hayashi, Eugenio Moggi, and Randy Pollack who have either directly or indirectly contributed their ideas and insights in various ways to the development of the type theory considered in this monograph. Thanks also go to, among others, Peter Aczel, Henk Barendregt, Stefano Berardi, Matt Fairtlough, Healfdene Goguen, Per Martin-Löf, Gordon Plotkin, Don Sannella, Thomas Streicher, Paul Taylor, and the members in the Lego club in Edinburgh for the helpful discussions we have had, and to my former teachers in China who have taught me the basic knowledge in computer science and logic.

Edinburgh Z.L.
December 1993

Contents

1 **Introduction** 1
- 1.1 Motivations in computer science 2
- 1.2 Basic concepts in type theory 3
  - 1.2.1 Objects and types 3
  - 1.2.2 Propositions as types 5
  - 1.2.3 Meaning and use 6
- 1.3 The conceptual universe of types 8
  - 1.3.1 Paradoxical type structures 9
  - 1.3.2 Martin-Löf's type theory 10
  - 1.3.3 Impredicative type theories 11
  - 1.3.4 Data types vs. logical propositions 12
- 1.4 Towards a unifying theory of dependent types 15

2 **The Extended Calculus of Constructions** 21
- 2.1 The language of ECC 21
  - 2.1.1 Terms and computation 21
  - 2.1.2 Judgements and inference rules 24
- 2.2 Informal explanations 26
  - 2.2.1 Computation and computational equality 26
  - 2.2.2 Judgements and context validity 28
  - 2.2.3 Types and their meaning explanation 29
  - 2.2.4 Non-propositional types 29
  - 2.2.5 Predicative universes and the reflection principle 32
  - 2.2.6 Propositions and the impredicative universe 34
  - 2.2.7 Type equality and the cumulativity relation 36
- 2.3 Further remarks and discussion 38
  - 2.3.1 Data types vs. logical propositions 38
  - 2.3.2 Σ-types and existential types 41
  - 2.3.3 Equalities: intensionality vs. extensionality 43
  - 2.3.4 Decidability issues 46
  - 2.3.5 On the use of the type theory 46

3 **Basic meta-theoretic properties** 49
- 3.1 Church-Rosser theorem and cumulativity 49
- 3.2 Derivable judgements and derivability 54
- 3.3 Principal types 61

4 **Strong normalisation** 65
4.1 The Girard–Tait reducibility method 66
4.1.1 The reducibility method and the notion of predicativity 66
4.1.2 Environments 69
4.1.3 Saturated sets and candidates of reducibility 71
4.2 Quasi-normalisation 74
4.2.1 Levels of types 74
4.2.2 Quasi-normalisation and degrees of types 76
4.2.3 The complexity measure of types 79
4.2.4 An inductive proof of the quasi-normalisation theorem 81
4.3 Strong normalisation 88
4.3.1 Possible denotations of objects 88
4.3.2 Assignments and valuations 90
4.3.3 The interpretation 92
4.3.4 Soundness of the interpretation 96
4.3.5 The strong normalisation theorem 100

5 **The internal logic and decidability** 103
5.1 The internal higher-order logic 103
5.1.1 The internal logic and its consistency 103
5.1.2 Understanding the logical operators 106
5.1.3 The Leibniz equality and equality reflection 109
5.2 Decidability of the type theory 112
5.2.1 Decidability of conversion and cumulativity 112
5.2.2 Decidability of type inference and type checking 112

6 **A set-theoretic model** 117
6.1 Understanding ECC in the ω-**Set** framework 118
6.2 Valid contexts and objects 120
6.3 Predicative universes and non-propositional types 121
6.4 The impredicative universe and propositions 123
6.5 Remarks 125

7 **Computational and logical theories** 127
7.1 Computational theories and inductive data types 128
7.1.1 The type of natural numbers 128
7.1.2 The type of lists of natural numbers 131
7.2 Abstract theories and abstract reasoning 132
7.2.1 A notion of abstract theory 133
7.2.2 Abstract reasoning 136
7.2.3 Theory morphisms and proof inheritance 136
7.3 Discussion 137

8 **Specification and development of programs** 139
8.1 A brief summary 140

8.2 Specifications and data refinement 141
8.2.1 Program specifications and their realisations 141
8.2.2 Specifications of abstract data types 144
8.2.3 Data refinement and implementation 146
8.3 Modular design and structured specification 149
8.3.1 Decomposition and sharing 150
8.3.2 Constructors and selectors 153
8.3.3 Constructor/selector implementation 156
8.4 Parameterised specification 156
8.4.1 Parameterised specifications 157
8.4.2 Implementation of parameterised specifications 159
8.5 Discussion 162

9 Towards a unifying theory of dependent types 165
9.1 A logical framework with inductive schemata 166
9.1.1 Martin-Löf's logical framework 166
9.1.2 Specifying type theories in LF 170
9.1.3 Inductive schemata 173
9.2 The formulation of UTT 175
9.2.1 SOL: the internal logical mechanism 175
9.2.2 Inductive data types 177
9.2.3 Predicative universes 182
9.2.4 A summary 185
9.3 Discussion 186
9.3.1 The internal logic and pure logical truths 186
9.3.2 Further separation of propositions and data types 195
9.3.3 Intensionality and η-equality rules 198
9.3.4 Understanding of the type theory 202
9.3.5 Inductive families of types 204
9.3.6 Subtyping and other implementation issues 208
9.4 Final remarks 209

Bibliography 211

Notation and Symbols 221

Index 225

1
Introduction

The study of type theory may offer an *adequate* computational and logical language for computer science. There are several compelling reasons supporting such a claim of adequacy. First, type theory offers a coherent treatment of two related but different fundamental notions in computer science: computation and logical inference. This makes it possible for one to program and to understand and reason about programs in a single formalism. Second, type theory can provide nice abstraction mechanisms which support conceptually clear (e.g. modular and structured) development of programs, specifications, and proofs. This makes it a promising candidate for a uniform language for programming, specification, and reasoning in the large as well as in the small. Finally, although type theory provides powerful and sophisticated tools, it is simple. Its simplicity is to be understood in two aspects: one is that it allows a direct operational understanding of the meanings of the constructions in its language, which gives a solid basis of its use in applications; the other is that it is manageable in the sense that there is a good way to implement it on the computer.

In this monograph, we develop a theory of dependent types, study its properties, and illustrate its uses in computer science. Besides its contribution to the studies of type theory, logic and computer languages in general, it is hoped that such an investigation will help to explain the theme and points summarised in the last paragraph, make explicit the advantages and possible limitations of using a type-theoretic language in pragmatic applications, and, therefore, stimulate further development in this area.

In this introduction, after a brief explanation of some viewpoints and motivations of studying type theory for computer science, the basic concepts in type theory and their relationship with logical inference and programming are explained intuitively, and a general inquiry into the underlying structures of various type theories is made to discuss several issues in the study of type theory, leading to an explication of the ideas based on which our type theory is developed. The type structure of the type theory is briefly described, followed by an overview of this monograph.

1.1 Motivations in computer science

Type theories have mainly been developed as foundational and logical languages by logicians who are interested in the foundation of mathematics. Why is type theory useful for computer science? Here, rather than discussing the possible applications of type theories in computer science, we briefly explain our particular motivations for studying and developing type theory as a promising computational and logical language.

The study of languages in computer science, most of which are necessarily formal in order to be implementable on the computer, is closely related to that of formal systems, including type theories, which may provide valuable insights and useful ideas in understanding and designing computer languages. In this respect, the study of logical systems is particularly important since logic plays an indispensable role in specifying and reasoning about programs. Besides such a general contribution, type theory has several features that are particularly interesting in computer science.

Computer languages have developed with their own distinguishing characteristics, and computer scientists have rather different concerns as compared with those in the traditional study of logical systems. For example, the notion of *computation* or computational behaviour of programs is the most basic and the most important in understanding a programming language. That is why the operational semantics which directly characterises the computational behaviour of programs has been essential for the programmer and prevailing in understanding and using a programming language, although other semantics such as denotational semantics may also help a great deal. Unlike the other logical or mathematical languages, type theory is essentially a computational language (in particular, a functional programming language) where computation is taken as the basic notion and its operational semantics is simple and allows a clear understanding of the language and its use. On the basis of that, type theory may be used as a uniform language for programming, specification, and reasoning.

Another important aspect in the study of computer languages is that computer scientists design and invent languages to be *used* in real applications to, for example, large software development. This leads to the particular interests of computer scientists in studying such issues as modularisation and abstraction, which are among the central concerns in the design of programming and specification languages. These concerns are rather different as compared with those of meta-mathematicians in studying formal systems for the foundation of mathematics where what seems to prevail is the theoretical *possibility* of formalisation and foundational understanding of mathematics. In the research of programming methodology, which is closely related to but has different emphasis from software engineering, computer scientists have been looking for theoretical foundations on the basis of which a science of programming or program development may be developed. The research on proof development systems or proof engineering has attracted more and more interest in computer science now that the need to verify various proof obligations in rigorous program development has been recognised. In these researches, people are interested not only in the fundamental understanding of the basic notions such as computation and proof, but in the methodological issues such as modularity which may lead to the design of good computer languages. Since types are useful tools in organising concepts, a type-theoretic language with a rich type structure can provide nice abstraction mechanisms for modular development of programs, specifications, and proofs.

Simplicity of languages is another issue considered by computer scientists as well as logicians. As logicians, computer scientists seek for simplicity for the fundamental understanding of the computer languages, but not just that. Furthermore, computer scientists are interested in the quality of software and the effectiveness of its production, where the simplicity of the languages in use (e.g. a simple semantics that makes it easier to learn and use a language) is important. Simplicity for a computer scientist also includes the implementability of the language. As we have remarked, type theory has a simple operational semantics, and it is a more manageable language as compared with classical set theory since its good proof-theoretic properties such as decidability provide a good basis for the computer implementation.

Looking for simplicity, the work by a theoretical computer scientist is in a certain sense 'foundational'. For instance, to study computer languages, he is usually working with a core language with essential constructions to explain the issues and problems of interest, which may be further developed into a full-scale language (e.g. with syntax sugar and other features) to be used in practice. However, doing so, he has a wider concern about the use of the language in practical applications since his study also involves the methodological issues mentioned above. Type theory may offer a computational and logical language for computer science, which is foundational in the above sense and adequate as claimed in the first paragraph of this chapter.

1.2 Basic concepts in type theory

1.2.1 Objects and types

Computer scientists and mathematicians consider various *constructions* or *objects*: computational objects like programs and specifications, and math-

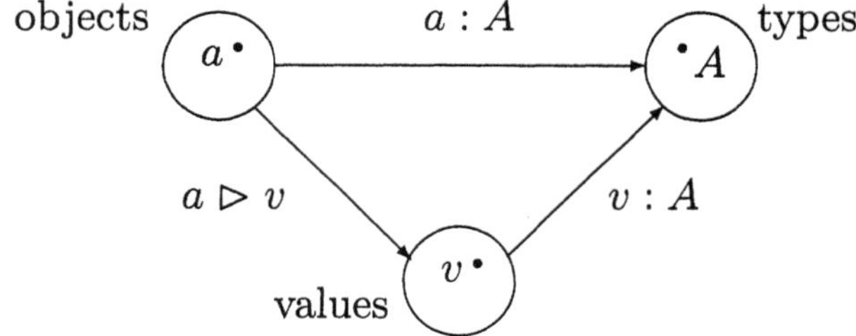

Fig. 1.1. Understanding the judgement $a : A$.

ematical objects like proofs and theorems. The world of objects under consideration may naturally be classified into *types*, to each of which some objects belong while the others do not. For example, the natural numbers constitute a type and the functions from type A to type B constitute the type of functions from A to B. We can therefore think of two *conceptual universes*, one of objects and the other of types (see Fig. 1.1). The relationship between (the representations of) objects and types is captured in type theory by the judgements of the form

$$a : A$$

that asserts that *object a is of type A*. Among the objects of a type, some are called *canonical objects*, which are the values of objects of the type under computation. For example, a canonical natural number is either zero or the successor of a (canonical) natural number. A canonical object of the type of functions is in the form of a λ-expression. In the presence of a (defined) operation of addition, the natural number $1+1$ is not canonical and computes with 2 as its value. A canonical object cannot be further computed and has itself as value.

The notion of *computation* is another basic concept in type theory, which generates an equivalence relation, the *computational equality* between the basic expressions in the language of type theory. For instance, applying a function $\lambda x{:}A.b[x]$ to an object a of type A yields $b[a]$. It is an important property of computation that *every object has a unique value under computation and the objects which are computationally equal have the same value.* As we shall see, this guarantees the harmony between the different uses of the entities in the type theory.

The distinction between canonical objects from the others, together with the above property of computation, is important in understanding the language of type theory.[1] It allows us to understand the meanings of judgements, objects, and types in a direct and simple way (see Fig. 1.1). In particular, an object a being of type A, as asserted by judgement $a : A$, means that a computes into a canonical object of type A. That is to say, $a : A$ can be correctly asserted if the value of a is of type A. A type may then be understood as consisting of its canonical objects, relative to the understanding of computation. For instance, the type of natural numbers is understood as consisting of the canonical natural numbers, while the other natural numbers like $1 + 1$ are understood as programs that produce canonical natural numbers as their values.

On the basis of such a treatment of objects and types, a type theory with a rich type structure is a typed functional programming language, where programs are objects and functions (or functional programs) are first-class citizens. The notions of computation and canonical object give a basis for an operational semantics which allows a direct understanding of the programs in the language.

1.2.2 Propositions as types

Types may be viewed as partial specifications of their objects (programs). To describe and reason about the objects in type theory, one also needs logical formulas or propositions and incorporates logical inference. The key idea that makes this possible is that of *propositions-as-types*, discovered by Curry [CF58] and Howard [How80].

The basic idea is that any proposition P corresponds to a type $\mathbf{Prf}(P)$, the type of its proofs, and a proof of P corresponds to an object of type $\mathbf{Prf}(P)$. Furthermore, one is able to assert a proposition to be true if and only if one has a proof of the proposition, that is, an object of the type of its proofs. The origin of this idea goes back to the intuitionistic philosophy and, in particular, comes from Heyting and Kolmogorov's intuitionistic interpretation of logical operators (see [Hey71, Kol32]). For example, according to Heyting's interpretation, one has a proof of $P \supset Q$ (P implies Q) if and only if one has a construction which, whenever given a construction that proves P, yields a construction that proves Q. To cast such an informal semantics into a formal setting, a construction that proves $P \supset Q$ may be represented as a function that maps the proofs of P to proofs of Q, and the type of the proofs of $P \supset Q$, $\mathbf{Prf}(P \supset Q)$, may then be represented by the type of functions from $\mathbf{Prf}(P)$ to $\mathbf{Prf}(Q)$.

Being considered in this way, the truth of a proposition is understood by the inhabitance of the type of proofs of the proposition. The notion

[1] The notion of canonical object is a key idea in the verificationistic meaning theory (cf., the forceful arguments by Dummett, Prawitz and Martin-Löf [Dum75, Dum91] [Pra73, Pra74][ML84, ML85]).

of canonical objects for type $\mathbf{Prf}(P)$ gives a notion of *canonical or direct proofs* of proposition P, while the non-canonical objects of type $\mathbf{Prf}(P)$ may be called *indirect proofs*. The understanding of propositions and their proofs (and hence their truth and falsity) is then given, as we have discussed briefly in the last section. To be explicit, an object being a proof of a proposition P means that it computes into a canonical proof of P, and a proposition is true if and only if there is a canonical proof of it.

The above type-theoretic conception of logical inference is also based on the important idea, as emphasised by Martin-Löf, that there is a fundamental distinction between propositions, which are formulas describing properties and facts, and judgements, which are assertions of whether formulas are true. On the basis of this distinction, a type theory with sufficient logical type structures has an internal logic and presents a logical language rather different from that of set theory or that of logic programming. It is not a logical theory in the traditional sense in that judgements and the notion of computation are not sentences in some base logic such as first-order logic, and many mathematical concepts such as the set of natural numbers are introduced as types rather than axiomatic logical theories. However, this does not mean that type theory is 'logic-free'; its internal logic can provide powerful tools to describe and reason about the entities in the type theory.

1.2.3 Meaning and use

As explained above, the language of a type theory consists of objects and types which are related by the assertive sentences called judgements of the form $a : A$ whose meaning can essentially be understood as that a computes into a value (canonical object) of type A. Such a meaning explanation is verificationistic since verification is taken as the central concept in the operational meaning theory.

It should be made clear that taking verification as the central concept in meaning explanations does *not* mean that to understand a judgement, one only has to know *when it can be correctly asserted*, although that is an important aspect of its use. Another equally important aspect of the use of a judgement is about *what consequences it has to accept that a judgement is correct*. An understanding of a judgement is not complete unless one has grasped both of these two complementary aspects of its use.[2]

In type theory, as in other logical systems in natural deduction style, the above two aspects of use are essentially reflected by the introduction rules

[2]It is still questionable whether it is possible to have a satisfactory theory of meaning on the basis of which one can obtain or derive a complete understanding of the other aspect of use from the understanding of the aspect chosen to be the central concept for meaning. See [Dum91] for a very interesting explication.

and the elimination and computation rules, respectively. For example, in a language with dependent types, a type N of natural numbers may have introduction rules informally described as follows:

1. 0 is of type N.
2. If n is of type N, so is $succ(n)$.

The introduction rules determine what the canonical natural numbers are, and hence govern whether a judgement $a : N$ can be correctly asserted. The elimination and computation rules for N allows one to define functional operations with domain type N by primitive recursion in the form

$$F(0) = c, \qquad F(n+1) = f(n, F(n)).$$

The elimination rule introduces a recursion operator Rec_N such that

- for any family of types $C[x]$ indexed by natural numbers, any object of type $C[0]$, and any functional operation f that returns an object $f(m, c)$ of type $C[succ(m)]$ for any objects m of type N and c of type $C[m]$, $Rec_N(c, f)$ is a functional operation which for any natural number n returns an object of type $C[n]$.

The meaning of the recursion operator is given by the computation rules:

1. $Rec_N(c, f)(0)$ computes to c.
2. $Rec_N(c, f)(succ(n))$ computes to $f(n, Rec_N(c, f)(n))$.

Therefore, the elimination and computation rules determine what one can do once a judgement $n : N$ is correctly asserted, that is, how one may use such a fact to assert other judgements such as $Rec_N(c, f)(n) : C[n]$.

The understanding of objects and types can also be analysed into two aspects and may be derived from the above explanation of the uses of judgements. To understand a type, one must know what objects it may have or how it may be inhabited, and how its objects may be used or how its inhabitance implies that of other types. To understand an object, one needs to know its type(s) and how it may be used to define other objects. When a judgement is of the form $p : \mathbf{Prf}(P)$ asserting that p is a proof of proposition P, the above analysis of use gives rise to an analysis of the use of logical propositions and their proofs. The two aspects of use concern mainly about *when a logical proposition can be proved* and *what the logical consequences are when a proposition is accepted to be true*; these two aspects are reflected by the introduction rules and the elimination rules of the logical operators concerned, respectively.

If one expects such an understanding of the language of a type theory to be coherent, there is a basic requirement on the language of the type theory, that is, the rules that govern the different uses of the types, objects and judgements must be in *harmony* with each other (cf. [Dum91]). For example, from a verificationistic point of view, it is the introduction rules that would determine the meaning of a type as they indicate what the canonical objects are and hence how it can be directly inhabited. If this view is taken, the elimination rules must be justified to be in harmony with the introduction rules in the sense that the elimination rules must not allow one to use the type and its objects to do what should not have been possible according to the meaning of the type given by the introduction rules. In other words, for instance, if in the type theory one can demonstrate that a proposition P is proved by p, then it should be the case that P is already provable directly in the sense that p gives rise to a canonical proof of P. More generally, if a is an object of type A, then a should have a value (a canonical object) of type A. Technically, this basic requirement may be formulated as that every object of some type must be able to be computed into a value of the same type. This is the property of the notion of computation we have mentioned in Section 1.2.1; its proof-theoretic justification by proving a normalisation property is therefore very important in understanding of the language of type theory.

1.3 The conceptual universe of types

In the literature, one can find various different type theories. The main differences between them are essentially reflected in the different structures of their conceptual universes of types. The structure of the conceptual universe of types of a type theory reflects the way one tries to understand and characterise the real world of objects. Supposing that we are creating a type theory, we may consider various types and type constructors of interest to study, examples of which include the finite types, the type of natural numbers, types of functions, types of object-pairs, etc. We may also consider more sophisticated types like those whose objects are (names of) certain types—type universes. For instance, one may take the view that the class of logical propositions forms a type whose objects are names of types of proofs. Organising the structure of the conceptual universe of types in different ways results in type theories which present different views and capture different aspects of the reality and provide means of description suitable for different pragmatic applications. An important point in understanding the conceptual universe of types is that the conceptual universe should be viewed as *open* in the sense that the formal type theory, at any stage of its development, can only capture part of the real world of objects (if it does) and, therefore, is subject to further extension to incorporate new types in the future.

In this section, we briefly discuss some of the existing type theories: the predicative type theories, represented by Martin-Löf's type theory [ML75, ML84, NPS90], and the impredicative type theories, developed by Girard [Gir72], Reynolds [Rey74], and Coquand [CH88] among others. The discussion is not meant to be complete in any way but to mention some of the issues in the study of type theory to motivate the development of the type theory in this monograph.

1.3.1 Paradoxical type structures

When formulating a type theory, one cannot expect that all intuitively acceptable conceptions are logically consistent; some of them, especially those that involve certain conceptual circularity, may lead to logical paradoxes. A typical example of paradoxical type structures is the imposition of a type of all types. In 1971, Martin-Löf [ML71] formulated a type system which consists of a type of all types that contains itself as an object and is closed under arbitrary dependent product. The strong impredicativity (circularity) in its type formation gives the system a very strong power. However, unfortunately this type system turns out to be logically inconsistent in the sense that every type is inhabited, a result due to Girard [Gir72] known as Girard's paradox, and therefore does not have a consistent internal logic according to the principle of propositions-as-types.

The idea of introducing a type of all types may be analysed into the following two basic ideas: (1) *impredicativity*: the class of all propositions forms a type over which universal quantification is allowed to form new propositions; (2) *identification of propositions and types*: every proposition is a type and *vice versa*. Now, suppose U is the type of all propositions, then U is also the type of all types by the identification of propositions and types. Therefore, type U of all types naturally occurs and, in particular, it is the type of itself. The first idea is behind the development of higher-order logics (e.g. in the simple type theory [Ram25][Chu40]) where, using a terminology of Russell, the range of significance of a propositional function forms a totality, while the second comes from the principle of propositions-as-types but takes a strong form in that not only propositions are regarded as types, but every type is viewed as corresponding to a logical proposition. If such an analysis is correct, there seems to be two ways to organise the structure of the conceptual universe of types in order to avoid such a paradox: either to abandon the impredicativity or to give up the strong principle of identification. Martin-Löf has since adopted the former and developed his predicative type theory, while along the other line, people have studied various impredicative type theories.[3]

1.3.2 Martin-Löf's type theory

The conceptual universe of Martin-Löf's predicative type theory [ML75, ML84, NPS90] can be understood in a hierarchical way: one starts by introducing various basic types (e.g. the finite types, the type of natural numbers, etc.), and then considers various type constructors like dependent product, strong sum and disjoint union which introduce more complex types formed from the simpler ones, and finally, one may introduce type universes which consist of names of types which have already been introduced into the theory. The type of all types does not exist anymore, but is replaced by an infinite sequence of universes $U_0 : U_1 : U_2 : ...$, introduced in a stratified way, to approximate the type of all types. Reflection principle is used to ensure that the introduction of universes gives a stronger power, for example, to define transfinite types. The theory is supposed to be open in the sense that new types and type constructors may be introduced when they are needed. Based on his intuitionistic philosophy, Martin-Löf has developed a verificationistic meaning-theory for his type theory [ML84], which strengthens in a great deal the position of the theory as a foundational language for constructive mathematics as, for example, described by Bishop [Bis67].

It is the view of intuitionists in the philosophy of mathematics that logic is a part of mathematics. In the context of Martin-Löf's type theory, types and propositions are identified and logical operators are represented by type constructors. For example, the existential quantifier is represented by the strong sum types whose objects are pairs (of proofs); this gives a stronger version of existential quantification (cf. [How80]) so that the axiom of choice holds in the theory (and because of this, Martin-Löf's type theory is not a conservative extension of the first-order intuitionistic logic). One cannot quantify over *all* propositions or relations, although quantification over each of the universes is allowed. Put in another way, the propositions do not form a totality in the language and hence there is no internal notion of predicate or relation, which is supposed to be a meta-level notion (as in first-order logic). Since the higher-order logical mechanism is not available, a new equality type constructor is also introduced. There are basically two versions of Martin-Löf's predicative type theory: the intensional version with weak (intensional) equality types [ML75, NPS90] and the extensional version with strong (extensional) equality types [ML84]. The weak equality type reflects the notion of computation given by computational equality,

[3]However, this is by no means to imply that avoiding paradox to ensure logical consistency is the main stimulus to the development of type theories, although it has been an important consideration.

while the introduction of the strong equality leads to an undecidable judgemental equality which does not capture the intended notion of computation anymore.

1.3.3 Impredicative type theories

Different from predicative type theories, impredicative type systems incorporate an important idea of polymorphic type which allows quantification and abstraction over all propositions (or types) to form a new proposition (or type). For example, in the calculus of constructions [CH88], propositions may be formed by universal quantification over any type including *Prop*, the type of all logical propositions. For instance, $\forall P{:}Prop.P$ is a proposition of type *Prop*. Such a formation of propositions is impredicative or circular since $\forall P{:}Prop.P$ is formed by quantifying over all propositions including itself. This conception of impredicative type formation gives a strong power to the impredicative type systems, and in particular, incorporates a strong logical power under the principle of propositions-as-types. (See Barendregt's analysis of type systems in λ-cube [Bar92].) For example, the calculus of constructions corresponds to the intuitionistic higher-order predicate logic; therefore, in contrast to predicative type theories, there is an internal notion of predicate and relation represented by propositional functions whose values range over the propositions.

The idea of polymorphic type in an impredicative type system may be analysed as being based on the view that the class of all logical propositions form a totality whose objects may be formed by arbitrary universal quantification. It is important that, to avoid logical paradox, this totality or any more complex type cannot contain itself as an object; for instance, the type of logical propositions itself does not correspond to a proposition. Therefore, types cannot be completely identified with logical propositions in a powerful impredicative setting, although propositions correspond to their proof types.

Besides the higher-order logical power, there is also a rather popular tendency of using propositions in impredicative type theories to represent data types and proofs to represent programs. In fact, the impredicative conception also incorporates a strong computational power [Gir73] and allows representation of many data types by a coding technique [BB85]; for example, a type of natural numbers may be represented by $\forall P{:}Prop.P \to (P \to P) \to P$, which has the Church numerals as its canonical objects. Because of this, although a complete identification of types and propositions is not possible in impredicative type theories, one might still view, for example, *Prop* as the (formal) universe of both logical propositions and computational data types.

However, it seems that the use of impredicative systems based on such a view has not been well-understood. In particular, there are problems and difficulties in the use of propositions as data types and in the view of identifying conceptually logical propositions with data types in impredicative type theories. The first problem concerns the adequacy of the Church-style representation of data types. It is known that such representations have some weaknesses. For example, the induction principle and the axiom of infinity (zero is not equal to one) are not provable for the Church numerals from the inference rules of the type theories. Therefore, to prove properties about the Church-style natural numbers, one has to *assume* these as 'extra-logical' axioms, but that would cause difficulties in the operational understanding of the type theory since the assumed proofs of these axioms are not in canonical forms. Another weakness of the impredicative representation of data types is that it excludes some straightforward and efficient computational algorithms. A typical example of this is that, for the Church-style natural numbers, there is no linear-time predecessor function. In comparison, these problems do not appear for the directly introduced types in Martin-Löf's type theory such as the type of natural numbers informally discussed in Section 1.2.3, which are superior formulations of data types in these aspects. The second problem is concerned with the essence of the view that in impredicative systems propositions and types can in some sense also be identified. Put in a simple way, since the formulations of impredicative type theories correspond to the logical systems (cf. [Bar92]), one would expect that the systems capture the corresponding logics in a nice way. However, the view of using propositions as data types fails to achieve that. An example of this is that the calculus of constructions is *not* a conservative extension of higher-order intuitionistic logic, if propositions are used to represent data types [Ber90, Luo90b].

An interesting note is that such a tendency of using impredicative systems, which is not necessarily held by the inventors of the impredicative systems, may be seen as influenced by that of logicists in the foundational study of mathematics, who believe that mathematics can be reduced to logic by definitions. This is not surprising because the impredicative type theories are in fact very close to, for example, Ramsey's simple type theory [Ram25]. In fact, some of the difficulties of such a use mentioned above already appeared in the context of logicist foundational study of mathematics.

1.3.4 Data types vs. logical propositions

It is the rather modern discovery by Curry and Howard of the possibility of viewing logical propositions as types of proofs that makes it possible to consider propositions and types to be the same entities. However, no matter how tempting it may be, it is still reasonable to question whether such an identification view is necessary or natural to take. Some of the technical issues and difficulties in the identification view have been mentioned above. To summarise, in predicative type theories, taking the identification view and insisting on predicativity, one loses the possibility to incorporate stronger logical mechanisms such as higher-order logic, which may provide powerful tools in pragmatic applications in computer science and mathematics (see Chapters 7 and 8); in impredicative type theories, the impredicative definitions of data types are too weak and the identification view leads to a possibly inadequate logic which seems difficult to understand.

It is our view that *it is not natural to identify types with propositions.* It seems to the author that there are apparent differences, both conceptual and structural, between the purely logical entities and the others such as computational and mathematical ones, although it is sometimes admittedly difficult to draw a clear line between them. Furthermore, besides its conceptual clarity, a distinction between logical propositions and computational data types is important in many applications in computer science.

This amounts to an argument for the independence in certain extent of logic with the world of objects to be reasoned about by means of the logic. Concerning type-theoretic languages, several points may be elaborated on this aspect. First of all, logic, in its pure sense, is a language that can be used to describe and reason about any class of objects which are of interest by the user of the language; in other words, logic has a trait of being universal and hence independent of the existence (or presence, if we want to avoid any ontological flavour) of the objects that particular applications may involve. Pure logical truths are established by the very meaning of the logical operators which is embodied in the form of propositions and the rules one accepts and uses to reason; therefore, they are true because one can establish their truth without worrying about what non-logical entities they may involve. Put in another way in the context of type theory, a true (i.e. inhabited) proposition is a pure logical truth if its truth is essentially determined by the meaning of the logical type constructors, and hence its inhabitability is invariant under reasonable changes of non-logical objects that occur in it. If such a view is taken correctly, it is very difficult to see how logical propositions can be identified with data types which are supposed to represent, for example, application-oriented objects. For otherwise, the independence of logic would be lost or, at least, compensated since there is then no such a thing of pure or universal logical truth—even the existence of logical operators in a language may then be dependent on the existence of certain classes of computational objects.

Secondly, there is a strong intuition that leads to a belief that although propositions can be viewed as types (of their proofs), it is not natural to view every type to be a logical proposition. One might say that data types like that of natural numbers are just true or provable propositions, but this seems to be enforced somehow by a brute force and is rather questionable. The intuition simply says that the data types such as the type of natural numbers are not logical propositions.

The third argument for a distinction between logical propositions and the other data types concerns about how we should view the philosophical openness of the conceptual universe of types. As remarked above, we very much appreciate and agree with Martin-Löf among many others that a formal type theory can only capture part of the real world and is subject to further extension, at least, philosophically. However, it seems natural to us that the philosophical openness should be mainly concerned with the ways in which the formal theory capture the concerned objects (computational or mathematical objects, in our case) rather than the form and the meaning of the logical propositions in the internal logic of the formal theory.[4] If the point of view that openness is mainly about the subject matter concerned instead of the logical apparatus is coherent and accepted, it is unnatural to accept the identification view, as the latter would lead to the unwilling commitment that the ways of forming logical propositions are left open for further extension, just as the ways of forming data types.

A particular aspect about impredicative type theories should be further discussed here. In the above, we have only discussed the problems with data types by impredicative definitions. What about having an impredicative system (e.g. the calculus of constructions) which is supposed to be open in such a way that new 'data types' are in the future added as propositions (e.g. of type *Prop*)? In other words, can we take an identification view for an impredicative system and make the impredicative universe of data types (propositions) as open? The answer seems to be negative, or putting in another way, this is not natural or satisfactory. First, intuitively, it is unnatural because one would then have to assume that the internal logical machinery is open for further extension. Besides this arguable intuitive reason, such a view has further pragmatic difficulties. In fact, some reasonable and pragmatically useful data types can not be consistently or reasonably added to an impredicative system without unpleasant side-effects. A typical example of such data types is the strong sum type constructor (Σ-types). It is known that the extension of the calculus of constructions by the large impredicative strong sum types is logically inconsistent (and leads to Girard's paradox [Coq86a, HH86]). However, the

[4]This is different from the pure intuitionistic view which takes logic as a part of mathematics. However, for us, either logic is not a part of the computational world or it is a very special part. Logic is for describing, understanding, and reasoning about the computational objects, but logical entities themselves are not necessarily computational entities in the application domain.

large Σ-types are essential for specification of abstract data types and abstract reasoning. Furthermore, the small impredicative Σ-types are also problematic; for example, adding them to the calculus of constructions is not logically conservative. (See Section 2.3.2 for a further discussion.) In fact, such problems seem to come from a more fundamental reason, that is, the impredicativity of a formal type universe such as that of all propositions has essentially 'closed' the world of propositions which is not free for further extensions without significant change of the meaning of the logical operators.

Therefore, on the basis of the above analysis, it is our view that, even in type theory, *a conceptual and formal distinction between the notions of logical formula and data type is both conceptually natural and pragmatically important.* There may be different ways to organise the structure of types to make such a distinction. The type theory to be studied in this monograph offers a particular proposal.

1.4 Towards a unifying theory of dependent types

The main goal of this monograph is to develop a theory of dependent types, explain the meaning of its language, study its meta-theory (in particular, its proof-theoretic properties), and show its uses in applications to computer science. The type theory is developed with the motivations explained above, aiming at the direction to develop type theory as a rich computational language with a powerful internal logic, good abstraction mechanisms, and a simple operational semantics (or meaning understanding), so that it can be effectively used as a uniform language in modular programming, structured specification and modular development of programs, and logical reasoning.

The conceptual universe of types of our type theory consists of two parts: the computational world of data types and the logical world of propositions (see Fig. 1.2). Intuitively, to grasp this conceptual universe, one considers various types and type constructors such as the dependent product types (Π-types), the strong sum types (Σ-types), the type of natural numbers, etc. In particular, we consider a type (*Prop*) of logical propositions which are themselves (names of) types of their proofs and provide the means to describe the logical properties of objects of any type. For any type A (including *Prop* and the more complicated ones) and any families of propositions $P[x]$ indexed by objects of type A, one can quantify over A to form a proposition $\forall x{:}A.P[x]$. We can also introduce predicative type universes in a stratified way, as in Martin-Löf's type theory, which consist of names of the types already introduced into the theory. The intended understanding (and use) of the language is based on this intuitive understanding,

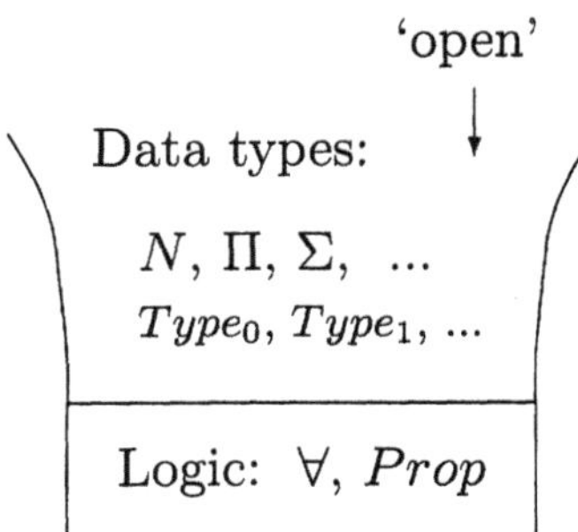

Fig. 1.2. The conceptual universe of types.

in which it is important to distinguish the roles of logical propositions and data types. More specifically, the data types which do not involve logical propositions in general represent classes of entities in the concerned world. For example, using the language in program development, they represent the data types whose objects are programs or program structures, etc. The logical propositions, on the other hand, represent the descriptions of properties of the concerned objects (for instance, programs). Such a view on the language makes a conceptual distinction between the notions of data type and logical proposition, which are formally represented in the language by different entities. Formally, this will essentially amount to a 'unification' of Martin-Löf's type theory and Coquand-Huet's calculus of constructions, with a distinction between logical propositions and data types.

Since we do not expect to exhaust the possible conceptions of type formation, the conceptual universe of types is supposed to be open. However, allowing impredicative formation of propositions, it is our intention to consider the world of logical propositions as relatively closed, in the sense that the ways (e.g. in the case of higher-order logic, the universal quantification) to form logical propositions are not supposed to be further extended. Therefore, the openness essentially concerns the predicative part of the theory, where the objects like programs and data types reside. This presents a coherent structure of types which incorporates a powerful internal logic relatively independent with the computational world and allows one to introduce and use the type constructors like strong sum (large Σ-types) in the computational world.

Based on the basic ideas as described above, the *Extended Calculus of Constructions* (ECC for short), has been developed in the author's PhD thesis [Luo90a]. ECC extends the calculus of constructions with Σ-types and predicative universes. One may also consider it as an impredicative extension of (the core of) Martin-Löf's type theory with universes by adding an impredicative universe of logical propositions. This monograph is based on the thesis work and the further research work that leads to the development of a unifying theory of dependent types.

In developing type theory as a computational language, it is one of our aims to obtain a language whose constructions have clear and comprehensible meanings on which their correct uses are based. Understanding a language requires an understanding of the basic meanings of its constructions, various essential properties of the language, and its pragmatic uses in its application. It is obvious that these aspects of understanding are intrinsically related: first, an understanding of the basic meanings is usually the starting point to use a language correctly; second, the meaning explanation is often justified by demonstration of the relevant properties of the language which give further or deeper understanding; third, on the one hand, the correct uses of a language are based on the correct understanding, but on the other hand, they also demonstrate extensively what the meaning explanations convey and how they should be applied in practice, which in return, extend or enrich one's knowledge of the language.

Besides the technical issues to be studied along the way of the development of the type theory, this book can be viewed as a study of how to understand and use its language. We first present the language of ECC, explain the basic meanings of its constructions, and discuss some of the issues about its intended uses. These explanations will be elaborated and justified by studying the proof-theoretic properties of ECC and its internal higher-order logic. The use of the language will be demonstrated by considering two notions of theory: computational theories as inductive data types and abstract logical theories for structured abstract reasoning in proof development, and by developing an approach to program specification and modular development of programs and proofs. Finally, we consider a further development of the language into a unifying theory of dependent types UTT which shows how computational theories (inductive data types) may be introduced in general. The following is an overview of the following chapters.

In Chapter 2, the language of ECC is presented and informal explanations are given to explain the basic meanings of the constructions in the language, their possible uses and the important proof-theoretic properties of the language. Some philosophical and technical issues concerning the structure of the conceptual universe of types, the intensionality and extensionality of equalities, and the use and computer implementation of the type theory, are also discussed to elaborate our points of view and to explain the particular design decisions made in the development of the type theory.

Chapter 3 studies the basic meta-theoretic properties of ECC, which include those about the notion of computation such as the Church-Rosser theorem and the extensionality of type equality, properties of correct (derivable) judgements, admissibility results such as subject reduction, and the typing properties such as those about principal types of objects.

The most important proof-theoretic property of ECC—strong normalisation—is proved in Chapter 4. It shows that every object computes into a (unique) value, and hence guarantees that the different aspects of use of entities in the language are in harmony. The proof of the strong normalisation theorem uses the Girard–Tait reducibility method and a new proof technique of 'quasi-normalisation' to deal with the extra complexity of the language, which is itself an interesting result since it makes explicit the predicativity of the computational world in the language.

On the basis of the normalisation theorem, Chapter 5 studies the internal higher-order logic and the decidability results. Besides the logical consistency, it is shown how the logical operators can be understood by grasping its two aspects of use; in particular, the definable propositional equality (the Leibniz equality) is studied and an equality reflection result is proved to show that the Leibniz equality reflects the computational equality. The decidability results include the decidability of the computational equality and that of type checking and type inference. An algorithm for type inference (and type checking) is given and proved to be correct, which directly establishes the basis for a computer implementation of the language.

Chapter 6, which is rather independent with the other chapters, describes briefly a set-theoretic (realisability) model of ECC in the constructive framework of ω-sets and modest sets, and explains how the type theory may be understood set-theoretically.

Pragmatic uses of the type theory in computer science are studied in Chapter 7 and Chapter 8. In Chapter 7, two notions of theory are considered: the computational theories represented by inductive data types and the abstract logical theories. The discussion of the former illustrates how to use the type theory as a functional programming language (and how to introduce basic mathematical theories) and to prove properties of programs (and mathematical structures). The development of the latter shows that the rich type structure and strong logical power of the type theory allow one to use the language to describe abstract structures and reason about classes of mathematical structures in an abstract way so that large proof development can be modularised.

Chapter 8 describes an important application of the type theory as a uniform language for modular development of programs, specifications, and proofs. A type-theoretic approach to program specification and data refinement is developed to show that the type theory, with its powerful internal logic and the useful abstraction mechanisms provided by dependent types (in particular, Π-types, Σ-types and universes), offers an adequate language for describing abstract data types, structured and parameterised specification, and modular program development by means of data refinement.

In the final chapter (Chapter 9), a further development of the type theory is considered by giving a formulation of a unifying theory of dependent types (UTT). It shows how a large class of inductive data types may be introduced into the type theory to incorporate a rich computational type structure (computational theories). The presentation of UTT uses Martin-Löf's logical framework as a meta-language and allows us to analyse the conceptual universe of types more explicitly and to discuss some philosophical and technical issues more clearly. It also suggests improvements to the formulation of the type theory and raises several interesting issues to be further studied.

2
The Extended Calculus of Constructions

The *Extended Calculus of Constructions* (ECC) is a type theory which is developed as an initial step towards a rich computational language with a powerful internal logic for modular development of programs, specifications, and proofs. The basic ideas incorporated in ECC, in particular, the idea that there should be a conceptual distinction between the notions of logical proposition and data type, have been explained in the Introduction. It is also based on those ideas that the study of ECC will lead to a unifying theory of dependent types which unifies Martin-Löf's type theory with universes [ML75, ML84] and Coquand-Huet's calculus of constructions [CH88] (see Chapter 9).

In this chapter, we introduce the language of ECC and give informal explanations of the constructions in the language and their meanings. Some of the issues on type theory mentioned in the Introduction are also discussed. The informal explanations and discussion may also be regarded as a more detailed overview of the following chapters.

2.1 The language of ECC

The language of ECC consists of an underlying calculus of terms and computation, and a set of rules for inferring judgements.

2.1.1 Terms and computation

The basic expressions of the language are called *terms*, given by the following definition.

Definition 2.1. ***(terms)*** Terms *are inductively defined as follows:*

- *The constants $Prop$ and $Type_j$ ($j \in \omega$), called* universes, *are terms;*
- *Variables (x,y,...) are terms;*

- *If M, N and A are terms, so are the following:*

$$\Pi x{:}M.N,\quad \lambda x{:}M.N,\quad MN,\quad \Sigma x{:}M.N,\quad \langle M,N\rangle_A,\quad \pi_1(M),\quad \pi_2(M).$$

We use $\mathcal{T}$ to denote the set of terms.

In $\Pi x{:}M.N$, $\Sigma x{:}M.N$, and $\lambda x{:}M.N$, the free occurrences of variable x in N (but not those in M) are bound by the binding operators Π, Σ, and λ, respectively. The usual conventions of parenthesis omitting are adopted; for example, $M_1M_2...M_n$ stands for $(...((M_1M_2)M_3)...M_{n-1})M_n$ and the scopes of the binding operators Π, Σ, and λ extend to the right as far as possible. For a term M, $FV(M)$ is the set of free variables occurring in M. When $x \notin FV(N)$, $\Pi x{:}M.N$ and $\Sigma x{:}M.N$ can be abbreviated as $M \to N$ and $M \times N$, respectively. We also often write $M_1M_2...M_n$ as $M_1(M_2, ..., M_n)$ for readability consideration.

α-convertible terms (i.e. terms which are the same up to changes of bound variables) are identified. $\equiv$ is used for the syntactical identity between expressions such as terms, i.e. $A \equiv B$ means that A and B are the same up to α-conversion. We shall use $[N/x]M$ to represent the term got from M by substituting term N for the free occurrences of variable x in M, defined as usual with possible changes of bound variables. Informally, we sometimes use $M[x]$ to indicate that variable x may occur free in M and subsequently use $M[N]$ to abbreviate $[N/x]M$, when no confusion may occur.

The following notions of reduction and conversion give the notions of computation and computational equality for ECC, respectively.

Definition 2.2. (reduction and conversion) Reduction *($\triangleright$) and* conversion *($\simeq$) are defined as usual with respect to the following contraction schemes:*

(β) $$(\lambda x{:}A.M)N \leadsto_\beta [N/x]M$$

(σ) $$\pi_i(\langle M_1, M_2\rangle_A) \leadsto_\sigma M_i \quad (i = 1, 2)$$

More precisely,

1. *The terms of the forms $(\lambda x{:}A.M)N$ and $\pi_i(\langle M_1, M_2\rangle_A)$ $(i = 1, 2)$ are called* β-redexes *and* σ-redexes, *with $[N/x]M$ and M_i being their* contractums, *respectively, and $\lambda x{:}A.M$ and $\langle M_1, M_2\rangle_A$ are called* major terms *of these redexes.*

2. *If a term M contains an occurrence of a redex R and we replace that occurrence by its contractum, and the resulting term is M', we say* M one-step reduces to M' *(notation $M \triangleright_1 M'$).*

3. *We say M* reduces to *M' (or M* computes to *M', notation $M \triangleright M'$) if and only if M' is obtained from M by a finite (possibly empty) series of contractions.*

4. *We say M* is convertible to *M' (or M and M' are* computationally equal, *notation $M \simeq M'$) if and only if M' is obtained from M by a finite (possibly empty) series of contractions and reversed contractions, i.e. there exist $M_1, ..., M_n$ $(n \geq 1)$ such that $M \equiv M_1$, $M' \equiv M_n$ and $M_i \triangleright_1 M_{i+1}$ or $M_{i+1} \triangleright_1 M_i$ for $i = 1, ..., n-1$.*

A term is in normal form *if and only if it does not contain any redex. A term M_1 is* strongly normalisable *if and only if every reduction sequence of the form $M_1 \triangleright_1 M_2 \triangleright_1 M_3 \triangleright_1 \dots$ is finite.*

The relationship between universes in ECC induces the type cumulativity (to be explained below in Section 2.2.7) that is syntactically characterised by the following relation.

Definition 2.3. (cumulativity relation) *The* cumulativity relation *$\preceq$ is defined to be the smallest binary relation over terms such that*

1. *$\preceq$ is a partial order with respect to conversion, that is,*

   (a) *if $A \simeq B$, then $A \preceq B$;*

   (b) *if $A \preceq B$ and $B \preceq A$, then $A \simeq B$; and*

   (c) *if $A \preceq B$ and $B \preceq C$, then $A \preceq C$.*

2. *$Prop \preceq Type_0 \preceq Type_1 \preceq \dots$;*

3. *if $A_1 \simeq B_1$ and $A_2 \preceq B_2$, then $\Pi x{:}A_1.A_2 \preceq \Pi x{:}B_1.B_2$;*

4. *if $A_1 \preceq B_1$ and $A_2 \preceq B_2$, then $\Sigma x{:}A_1.A_2 \preceq \Sigma x{:}B_1.B_2$.*

Furthermore, $A \prec B$ if and only if $A \preceq B$ and $A \not\simeq B$.

Remark The well-definedness (i.e. the existence) of the cumulativity relation will be justified in Section 3.1 by giving an alternative inductive definition.

2.1.2 Judgements and inference rules

We now describe the form of judgements, which are sentences in our language, and the inference rules for inferring judgements.

Definition 2.4. (contexts) Contexts *are finite sequences of expressions of the form $x{:}M$, where x is a variable and M is a term. The empty context is denoted by $\langle\rangle$.*

The set of free variables in a context $\Gamma \equiv x_1{:}A_1, ..., x_n{:}A_n$, $FV(\Gamma)$, is defined as $\bigcup_{1\leq i\leq n}(\{x_i\} \cup FV(A_i))$.

Definition 2.5. (judgements) Judgements *are of the form*

$$\Gamma \vdash M : A,$$

where Γ is a context and M and A are terms. The judgement above is read as 'M is of type A in Γ'.

A judgement $\Gamma \vdash M : A$ is called non-hypothetical *if Γ is the empty context, and called* hypothetical, *otherwise. We shall write $\vdash M : A$ for non-hypothetical judgement $\langle\rangle \vdash M : A$.*

The inference of correct judgements is governed by *inference rules*. In general, an inference rule of judgements is of the form

$$\frac{J_1 \quad ... \quad J_n}{J} \quad (\textit{side conditions})$$

where J_1, ..., J_n $(n \geq 0)$ are judgements called *premises*, and J is the judgement called *conclusion*. There may be some side conditions on the application of an inference rule.

The inference rules of ECC are listed in Fig. 2.1, where j stands for an arbitrary natural number. The inference of correct judgements in ECC according to the rules is given by the following notions of derivation and derivability.

Definition 2.6. (derivations) *A* derivation *of a judgement J is a finite sequence of judgements $J_1, ..., J_n$ with $J_n \equiv J$ such that, for all $1 \leq i \leq n$, J_i is the conclusion of some instance of an inference rule whose premises are in $\{\, J_j \mid j < i \,\}$.*

A judgement J is derivable *if there is a derivation of J. We shall write $\Gamma \vdash M : A$ for '$\Gamma \vdash M : A$ is derivable', and $\Gamma \not\vdash M : A$ for '$\Gamma \vdash M : A$ is not derivable'.*

This completes our formal presentation of ECC. In the following definitions, we introduce some terminology to be used later.

$$(Ax) \qquad \frac{}{\vdash Prop : Type_0}$$

$$(C) \qquad \frac{\Gamma \vdash A : Type_j}{\Gamma, x{:}A \vdash Prop : Type_0} \quad (x \notin FV(\Gamma))$$

$$(T) \qquad \frac{\Gamma \vdash Prop : Type_0}{\Gamma \vdash Type_j : Type_{j+1}}$$

$$(var) \qquad \frac{\Gamma, x{:}A, \Gamma' \vdash Prop : Type_0}{\Gamma, x{:}A, \Gamma' \vdash x : A}$$

$$(\Pi 1) \qquad \frac{\Gamma, x{:}A \vdash P : Prop}{\Gamma \vdash \Pi x{:}A.P : Prop}$$

$$(\Pi 2) \qquad \frac{\Gamma \vdash A : Type_j \quad \Gamma, x{:}A \vdash B : Type_j}{\Gamma \vdash \Pi x{:}A.B : Type_j}$$

$$(\lambda) \qquad \frac{\Gamma, x{:}A \vdash M : B}{\Gamma \vdash \lambda x{:}A.M : \Pi x{:}A.B}$$

$$(app) \qquad \frac{\Gamma \vdash M : \Pi x{:}A.B \quad \Gamma \vdash N : A}{\Gamma \vdash MN : [N/x]B}$$

$$(\Sigma) \qquad \frac{\Gamma \vdash A : Type_j \quad \Gamma, x{:}A \vdash B : Type_j}{\Gamma \vdash \Sigma x{:}A.B : Type_j}$$

$$(pair) \qquad \frac{\Gamma \vdash M : A \quad \Gamma \vdash N : [M/x]B \quad \Gamma, x{:}A \vdash B : Type_j}{\Gamma \vdash \langle M, N \rangle_{\Sigma x:A.B} : \Sigma x{:}A.B}$$

$$(\pi 1) \qquad \frac{\Gamma \vdash M : \Sigma x{:}A.B}{\Gamma \vdash \pi_1(M) : A}$$

$$(\pi 2) \qquad \frac{\Gamma \vdash M : \Sigma x{:}A.B}{\Gamma \vdash \pi_2(M) : [\pi_1(M)/x]B}$$

$$(\preceq) \qquad \frac{\Gamma \vdash M : A \quad \Gamma \vdash A' : Type_j}{\Gamma \vdash M : A'} \quad (A \preceq A')$$

Fig. 2.1. The inference rules of ECC.

Definition 2.7. *Let* Γ *be a context.*

- Γ *is a* valid context *if and only if* $\Gamma \vdash Prop : Type_0$.
- *A term* M *is called an* object in Γ *(or* Γ-object*) if* $\Gamma \vdash M : A$ *for some* A.
- *A term* A *is called a* type in Γ *(or* Γ-type*) if* $\Gamma \vdash A : U$ *for some universe* U.
- *A* Γ*-type* A *is called a* proposition in Γ *(or* Γ-proposition*) if* $\Gamma \vdash A' : Prop$ *for some* $A' \simeq A$*, and called* non-propositional, *otherwise.*
- *A term* M *is called a* proof in Γ *(or* Γ-proof*) if* $\Gamma \vdash M : P$ *for some* Γ*-proposition* P.
- *A term* A *is* inhabited in Γ *(or* Γ-inhabited*) if* $\Gamma \vdash M : A$ *for some* M.

A term is called well-typed *if it is a* Γ*-object for some* Γ.

2.2 Informal explanations

As presented above, the type theory ECC incorporates a higher-order logic whose propositions reside in type universe *Prop*, and non-propositional data types including the non-propositional dependent product types (Π-types) and the strong sum types (Σ-types) which reside in predicative universes $Type_j$. As a formal system, ECC extends the calculus of constructions with Σ-types and predicative universes. One may also consider it as an impredicative extension of (the core of) Martin-Löf's type theory with universes by adding an impredicative universe of logical propositions.

In this section, we explain informally the basic meanings of the constructions in the language of ECC. To understand the meanings is essential in learning and using the language. Furthermore, the meta-theoretic properties of the language to be studied in the following chapters show that our rules of inference do conform with the intended meaning explanations of the language and give more formal justifications of the adequacy of the language.

2.2.1 Computation and computational equality

Computation is a basic notion whose understanding underlies the understanding of the other constructions in the language, in particular, of judgements and types. The notions of computation and computational equality are formally captured by reduction and conversion (see Definition 2.2), respectively, defined as relations between the basic expressions—terms. The computation (contraction) rules may be regarded as formally expressing certain schemata of definitions[5] usually used in functional programming and mathematical definitions, and computation may be regarded as evaluation of the defined function when applied to its arguments. More precisely, given the specific contraction rules such as (β) and (σ) to be explained in more detail below, *one-step computation* (or one-step reduction) captures the process of replacing a definiendum by its definiens, the relation that a term *computes* (or reduces) to another is the reflexive and transitive closure of one-step computation, and the *computational equality* (or the conversion relation) is the reflexive, symmetric, and transitive closure of one-step computation.

Talking about computation, we need a notion of *values*—expressions with which computation terminates. We identity the notion of value with that of normal form. In other words, a value is a term that can only compute to itself. We say that a computation starting from a term *terminates* if it arrives at a value, which is then called a value of the term.

We remark that the notion of computation in our language satisfies several important properties, among which are

- the *Church-Rosser property* (see Theorem 3.1): *any two computationally equal terms can be reduced to a common term*, which in particular guarantees the uniqueness of value of a term, if it exists;
- the *property of subject reduction* (see Theorem 3.16), which says that *computation is type-preserving*;
- the *strong normalisation property* (see Chapter 4), which says that *every well-typed term is strongly normalisable* (i.e. every computation starting from a well-typed term terminates).

These properties of computation guarantee, in particular, that *every well-typed term computes to a unique value of the same type and that two well-typed terms are computationally equal if and only if they compute into the same value.* Therefore, together with other properties of the language, they provide a formal (proof-theoretic) justification of the inference rules by showing that they are in harmony with each other and in accord with the meaning explanation of judgements and type constructors to be given below.

---

[5]However, different from meta-level *abbreviational* definitions which may be eliminated and hence inessential for the use of a language, the computational rules for a type are *meaning-giving* and essential. (See Chapter 9 for a further discussion.)

2.2.2 Judgements and context validity

The sentences in the language are the judgements, whose formal correctness is given by the notion of derivability. A non-hypothetical judgement

$$\vdash a : A$$

asserts that a is an object of type A (in the empty context); its basic meaning is that *a computes to a value which is of type A*. The meta-theoretic properties of computation (in particular, subject reduction and strong normalisation) justify that a does compute to its value which is of type A if the above judgement is derivable.

The meaning of a hypothetical judgement can be explained by means of those of non-hypothetical ones. A context $\Gamma \equiv x_1{:}A_1, ..., x_n{:}A_n$ is informally viewed as a list of assumptions that x_i is an arbitrary object of type A_i in Γ (cf. the assumption rule (var)). A hypothetical judgement

$$\Gamma \vdash a : A$$

asserts that a is an object of type A in context Γ; its basic meaning is that, *in the empty context, a' is an object of type A' for any objects a_i of type A'_i $(i = 1, ..., n)$*, where a' and A' are the terms got from a and A with the free occurrences of $x_1, ..., x_n$ substituted by $a_1, ..., a_n$, respectively, and A'_i is the term got from A_i with the free occurrences of $x_1, ..., x_{i-1}$ substituted by $a_1, ..., a_{i-1}$, respectively. The justification of the formal correctness of non-hypothetical judgements can be given using a property about substitution (Theorem 3.14), which guarantees that, under the above assumptions, $\vdash a' : A'$ is derivable if $\Gamma \vdash a : A$ is.

The only axiom of the system is $\vdash Prop : Type_0$. Besides asserting that $Prop$ is of type $Type_0$ in Γ, the judgement $\Gamma \vdash Prop : Type_0$ also plays the role of asserting that Γ is a valid context. The meaning of a context being valid is reflected by the rules (Ax) and (C). We may replace the rules $(Ax)(C)(T)(var)$ in the above presentation of ECC by the following ones, with an additional judgement form 'Γ **valid**':

$$\frac{}{\langle\rangle\ \textbf{valid}} \qquad \frac{\Gamma \vdash A : Type_j \quad x \notin FV(\Gamma)}{\Gamma, x{:}A\ \textbf{valid}}$$

$$\frac{\Gamma\ \textbf{valid}}{\Gamma \vdash Prop : Type_0} \qquad \frac{\Gamma\ \textbf{valid}}{\Gamma \vdash Type_j : Type_{j+1}} \qquad \frac{\Gamma, x{:}A, \Gamma'\ \textbf{valid}}{\Gamma, x{:}A, \Gamma' \vdash x : A}$$

Then we get an equivalent system as presented in [Luo89], in which the only axiom is the judgement asserting that the empty context is valid. These rules may give a clearer picture of context validity in the language.

2.2.3 Types and their meaning explanation

Types are entities which may be inhabited by objects. In the above presentation of ECC, we do not formally distinguish types from their names and types are special objects whose types are universes. Therefore, for example, the type of proofs of a proposition P of type *Prop* is identified with P, which as a type symbol has a 'double identity' of being a proposition (i.e. an object of type *Prop*) and the proof type of itself. Such a treatment of types and universes is called by Martin-Löf as 'formulation à la Russell', as opposed to the 'formulation à la Tarski', where types are distinguished from their names and the former are related to the latter by explicit operators (for example, for a proposition P, $\mathbf{Prf}(P)$ is the type of proofs of P).[6]

The basic meaning of a type (or types formed by a type constructor) can be understood by grasping how the type (and its objects) can be used. Here, use may be understood by grasping two of its basic aspects (cf. Section 1.2.3); they are

1. how values of the objects of the type, i.e. *canonical objects*, can be introduced, which logically corresponds to how a proposition as a conclusion may be arrived at, and

2. how operations can be defined by analysing the objects of the type, which logically corresponds to how a proposition can be used to derive other logical consequences.

Once again, we emphasize, as we shall see below, that such an understanding is based on our understanding of the notion of computation whose basic rules (contraction rules) determine the meanings of the definable operations with the concerned types as domains.

As we have emphasized in the introduction, we classify types into (logical) propositions and non-propositional types, the latter of which include some special types called universes which have (names of) types as their objects. Furthermore, these classes of types are related to each other so that they form a coherent structure in our conceptual universe of types. In the following, we shall explain each class of these types by showing how their basic meanings should be understood and explaining the intended roles they play in the language (that is, their intended uses).

2.2.4 Non-propositional types

We start by explaining non-propositional types. In ECC, besides type universes, we have only included dependent product types and strong sum

[6] See Chapter 9 for a formulation of our type theory in such a style.

types, leaving other possible non-propositional data types to be considered and discussed when we extend the system with more inductive data types (see Section 7.1 and Chapter 9). Although these non-propositional types play special roles both in pragmatic applications (e.g. those to be considered in Section 7.2 and Chapter 8) and in theoretical studies (cf. Section 2.3.2), we should point out that Π-types and Σ-types are special cases of inductive data types and should not be regarded as more basic than the others.

Dependent product types (Π-types)

Dependent product types, or Π-types, are types with functions (functional programs) as objects. For any type A and any family of types $B[x]$ indexed by arbitrary object x of type A, $\Pi x{:}A.B[x]$ is the type of functions f such that for any object a of type A, applying f to a yields an object of type $B[a]$. Intuitively, it represents the set of (dependent) functions from A to $B[x]$:

$$\{ f \mid f(a) \in B[a] \;\; for\ all\ a \in A \}.$$

When B is not dependent on the objects of A, i.e. x does not occur free in B, $\Pi x{:}A.B$ (abbreviation $A \to B$) is the type of functions from A to B.

The canonical objects of a Π-type are introduced formally as λ-terms by the introduction rule (λ). If A computes to the value A' (in the empty context) and b is a value of type B in context $x{:}A$, then $\lambda x{:}A'.b$ is a value of type $\Pi x{:}A.B$, and any value of type $\Pi x{:}A.B$ is of such a form. Functional application is governed by the elimination rule (*app*), which shows how a function may be used (i.e. applied to an object of its domain type) to obtain objects of its range types. The meaning of functional application is given by the computation (contraction) rule (β) which shows how functional application operates on the canonical objects of a Π-type.

λ-abstraction and the computation rule (β) are related to the following schema of definitions: if a term b is of type B assuming variable x is an arbitrary object of type A, we can define a function f of type $\Pi x{:}A.B$ by

$$f(x) =_{\mathrm{df}} b.$$

f thus defined is formally expressed by $\lambda x{:}A.b$. Then a β-reduction step contracting $f(a)$ to $[a/x]b$ corresponds to an evaluation step of the function f applied to an object a of type A.

Viewing the type theory as a functional programming language, functions of Π-types are the basic functional programs which play an essential role in programming. Besides this, in the presence of the other type constructors in the language (Σ-types and universes, in particular), functions also provide important mechanisms for, for example, parameterisation in modular programming and parameterised specifications.

Strong sum types (Σ-types)

Strong sum types, or Σ-types, are types of pairs of objects. For any type A and any family of types $B[x]$ indexed by arbitrary object x of type A, $\Sigma x{:}A.B[x]$ is the type of pairs (a, b) where a is an object of type A and b is of type $B[a]$. Intuitively, it represents the set of (dependent) pairs of elements of A and B,

$$\{\,(a,b) \mid a \in A,\ b \in B[a]\,\}.$$

When B is not dependent on the objects of A, $\Sigma x{:}A.B$ (abbreviation $A\times B$) is the usual product type of pairs of objects of A and B.

The canonical objects of a Σ-type are introduced formally by the introduction rule (*pair*). If a is a value of type A, b is a value of type $B[a]$, and $\Sigma x{:}A.B[x]$ computes to the value C, then $\langle a, b\rangle_C$ is a value of type $\Sigma x{:}A.B[x]$, and any value of type $\Sigma x{:}A.B[x]$ is of such a form. Objects of type $\Sigma x{:}A.B$ can be analysed by using the two operations of projection (π_1 and π_2) governed by the elimination rules ($\pi 1$) and ($\pi 2$). The meanings of the projection operations are given by the computation rules (σ), which shows how to extract the components from a pair by evaluating the projection operations.

Pairing and the computational rules (σ) can be explained by considering the following schema of definitions: for a binary function g of type $\Pi x{:}A\Pi y{:}B[x].C[x,y]$, we can define a unary function f of type $\Pi z{:}(\Sigma x{:}A.B[x]).\ C[\pi_1(z), \pi_2(z)]$ by

$$f(z) =_{\mathrm{df}} g(\pi_1(z), \pi_2(z)).$$

Formally, $f =_{\mathrm{df}} \lambda z{:}(\Sigma x{:}A.B[x]).g(\pi_1(z), \pi_2(z))$. Then, by the computation rule (σ) (together with (β)), we have that $f(\langle a, b\rangle_{\Sigma x:A.B})$ computes to $g(a, b)$. For example, with Σ-types, a binary relation (i.e. a propositional function with two arguments) of type $\Pi x{:}A.(B[x] \to Prop)$ can be viewed as an 'equivalent' predicate of type $(\Sigma x{:}A.B[x]) \to Prop$.

Note that the formal objects for pairs in our language are 'heavily typed'. We use $\langle M, N\rangle_A$ instead of the usual untyped term $\langle M, N\rangle$. This avoids the undesirable type ambiguity which would make type inference and type checking difficult (perhaps impossible). For example, if untyped pairs were used, $\langle Type_0, Prop\rangle$ would have both $\Sigma X{:}Type_1.X$ and $Type_1 \times Type_0$ as its types which are incompatible.

The basic constructions that Σ-types provide are tuples which can be analysed by extracting their components. Based on this basic functionality, Σ-types provide a nice structuring mechanism in various pragmatic applications. In the presence of other type constructors (universes, in particular), Σ-types can be used as types of program modules or abstract structures, which are essential for modular programming, specification of abstract data types, and structured abstract reasoning in proof development. Furthermore, since propositions are also lifted to the predicative levels (see below), Σ-types in ECC can also be used to express the intuitionistic notion of 'subset' [Bis67, Kre68, ML75, ML84]; i.e. $\Sigma x{:}A.P[x]$ expresses the set of objects a of type A such that the proposition $P[a]$ holds, as from the intuitionistic point of view, to give an object of type A such that $P[a]$ is to give a together with a proof of $P[a]$.

2.2.5 Predicative universes and the reflection principle

Universes are special non-propositional types which have (names of) types as their objects. The underlying idea of introducing universes may be explained as follows. The development of a type theory is considered as a progressive process of grasping and understanding the conceptual universe of types. At a certain stage of the development of the language, certain types have been introduced and, after that, a universe may be introduced to collect some or all of the existing types into a totality by introducing (the names of) them as objects of the universe so that they can be talked about in general and used collectively. This was called by Martin-Löf as the *reflection principle* [ML75, ML84]. The introduction of such a universe is *predicative* in the sense that only the existing types are reflected, but not those types which are introduced afterwards. In particular, a predicative universe does not reflect itself—it does not have a name of itself, and it is not allowed to quantify over the universe to form an object in itself, either. After introducing a universe (and some other types), we may then add another (stronger) universe to reflect the existing types, including the previous universe. Such a development can continue to introduce infinitely many universes.

In ECC, besides the impredicative universe *Prop* of logical propositions to be explained below, we introduce predicative universes $Type_i$ $(i \in \omega)$ in such a way that the logical universe *Prop* is an object of $Type_0$ (by rule (Ax)) and $Type_i$ is an object of $Type_{i+1}$ (by rule (T)). Intuitively, viewing types as sets, we have

$$\text{(1)} \qquad Prop \in Type_0 \in Type_1 \in Type_2 \in \ldots .$$

Note that a universe is not an object of itself or any universe lower than it. With infinite universes, every object in ECC has a type and, in particular, types have universes as their types. Furthermore, any type that is reflected in a lower universe is also reflected in a higher universe; more precisely, by rule $(\preceq)$, every object of type *Prop* is an object of type $Type_0$ and every object of type $Type_i$ is an object of type $Type_{i+1}$. Intuitively, we have

(2) $$Prop \subseteq Type_0 \subseteq Type_1 \subseteq Type_2 \subseteq \ldots .$$

In general, one only works with finitely many universes. With universe inclusions, one can work uniformly in a universe large enough without worrying about indices of universes.

The universes $Type_i$ are predicatively closed under the formation of dependent product types and the strong sum types. According to rules $(\Pi 2)(\Sigma)$, for any type A in $Type_i$ and any family of types $B[x]$ in $Type_i$, $\Pi x{:}A.B[x]$ and $\Sigma x{:}A.B[x]$ are objects of type $Type_i$. In fact, because of the type inclusions between universes ((2) above), rules $(\Pi 2)(\Sigma)$ are the more economic expressions of the following rules:

$$\frac{\Gamma \vdash A : U \quad \Gamma, x{:}A \vdash B : U'}{\Gamma \vdash \Pi x{:}A.B : U_{max}} \qquad \frac{\Gamma \vdash A : U \quad \Gamma, x{:}A \vdash B : U'}{\Gamma \vdash \Sigma x{:}A.B : U_{max}}$$

where U and U' are arbitrary universes (including *Prop*), and $U_{max} \equiv max_{\preceq}\{Type_0, U, U'\}$ is the maximum universe among $Type_0, U$ and U' subject to the cumulativity relation $\preceq$. In other words, the dependent product/sum of any two types which are in universes lower than or the same with $Type_i$ is an object of $Type_i$. For example, $Type_0 \to Prop$ is of type $Type_i$ for $i \geq 1$ but not of type *Prop* or $Type_0$.

To emphasize, the universes $Type_i$ are predicative in the sense that there is no circularity in formations of non-propositional types. This predicativity will be made explicit formally in Section 4.2 and is essential for ECC to be logically consistent and not to suffer from logical paradox. In contrast, as to be explained below, the universe *Prop* of logical propositions is impredicative in the sense that propositions can be formed by quantifying over arbitrary types. If, for instance, $Type_0$ were similarly impredicative as *Prop* is, ECC would suffer Girard's paradox [Gir72, Coq86a] to become logically inconsistent.

It is our intention that in the predicative universes reside the types of computational objects, for example, Π-types of functional programs and Σ-types of program modules. In ECC, we have not yet considered various other data types such as types of natural numbers, lists, trees, etc., which will be introduced when we consider further extensions of the system in Chapter 9. In pragmatic uses, the reflection principle embodied in universes allows us to talk internally in the language about 'arbitrary types' of a certain class. This is an essential abstraction mechanism (predicative polymorphism) useful in applications such as describing abstract structures like program modules and parameterised specifications. It also allows the possibility of inductive definition of transfinite types when the language is further extended by other inductive types.

2.2.6 Propositions and the impredicative universe

In our language, propositions are logical formulas used to talk about and represent properties of the computational objects in the language. Inheriting the impredicative type structure from the calculus of constructions, our language has an internal intuitionistic higher-order logic, whose detailed description and properties will be discussed in Chapter 5. Here, we give a brief and informal discussion on several issues concerned about propositions and their role in the language.

The universe *Prop* is the logical universe where propositions reside; in other words, a proposition is (essentially) an object of type *Prop*. In type theory, according to the principle of propositions-as-types, propositions are viewed as (names of) types of proofs and provability of a proposition corresponds to the inhabitation of its proof type. In ECC, without distinguishing types from their names, proof types are not distinguished from propositions; a proposition is a type and it is provable if and only if it is inhabited.

The propositions in our language are formed by a single logical operator —the universal quantifier, represented by the type constructor Π. For any type A and any family of propositions $P[x]$ indexed by objects of type A, $\Pi x{:}A.P[x]$ (or we may better use another notation $\forall x{:}A.P[x]$) is a proposition, stating informally that 'for all objects a of type A, $P[a]$ holds'. The formation rule for propositions is (Π1):

$$(\Pi 1) \qquad \frac{\Gamma, x{:}A \vdash P : Prop}{\Gamma \vdash \Pi x{:}A.P : Prop}$$

A proof of proposition $\Pi x{:}A.P[x]$ is a function which given any object of type A, yields a proof of $P[a]$. The canonical proofs of $\Pi x{:}A.P[x]$ are just its canonical objects, as introduced by the introduction rule (λ), and the elimination rule for universal quantification is simply given by (*app*).[7] This gives an intuitionistic meaning to universal quantification.

Note that, different from rule (Π2) for formation of non-propositional Π-types, in the above rule (Π1) there is no restriction on A (except that it is a Γ-type). This reflects our intention of using propositions to describe *all* possible objects in the conceptual world of objects, that is, not only the objects that have been representable in our language but those to be introduced in the future. Also, it is worth mentioning that in our conception, logical propositions and their proofs are also objects in the conceptual world and can be reasoned about. For instance, we can quantify over the

[7] In ECC we do not distinguish the introduction and elimination operators for the non-propositional Π-types and the logical propositions. This is notationally more economic, but conceptually less clear. For such a distinction, see Chapter 9.

$$\begin{array}{rcl}
\forall x{:}A.P[x] & =_{\rm df} & \Pi x{:}A.P[x] \\
P_1 \supset P_2 & =_{\rm df} & \forall x{:}P_1.P_2 \\
\mathbf{true} & =_{\rm df} & \forall X{:}Prop.\ X \supset X \\
\mathbf{false} & =_{\rm df} & \forall X{:}Prop.X \\
P_1\ \&\ P_2 & =_{\rm df} & \forall X{:}Prop.\ (P_1 \supset P_2 \supset X) \supset X \\
P_1 \vee P_2 & =_{\rm df} & \forall X{:}Prop.\ (P_1 \supset X) \supset (P_2 \supset X) \supset X \\
\neg P_1 & =_{\rm df} & P_1 \supset \mathbf{false} \\
\exists x{:}A.P[x] & =_{\rm df} & \forall X{:}Prop.\ (\forall x{:}A.(P[x] \supset X)) \supset X \\
a =_A b & =_{\rm df} & \forall P{:}A \to Prop.\ P(a) \supset P(b)
\end{array}$$

Fig. 2.2. Definitions of logical operators in ECC.

proofs of a proposition to form propositions and describe properties of and reason about them.

Using the operator of universal quantification, we can define the other usual logical operators as in higher-order logic (cf. [Pra65, CH85]), including truth, falsity, implication, conjunction, disjunction, existential quantifier, and in particular, a notion of propositional equality, as given in Fig. 2.2. Note that most of the definitions are essentially the higher-order coding of the elimination rule for the corresponding logical operators; in other words, the definitions embody how the propositions formed by the logical operator are supposed to be used to infer further logical consequences. The notion of propositional equality is defined by the Leibniz principle, which says that two objects (of the same type A) are propositionally equal if and only if they are indiscernible from each other with respect to all predicates (logical properties). An equality reflection result (see Theorem 5.9) shows that (in the empty context) two objects are computationally equal if and only if they are provably equal under the Leibniz principle. For details and justifications of the adequacy of the definitions, see Chapter 5.

From the above, it is clear that in the language all of the propositions constitute a totality—the universe *Prop*. Likewise, there are *internal* notions of predicates and relations which form totalities represented by types of propositional functions; for example, the type of (internal) predicates over type A is $A \to Prop$ and the type of (internal) binary relations over A is $A \to A \to Prop$. This logical universe *Prop*, unlike the other universes $Type_i$, is *impredicative* in the sense that it is allowed to quantify over any type, including *Prop* itself and types of higher logical complexity such as types of predicates and higher universes etc., to form 'new' propositions in this very universe. For example, $\Pi X{:}Prop.X$ is a proposition. The circularity in such a formation of propositions is clear: $\Pi X{:}Prop.X$ is formed by quantifying over the type $Prop$ which has $\Pi X{:}Prop.X$ as its object. Therefore, propositions in the language have rather special status due to such an impredicative polymorphism. However, such a circularity in forming logical propositions, which represent one's conceptual descriptions of properties of objects of interest, is not in any way *vicious*. (This will be further discussed in Section 2.3.1.)

Although we have emphasized the distinction between logical propositions and 'ordinary' data types, the logical propositions in ECC are still regarded as data types, and the proofs of propositions as computational objects (programs). The idea is that propositions are data types and proofs are programs, *but not vice versa in general*. This is reflected in the decision of lifting every proposition into the predicative universes by imposing that

$$Prop \subseteq Type_0.$$

Furthermore, we have also regarded types of propositions, predicates, etc., as computational types as well; this is reflected in having $Prop$ as an object of $Type_0$. Therefore, we have not only included in the computational world the usual data types such as types of natural numbers, of functional programs, etc., but the 'logical' types. This reflects our intention of regarding, for example, program specifications and mathematical theorems as objects to be manipulated internally in the computational world. Such a decision seems to be justified by various application examples we are going to discuss, although there are alternatives which we shall discuss in Section 2.3.1 and Section 9.3.2.

2.2.7 Type equality and the cumulativity relation

The cumulativity relation $\preceq$ (Definition 2.3) is a partial order over terms with respect to conversion. It subsumes the conversion relation and reflects the type inclusions between universes, and hence embodies several design decisions (such as that proofs are programs). Splitting the cumulativity relation into conversion and strict cumulativity, the cumulativity rule ($\preceq$) in fact stands for the following two rules:

$$(conv) \qquad \frac{\Gamma \vdash M : A \quad \Gamma \vdash A' : Type_j}{\Gamma \vdash M : A'} \quad (A \simeq A')$$

$$(cum) \qquad \frac{\Gamma \vdash M : A \quad \Gamma \vdash A' : Type_j}{\Gamma \vdash M : A'} \quad (A \prec A')$$

The first may be called the *rule of type equality*, reflecting the idea that two inhabited types are equal if and only if they have the same objects. In other words, the computational equality, being intensional itself, induces an essentially extensional equality between types. We shall discuss this further in Section 2.3.3.

The rule of strict cumulativity (*cum*) generalises the universe inclusions coherently to Π-types and Σ-types. Because of the universe inclusions, a well-typed term may have different types which are not computationally equal. For example, the following terms

$$M \equiv \lambda X{:}Type_1.X \quad and \quad N \equiv \langle Type_0, Prop\rangle_{Type_1 \times Type_0}$$

have types $Type_1 \to Type_i$ for $i \geq 1$ and $Type_j \times Type_k$ for $j \geq 1$ and $k \geq 0$, respectively. However, the cumulativity relation allows us to define a simple notion of *principal type* (or the most general type) which characterises the set of types of any object in a simple way (see Definition 3.22 and Theorem 3.23). For example, the principal types of M and N above are $Type_1 \to Type_1$ and $Type_1 \times Type_0$, respectively.

The generalisation of universe inclusions to the other types clarifies the feature of type inclusions in a type system with universes and leads to a simple implementation of the type hierarchy of ECC. If one had introduced the universe inclusions directly without this generalisation (cf. [ML84, Coq86a]) by the following rules:

$$\frac{\Gamma \vdash A : Type_j}{\Gamma \vdash A : Type_{j+1}}$$

the minimum type of a well-typed term, although it exists [Luo88a], is sometimes not the most general one; for example, it would be easily shown by induction on derivations that, in such a system, $X{:}Type_0 \to Type_0 \not\vdash X : Type_0 \to Type_1$.

The cumulativity relation $\preceq$ is *not* completely contravariant when universe inclusions are generalised to Π-types: for $\Pi x{:}A_1.A_2$ to be less than or equal to $\Pi x{:}B_1.B_2$, A_1 is required to be *convertible* to B_1 instead of $B_1 \preceq A_1$. One may take the latter decision and the proof-theoretic properties will still hold. The only difference from the proof-theoretic point of view is that some terms would get more types. For example, $\lambda X{:}Type_1.X$ would not only have types $Type_1 \to Type_j$, but have $Prop \to Type_j$ and $Type_0 \to Type_j$ ($j \geq 1$) as its types as well. However, from a set-theoretic semantic point of view, the type inclusions with a cumulativity relation being completely contravariant would be reflected by coercions instead of by set inclusions if we think of functions as relations.

A final remark is that, in the cumulativity rule ($\preceq$), $A \preceq A'$ is a *side condition*, whose justification is not internally governed by the inference rules of the system. Such a treatment takes computation and the cumulativity relation as meta-level notions and is in accord with a computer implementation of the language where computing and testing whether two well-typed terms are computationally equal (or have the cumulativity relation) are automatedly carried out by the machine while programming and logical inference are controlled by the user interactively.

2.3 Further remarks and discussion

Having presented the language of ECC and given informal explanations of the meanings of its basic constructions, we are now in a position to discuss some philosophical and technical issues concerning the type structure we have considered above, and in particular, the design decisions we have made in the language of ECC and the intended uses of the language.

2.3.1 Data types vs. logical propositions

The relationship between logical propositions and data types in the particular type structure of our type theory (ECC and the type theory to be considered in Chapter 9) may be summarised as *propositions are data types, but not vice versa.* In the following, we discuss this topic, taking into the account of the more technical issues concerned with ECC.

The logical propositions in ECC reside in the logical universe *Prop*, while the non-propositional types in the predicative universes. In our conception, logic is independent on the existence of particular non-logical (e.g. computational) entities one may consider in a language. The logical operations, the universal quantification, and the other definable logical operations, have definite basic meanings which should be independent with the meanings of non-logical entities. In other words, some propositions are *pure logical truths* in the sense that they are true (or inhabited) essentially because of the very meanings[8] of the logical operations occurring in them, regardless of the properties of the non-logical entities involved. For example, the propositions such as

$$\forall X{:}Prop.(X \supset X), \quad \forall a{:}A.(\forall x{:}A.P[x]) \supset P[a], \quad \textit{and} \quad \forall x{:}A.(x =_A x)$$

are pure logical truths in the above sense. In particular, changing type A or predicate P above does not change the inhabitability of the last two propositions. The provable propositions in the language that are not purely logical are those whose inhabitance can only be shown by means of the particular properties of some of the non-logical entities involved. For instance, we do *not* regard the following as a pure logical truth:

[8] We have informally explained the meaning of universal quantification. For the other defined logical operations, see Section 5.1.

$$\forall x_1{:}A\forall x_2{:}A.(\pi_1(\langle x_1, x_2\rangle_{A\times A}) =_{A\times A} x_1),$$

since its inhabitance depends essentially on the meaning of the non-logical constant π_1 as given by the computation rules for the non-propositional type $A \times A$. Similarly, for a non-propositional type of natural numbers, the Peano axioms are provable (see Section 7.1.1), but they are not pure logical truths since their inhabitability depends on the particular computational theory of natural numbers. The possibility to consider a notion of pure logical truth is in accord with our conception of universality and independence of logic and will be further discussed in more detail in Chapter 9.

In regard to the type structure of the language, one may ask: *why* is the type structure organised in such a way? In particular, in order to achieve a conceptual distinction between logical propositions and computational data types, why should one conceive of the logical universe as impredicative but the non-logical entities predicatively? Concerning these questions, we should first remark that what we hope to deliver is *a particular* structure of types which is coherent in the sense that its structural harmony can be justified by means of meta-theoretic arguments and its usefulness justified in pragmatic applications, as we shall study in the following chapters. In other words, it may not be the only type structure that can realise the conceptual distinction, although we view that it is a coherent one. Having said that, it seems necessary to consider the naturality of the conception in structuring the conceptual universe of types in such a way and several remarks are needed.

Considering the computational world predicatively, the author is very much influenced by Martin-Löf. There are two relevant points to be made. First, it is our view that the computational objects and their types represent objects and types in the real world (of particular applications, for example). Second, we think that the conceptual universe of types is open and the real world of objects and its possible conceptual classifications can not be exhausted. Starting from the first point and recognising the second, it seems to be natural for one to consider the conceptual universe of types (and hence that of objects) as being gradually developed to capture or reflect the reality in a stepwise way and, at any stage of this development, one may only mentally know a part of the reality and construct the representations of that known part. This seems to imply that, when we try to understand collections of types, the only reasonable thing to do is to collect some of the types that are already known into a totality (formally, a universe). Therefore, we conceive of the computational world as reflected in the language predicatively, and in ECC, they reside in the predicative universes.

The matter becomes quite different when one considers the logical entities. In a formal language, the logical propositions, predicates, and relations are internal entities representing our thoughts about and mental descriptions of properties of (the representations of) objects in the real world. Intuitively and from the tradition of logic, we may argue that there is a province of logic where the essence of (deductive) reasoning is captured or reflected; in particular, the essential forms of reasoning are rather independent of the variety of real-world objects (and their representations). Therefore, it seems natural to think that the logical propositions constitute a totality[9] which has a fixed number of formation rules and whose understanding is based on the understanding of the forms and the meanings of the propositions. In particular, the general (or basic) understanding of the logical machinery is independent of the understanding of the particular non-logical entities (cf. the above discussion on pure logical truths). To summarise, from such a perspective, once a logic is chosen, the logical universe may be viewed as *relatively closed*[10] in the sense that the ways of formulating logical propositions are fixed and their basic understanding is general and essentially independent of the non-logical entities.

On the basis of such a consideration, it does not seem unnatural to conceive of second-order or higher-order logics as good candidates for the internal logical machinery, as embedded in ECC. The internal higher-order logic provides a useful logical power in reasoning. The impredicativity of the logical universe is not in disaccord with the independence of logic and its relative closedness. In particular, a logical formula can be formed by universal quantification over an arbitrary totality. It also allows impredicative definitions of logical properties to express our thoughts, and we argue, as Ramsey once did [Ram25], that such an impredicativity does not contain any vicious circle as conceived of by Russell. It should be noted that the impredicativity of the logical universe does give certain special status to the logical propositions in our language. A particular aspect is that they could not be understood as arbitrary sets, which pragmatically prevents us from considering *Prop* as the universe of data types (cf. the discussions in the Introduction and the problems with Σ-types to be discussed below).

As mentioned at the end of Section 2.2.6, in ECC we have incorporated a further relationship between logical propositions and the computational entities, that is, we have regarded logical propositions and large logical types ($Prop$, $A \to Prop$, etc.) as data types as well. These are reflected by $Prop \subseteq Type_0$ and $Prop : Type_0$, respectively. These two decisions

[9]The conception of having a totality of logical propositions is not new and at least goes back to Russell [Rus03] in his early work.

[10]The closedness is relative because there are 'new' propositions (but not new *forms* of propositions) when new entities are introduced into the open computational world. It is also worth remarking that the notion of closedness here is different from, although related to, the more formal notion of inductive closedness of universes which is realised by assuming an induction (elimination) rule for the universe.

reflect our intentions of considering proofs and entities such as program specifications as computational objects to be manipulated. One may argue that they somehow blur out the distinction between logical propositions and computational data types, although they are coherent with the idea that propositions (proofs) are types (programs) but not vice versa. We remark that it is possible and equally reasonable to make a further and sharper distinction between logical and non-logical entities by omitting either or both of the above commitments. We postpone this discussion to Chapter 9, where when logical framework is used to formulate the type theory, these choices and their mutual independence will become clearer.

Another small point concerning about the lifting of propositions into predicative universes is that it does not propagate the impredicativity of the logical universe into the predicative universes, although in appearance, we can now derive judgements such as

$$\vdash \Pi X{:}Type_j \Pi P{:}Type_j \to Prop.P(X) : Type_j.$$

The type hierarchy, except the lowest level *Prop*, is still stratified (predicative) in the sense that the types can be ranked in such a way that the formations of non-propositional types are only dependent on the types with lower ranks (see Section 4.2).

2.3.2 Σ-types and existential types

The Σ-types in ECC are *non-propositional* types. Different from Martin-Löf's type theory, they are not viewed as logical propositions; logical existential quantifier is represented by $\exists x{:}A.P[x]$ as defined in Fig. 2.2 rather than Σ-types. Based on our conception of universality and independence of logic, the more traditional logical operator $\exists$ is in our opinion more faithful in representing the notion of existential quantification. Furthermore, since propositions are lifted to higher universes, Σ-types in ECC can still be used to express the intuitionistic notion of subset (of object-proof pairs).

Here, we discuss the problem of considering strong sum as a propositional type constructor in impredicative type theories such as ECC and the relationship between Σ-types and various existential types (see below). First, there is a known problem for extending impredicative type theories by strong sum; that is, arbitrary strong sum is logically inconsistent with impredicativity. Adding arbitrary type-indexed Σ-types to the impredicative level of the calculus of constructions would produce an inconsistent system in which Girard's paradox can be derived. In other words, the following inference rule of introducing *large impredicative* Σ-types is problematic and, together with the rules for two projections, inconsistent with the impredicativity of *Prop*:

$$(*)\qquad \frac{\Gamma, x{:}A \vdash P : Prop}{\Gamma \vdash \Sigma x{:}A.P : Prop}$$

Bearing in mind that the impredicative system with *Prop* being an object of itself is logically inconsistent, we may consider a simple and intuitive (but informal) argument to see the problem of rule $(*)$: if $(*)$ were allowed, then we would be able to derive $\vdash \Sigma x{:}Prop.u : Prop$, where u stands for an inhabited proposition, say a proposition with only one proof. Then, since intuitively $\Sigma x{:}Prop.u$ is 'isomorphic' to *Prop*, we would essentially have *Prop* : *Prop*! For formal proofs of this paradox, see [Coq86a, HH86, ML72].

The paradoxical nature of large impredicative Σ-types shows that large Σ-types have essential structural differences with the logical propositions in the impredicative universe, and they should not be viewed as entities at the same level. For impredicative type systems like the calculus of constructions, especially when people want to use propositions in the impredicative universe to represent both logical formulas and data types, this appears to be a serious problem and has prevented people from using such Σ-types to express abstract structures such as abstract data types and abstract algebras, since the largeness is essential for such a purpose (in particular, one needs Σ-types of the form $\Sigma X{:}U.B(X)$ with U being a universe). However, the above paradox does *not* prevent us from having Σ-types as large types (non-propositional types) as we do for ECC; Σ-types in our language are essential to express program specifications and abstract mathematical theories.

Note that the Σ-types introduced by the above rule $(*)$ are 'large' in the sense that A may be a type whose logical complexity may be the same or higher than *Prop*. What if we restrict A to small types, i.e. propositions? If we add such a premise, we get the following rule for introducing *small* Σ-types:

$$(**)\qquad \frac{\Gamma \vdash A : Prop \quad \Gamma, x{:}A \vdash P : Prop}{\Gamma \vdash \Sigma x{:}A.P : Prop}$$

We do *not* have small Σ-types in ECC, either, although the extension by them is logically consistent. In our setting, we do not know of any use of small Σ-types as they could not play the role to express abstract structures and we would not intend to use strong sum as (strong) existential quantifier, either.

In fact, adding small Σ-types to ECC would result in a non-conservative extension to the internal logic, which has unexpected and undesirable side effects. This is due to a less known problem about the relationship between Σ-types and the weak existential types.[11] The problem can be stated generally in the following way. Let U and V be universes and $\exists_U$ be the

[11] I learned this from a discussion with Dr Stefano Berardi.

existential type constructor defined as (cf. the logical existential quantifier $\exists$ which is equivalent to $\exists_{Prop}$ with no restriction on V)

$$\begin{aligned}\exists_U \quad =_{\text{df}} \quad & \lambda A{:}V\ \lambda B{:}A \to U. \\ & \Pi C{:}U.(\Pi x{:}A.(B(x) \to C)) \to C.\end{aligned}$$

Then, for any type A in V and any type-valued function $B : A \to U$, in the presence of the strong sum type $\Sigma x{:}A.B(x)$ in universe U, $\exists_U(A, B)$ becomes strong in the sense that we can *define* two projection functions p_1 and p_2 for the weak existential type. In fact, we can define a function p from $\exists_U(A, B)$ to $\Sigma x{:}A.B(x)$ as

$$p(h) =_{\text{df}} h(\Sigma x{:}A.B(x),\ \lambda x{:}A\lambda y{:}B(x).\langle x, y\rangle_{\Sigma x:A.B(x)}),$$

and take $p_1(h) =_{\text{df}} \pi_1(p(h))$ and $p_2(h) =_{\text{df}} \pi_2(p(h))$. In the case of small Σ-types, taking V to be *Prop*, we would have that the logical existential quantifier becomes strong when its quantification domain is a proposition; in other words, information hiding of the witnesses would be lost.

The above general argument also shows that, in ECC, when A is in $Type_i$, $\exists_{Type_i}(A, B)$ (in universe $Type_{i+1}$) is in fact equivalent to a strong sum type and cannot be used for information hiding. However, as considered in [Luo90a], when A is of the same or higher complexity than U, for example when A is U, the existential types such as $\exists_U(U, B)$ can be used for information hiding as considered in [MP85] for the second-order λ-calculus. It is easy to check that, in such a case, the projection functions for the existential type defined as above fail to be well-typed.

2.3.3 Equalities: intensionality vs. extensionality

Equality is one of the most important constructions in the study of logics and formal systems for formalisation of mathematics. In particular, the problem concerning the extensionality or intensionality of equality has been of long-standing interest in the research of logical systems. The issues about equality are equally and perhaps more important in studying computational languages, since the notion of computation is most central here and a faithful and correct characterisation of the notion of computational equality is essential. As we are interested in reasoning about the computational behaviour of programs, it is also necessary to have the corresponding logical notion of equality that faithfully reflects the computational equality.

The notion of computational equality in our language is intensional; two objects are equal if and only if they have the same meaning, that is, they have the same value, as explained in Section 2.2.1. The intensionality of computational equality reflects the idea that computation is a mechanizable process. From a computational point of view, the computational equality between objects (say, natural numbers, functions of Π-types) should be intensional. By this, we mean that neither the strong extensionality (for example, formulated by the strong equality types in [ML84]) nor the weak extensionality as expressed by the η-equality rules should be viewed as computational. The intensionality of the theory is important in at least two aspects. In our view, an extensional equality does not capture the notion of computation adequately, while the intensional equality does. Furthermore, when we have a suitable intensional notion of computational equality (and computation), it is easier to obtain a good operational understanding of the language.

To understand intensionality of the computational equality, we need to understand the notion of extensionality and in what sense the computational equality is not extensional. The notion of extensionality of equality concerns equality between functions, that is, in our language, objects of Π-types. In general, a notion of equality is extensional if for any functions f and g of the same type, f equals g provided that $f(a)$ and $g(a)$ are equal for every object a of the (common) domain type. The computational equality is not extensional in this sense. For instance, the binary numerical functions $add_1 =_{\mathrm{df}} \lambda x{:}N\lambda y{:}N.x + y$ and $add_2 =_{\mathrm{df}} \lambda x{:}N\lambda y{:}N.y + x$ return the same value for every two natural numbers m and n, but they are not computationally equal as they in fact are themselves different values.

Why is an extensional equality interesting? The above notion of extensionality comes from the desire of considering propositional functions (predicates and relations) as representing sets (or classes, cf. [WR25, Ram25, Chu40]). In classical mathematics, two sets are equal if and only if they have the same elements. Representing sets as propositional functions (as the characterisation functions), it would be natural and necessary to consider that two propositional functions are equal if they have the same truth value (either true or false) for every argument. For instance, two propositional functions over natural numbers expressing respectively, for any number x, 'x is an even prime' and 'x is identical to 2', are extensionally equal (have the same truth value), although they have different meanings. Different from such a use of propositional functions, in our language propositional functions are *not* meant to be used to represent sets; they represent (intensional) properties of objects. Therefore, it does not make sense to consider extensionally equal functions as identical. Furthermore, as explained above, the nature of computation requires an intensional treatment of computational equality and it is our view that computational equality should be intensional.

However, this does not mean that the notion of equality between types is non-extensional subject to what objects they have. As types are objects, two types are computationally equal if and only if they compute to the same value. But, since types are special objects which may be inhabited, there is a further (extensional) meaning attached to type equality, that is, *that two types are computationally equal means that they have the same objects.* This meaning of type equality is formally reflected in the inference rule ($\preceq$), which has the following rule of type equality as a special case:

$$(conv) \qquad \frac{\Gamma \vdash M : A \quad \Gamma \vdash B : Type_j}{\Gamma \vdash M : B} \quad (A \simeq B)$$

In particular, if two types are computationally equal, they have the same objects. It would also be natural to ask whether the converse is true, i.e. is it the case that two types having the same objects are necessarily computationally equal? To this question, the answer is 'yes', as soon as the types concerned are inhabited (see Theorem 3.26). (In the language, there are non-inhabited types which are not computationally equal, although they may be regarded to have 'the same objects' as they have none.) The extensionality of type equality is essential in using data types to formalise mathematical and computational structures.

The notion of computational equality in our language is not even weakly extensional in the sense that the η-equalities such as $\lambda x{:}A.f(x) \simeq f$ if $x \notin FV(f)$ and $\langle \pi_1(M), \pi_2(M) \rangle_A \simeq M$ do not hold in general. The meanings of such equality rules should in fact be understood as saying that every Γ-object of certain type is equal to a canonical Γ-object (if one reads the rules from the right to the left). We do not regard these as computational rules. Furthermore, it should be clear by the normalisation theorem that for objects (with no free variables), the above rules do hold. It may also be worth remarking a technical point, although it is not the reason that we omit them: such η-rules are incompatible in dependent type theories with type inclusions. Either of the above rules would make the Church-Rosser property fail to hold (see Section 3.1).

So far, we have only discussed the notion of computational equality. Since Frege, equality has been considered as a basic logical operator to form logical propositions. In type theory, the distinction and connection between computational equality and propositional equality are important issues. As computational equality is not propositional, it is important that one should be able to describe and reason about the notion of computational equality in the internal logic of the language. The Leibniz equality does have this property. It reflects the computational equality in the sense that every two objects are computationally equal if and only if they are provably Leibniz equal. This implies that the Leibniz equality is also intensional. (See Section 5.1.3.)

The formulation of Π-types and Σ-types as given in ECC has some defects in that the elimination operators are not strong enough to allow the η-rules to be logically provable in general (e.g. in the sense of the Leibniz equality). We shall come to these points in Chapter 9.

2.3.4 Decidability issues

Various issues of decidability about the type theory are closely related to the design decisions made in its development. The particular decidability problems of interest include those concerning the decidability of

1. the computational equality (and the cumulativity relation),
2. type checking (the correctness or derivability of judgements),
3. the well-typedness of a term in a context, and
4. the inhabitability of types.

Since in our presentation the computational equality and the cumulativity relation are defined for terms which are not necessarily well-typed, none of them is decidable for arbitrary terms. However, in the language, they only play an essential role for well-typed terms, and in this case, that they are decidable follows easily from the Church-Rosser and strong normalisation properties (Lemma 5.11). That computational equality is decidable is in accord with our understanding that computation is mechanizable and computational equality should be intensional. (An extensional equality would be undecidable.)

The second problem of decidability, that of type checking, corresponds to the problem of proof-checking in logical systems, i.e. whether a given proof is indeed a proof of a given proposition. As a well-formulated system, this should be decidable. In fact, this is also a most important property to implement a proof-checker for interactive theorem proving. Type checking is decidable for our language. This is a consequence of the positive answer of the third and the first decidability problems. In fact, there is a simple algorithm for type inference, i.e. given any term and any context, the algorithm checks whether the term is well-typed in the context, and if so, it computes the principal type of the term in the context (Definition 5.12 and Theorem 5.13).

The problem of whether any given type is inhabited is obviously undecidable, as it corresponds to the problem of deciding whether any proposition is provable.

2.3.5 On the use of the type theory

As a formal system, the language of the type theory presented in this monograph may be used in different ways in different applications. However, in this monograph, we emphasize an intended use of it, that is, the use as a uniform computational language for programming, specification, and reasoning, where the basic computational or mathematical structures are supposed to be introduced into the language as (non-propositional) inductive data types such as Π-types, Σ-types and the type of natural numbers (see Section 7.1 and Chapter 9), which may be called *computational theories*, as opposed to the traditional notion of logical (axiomatic) theories. The internal higher-order logic provides means of describing and reasoning about the objects in the language. The computational use emphasized here is different from the use of type theory as a pure logical system (higher-order logic in the case of ECC), where one formalises mathematical theories as contexts which consist of declarations of symbols and assumptions of logical axioms. Note that the computational use is in accord with the conceptions about type theory as explained in the above sections and reflects the advantages of type theory as a computational language (rather than a pure logical system). First of all, it is the computational features that allow us to use type theory as a programming language. Furthermore, in the computational use, one can understand the language of type theory by its operational semantics, as informally explained above. However, emphasizing the computational use is by no means to render the type theory as 'logic-free' in the sense that logic is of no or less use. On the contrary, the rich type structure (in particular, Π-types, Σ-types and universes) and the strong internal logic also allow one to consider interesting applications to computer science such as structured specifications of programs, modular program development, and abstract reasoning (see, for example, Chapter 8 and Section 7.2).

The proof development system Lego

An obvious direct application of type theory is in interactive theorem proving, an interesting application closely related to the study of programming methodology where people want to develop tools to support verification of crucial properties of programs. Various proof development systems have been developed based on type theories to support the formalisation of mathematical problems and reasoning about them. These include, to mention a few, Automath [dB80], NuPRL [C^+86], ALF [ACN90], Coq [D^+91], and Lego [Pol89, LP92].

Lego is an interactive proof development system (proof checker) designed and implemented by Randy Pollack in Edinburgh [Pol89, LP92]. It implements several related type systems—the Edinburgh Logical Framework [HHP87], the calculus of constructions [CH88], and the Extended Calculus of Constructions, as presented in this monograph. Lego is a powerful tool for interactive proof development in the natural deduction style and supports refinement proof as a basic operation and a definitional mechanism to introduce definitional abbreviations. The system design of Lego emphasizes removing the more tedious aspects of interactive proofs. For example, algorithms are implemented in the system to support argument synthesis [Pol90a, CH88] and universe polymorphism [Pol90a, HP91, Hue87] which make proof development more practical. In particular, the feature of universe polymorphism allows the user to omit the universe levels in ECC to write *Type* instead of $Type_i$. With such a facility, to assume $X{:}Type$ in a context is in some sense equivalent to assume that X be an arbitrary type. One can also quantify over *Type* to talk about 'all types', bearing in mind that it is the machine who does the work to avoid universe circularity (by giving an error message when it occurs). Lego also allows the user to specify new inductive data types (computational theories), which supports the computational use of the type theory as explained above. The inductive data types described in Chapter 9 have been implemented in Lego by Claire Jones.

The implementation of ECC in Lego has in a great deal enhanced the use and understanding of the type theory and is very important both in practical applications such as development of programs and proofs (e.g. all of the examples and propositions in Chapter 8 have been formally developed and proved in Lego) and in theoretical studies of type theory (e.g. we have used the implementation of the Edinburgh LF in Lego to testify formally many ideas to be explained in Chapter 9). Of course, implementations of type theories in proof development systems are not particularly oriented to programming and program specification. In order to develop type theory into a language for real application of programming and program development, there are a lot of implementation (and theoretical) issues to be further studied.

3

Basic meta-theoretic properties

This chapter studies the basic meta-theoretic properties of the language of ECC. We first consider the Church-Rosser theorem about the notion of computation and the basic properties of the cumulativity relation. Properties about derivable judgements and some important admissibility results for derivability are proved in Section 3.2. In Section 3.3, a notion of principal type characterising the type cumulativity in the language is studied and the extensionality of type equality is proved.

3.1 Church-Rosser theorem and cumulativity

The Church-Rosser theorem shows that computationally equal (convertible) terms can always be computed (reduced) to a common term, and therefore guarantees the uniqueness of the vlaue (normal form) of any term.

Theorem 3.1. ***(Church-Rosser theorem)*** *If $M_1 \simeq M_2$, then there exists M such that $M_1 \rhd M$ and $M_2 \rhd M$.*

Proof sketch By the definition of conversion, we only have to show that reduction has the diamond property, i.e. if $M \rhd M_1$ and $M \rhd M_2$, then $M_1 \rhd M'$ and $M_2 \rhd M'$ for some M'. Following [ML72], we give a proof sketch of the diamond property as follows.[12]

1. Definitions:

   (a) *Parallel one-step reduction:* $M \rhd^1 N$ if and only if N is got by contracting some (possibly all or none) of the redexes in M, starting from within and proceeding outwards.

[12]Martin-Löf in [ML72] refers to Tait for the basic ideas of the proof. Similar proofs for simpler λ-calculi can be found in other places, e.g. Appendix 1 of [HS87].

(b) *Parallel n-step reduction:* $M \rhd^0 N$ if and only if $M \equiv N$; $M \rhd^{n+1} N$ if and only if $M \rhd^n M' \rhd^1 N$ for some M'.

Note that $M \rhd N$ if and only if $M \rhd^n N$ for some $n \in \omega$.

2. Lemma: $M \rhd^1 M'$ implies $[N/x]M \rhd^1 [N/x]M'$. (Obvious by the definition of $\rhd^1$.)
3. Lemma: If $M \rhd^1 M_1$ and $M \rhd^1 M_2$, then $M_1 \rhd^1 M'$ and $M_2 \rhd^1 M'$ for some M'. (By induction on the structure of M and using the above lemma.)
4. Lemma: If $M \rhd^m M_1$ and $M \rhd^n M_2$, then $M_1 \rhd^n M'$ and $M_2 \rhd^m M'$ for some M'. (By $m \times n$ times applications of the above lemma.)

From the last lemma above, the diamond property for reduction holds, and hence the theorem. □

Corollary 3.2. (uniqueness of normal forms) *The normal form of a term is unique (up to the syntactical identity $\equiv$), if it exists.*

Remark Note that ECC does *not* include the η-contraction scheme

$$(\eta) \qquad \lambda x{:}A.Mx \leadsto_\eta M \quad (x \notin FV(M)),$$

or the contraction scheme of surjective pairing

$$(\pi) \qquad \langle \pi_1(M), \pi_2(M)\rangle_A \leadsto_\pi M,$$

either of which would make the Church-Rosser property fail to hold [vD80, Klo80]. The examples to show this would be, with $A \not\preceq B$,

$$\lambda x{:}A.(\lambda x{:}B.x)x \quad and \quad \langle \pi_1(\langle a,a\rangle_{A\times A}), \pi_2(\langle a,a\rangle_{A\times A})\rangle_{B\times B}.$$

The first would reduce to $\lambda x{:}A.x$ by (β) and to $\lambda x{:}B.x$ by (η); the second would reduce to $\langle a,a\rangle_{B\times B}$ by (σ) and to $\langle a,a\rangle_{A\times A}$ by (π). It is also worth remarking that, with either of them, Church-Rosser even fails for well-typed terms of ECC because of the existence of type inclusions induced by universes. In fact, whenever $x{:}A \vdash x : B$ and $\vdash a : A$, the above two terms are well-typed.

In the rest of this section, we prove the existence of the cumulativity relation as defined in Definition 2.3 and some of its properties. We will show in Section 3.3 that the cumulativity relation does characterise the type cumulativity in the language.

We first give an inductive definition of a binary relation over terms which will be shown to be the cumulativity relation as defined in Definition 2.3.

Definition 3.3. (cumulativity relation: inductive definition) *Let $\preceq_i \subseteq \mathcal{T} \times \mathcal{T}$ $(i \in \omega)$ be the relations over terms inductively defined as follows:*

1. *$A \preceq_0 B$ if and only if one of the following holds:*
   - *(a) $A \simeq B$; or*
   - *(b) $A \simeq Prop$ and $B \simeq Type_j$ for some $j \in \omega$; or*
   - *(c) $A \simeq Type_j$ and $B \simeq Type_k$ for some $j < k$.*
2. *$A \preceq_{i+1} B$ if and only if one of the following holds:*
   - *(a) $A \preceq_i B$; or*
   - *(b) $A \simeq \Pi x{:}A_1.A_2$ and $B \simeq \Pi x{:}B_1.B_2$ for some $A_1 \simeq B_1$ and $A_2 \preceq_i B_2$; or*
   - *(c) $A \simeq \Sigma x{:}A_1.A_2$ and $B \simeq \Sigma x{:}B_1.B_2$ for some $A_1 \preceq_i B_1$ and $A_2 \preceq_i B_2$.*

Define $\preceq$ as

$$\preceq \;=_{\mathrm{df}}\; \bigcup_{i \in \omega} \preceq_i .$$

And, $A \prec B$ $(A \prec_i B)$ if and only if $A \preceq B$ $(A \preceq_i B)$ and $A \not\simeq B$.

We show below that $\preceq$ defined above is the smallest binary relation over terms such that the four conditions in Definition 2.3 are satisfied; in other words, the above is in fact an alternative definition of the cumulativity relation (Corollary 3.7).

Lemma 3.4. *Let $\preceq$ be the relation defined by Definition 3.3. Then, $A \preceq B$ if and only if one of the following holds:*

- *$A \preceq_0 B$;*
- *$A \simeq \Pi x{:}A_1.A_2$ and $B \simeq \Pi x{:}B_1.B_2$ for some $A_1 \simeq B_1$ and $A_2 \preceq B_2$;*
- *$A \simeq \Sigma x{:}A_1.A_2$ and $B \simeq \Sigma x{:}B_1.B_2$ for some $A_1 \preceq B_1$ and $A_2 \preceq B_2$.*

Remark We may define a relation $\approx$ between terms as follows: $A \approx B$ if and only if there exists a sequence of terms $M_0, ..., M_n$ such that $A \equiv M_0$, $B \equiv M_n$, and $M_i \preceq M_{i+1}$ or $M_{i+1} \preceq M_i$ for $0 \leq i < n$. Then, the relationship between $\approx$ and $\preceq$ is similar to that between $\simeq$ and $\rhd$. Lemma 3.4 implies that, if $A \approx B$, then A and B have the same *sort* of forms up to conversion.

The following lemma will be used to prove that the relation defined in Definition 3.3 is a partial order (Lemma 3.6) and that the cumulativity relation is well-founded (Corollary 3.8).

Lemma 3.5. *Let A, B, C and D be terms, $i \in \omega$, and $\preceq$ be the relation defined in Definition 3.3. If $D \preceq A \prec_i B \preceq C$, then $D \preceq_i A$ and $B \preceq_i C$.*

Proof By induction on $i \in \omega$ and the Church-Rosser theorem. See [Luo90a] for details. □

Lemma 3.6. *The relation $\preceq$ defined in Definition 3.3 is a partial order with respect to conversion; that is,*

1. *if $A \simeq B$, then $A \preceq B$,*
2. *if $A \preceq B$ and $B \preceq A$, then $A \simeq B$, and*
3. *if $A \preceq B$ and $B \preceq C$, then $A \preceq C$.*

Proof We only have to show that every $\preceq_i$ is a partial order with respect to conversion. By induction on i. The base case for $\preceq_0$ can readily be verified. Consider $\preceq_{k+1}$. Reflexivity is obvious from Definition 3.3. The proofs of its anti-symmetry and transitivity with respect to conversion are similar; we consider only the case for anti-symmetry here.

Suppose $A \preceq_{k+1} B$ and $B \preceq_{k+1} A$. As $A \preceq_{k+1} B$, we have two cases to consider.

1. $A \preceq_k B$;
2. $A \not\preceq_k B$ and $A \prec_{k+1} B$.

For the first case, either $A \simeq B$ or $A \prec_k B$, and we have $B \preceq_k A$ by the definition of $\preceq_k$ and Lemma 3.5. Therefore, $A \simeq B$, by induction hypothesis. For the second case, $A \simeq Qx{:}A_1.A_2$ and $B \simeq Qx{:}B_1.B_2$ for some $Q \in \{\Pi, \Sigma\}$, A_i and B_i such that

- $A_1 \simeq B_1$ and $A_2 \prec_k B_2$, if $Q \equiv \Pi$,
- $A_1 \prec_k B_1$ and $A_2 \preceq_k B_2$, or $A_1 \preceq_k B_1$ and $A_2 \prec_k B_2$, if $Q \equiv \Sigma$.

By the Church-Rosser theorem and Lemma 3.5, the assumption $B \preceq_{k+1} A$ is also due to the same reason, i.e. $B \simeq Qx{:}B_1'.B_2'$ and $A \simeq Qx{:}A_1'.A_2'$ for some $B_1' \begin{cases} \simeq A_1' & \text{if } Q \equiv \Pi \\ \preceq_k A_1' & \text{if } Q \equiv \Sigma \end{cases}$ and $B_2' \preceq_k A_2'$. By the Church-Rosser theorem, $A_j \simeq A_j'$ and $B_j \simeq B_j'$ $(j = 1, 2)$, and hence, $B_1 \begin{cases} \simeq A_1 & \text{if } Q \equiv \Pi \\ \preceq_k A_1 & \text{if } Q \equiv \Sigma \end{cases}$ and $B_2 \preceq_k A_2$. By induction hypothesis, $A_j \simeq B_j$ $(j = 1, 2)$ and hence $A \simeq B$. □

Corollary 3.7. *The relation $\preceq$ defined in Definition 3.3 is the smallest partial order over terms with respect to conversion such that*

1. *$Prop \preceq Type_0 \preceq Type_1 \preceq ...$;*
2. *if $A \simeq A'$ and $B \preceq B'$, then $\Pi x{:}A.B \preceq \Pi x{:}A'.B'$;*
3. *if $A \preceq A'$ and $B \preceq B'$, then $\Sigma x{:}A.B \preceq \Sigma x{:}A'.B'$.*

Proof By Lemma 3.6, $\preceq$ is a partial order w.r.t. conversion and it obviously satisfies the three conditions. For minimality, suppose $R \subseteq \mathcal{T} \times \mathcal{T}$ to be a partial order w.r.t. conversion satisfying the conditions. We only have to show that $\preceq_i \subseteq R$ for every $i \in \omega$, which can easily be done by induction on i. □

Remark Definition 3.3 and the above corollary show that the cumulativity relation (Definition 2.3) is well-defined; in other words, Definition 3.3 gives an alternative inductive definition of the cumulativity relation.

Using Lemmas 3.5 and 3.4, we can also show that the cumulativity relation is well-founded.

Corollary 3.8. (well-foundedness of $\preceq$) *The cumulativity relation $\preceq$ is well-founded in the sense that there is no infinite decreasing sequence of the form $A_0 \succ A_1 \succ A_2 \succ ...$.*

Proof If there exists an infinite sequence $A_0 \succ A_1 \succ A_2 \succ ...$, we have by Lemma 3.5, $A_0 \succ_i A_1 \succ_i A_2 \succ_i ...$ for some $i \in \omega$. So, we only have to show that $\preceq_i$ is well-founded for every $i \in \omega$.

By induction on i. $\preceq_0$ is obviously well-founded. Consider $\preceq_{i+1}$. If $A \succ_{i+1} B$, then there are three possibilities:

1. $A \succ_i B$,
2. $A \simeq \Pi x{:}A_1.A_2$ and $B \simeq \Pi x{:}B_1.B_2$ for some $A_1 \simeq B_1$ and $A_2 \succ_i B_2$, or
3. $A \simeq \Sigma x{:}A_1.A_2$ and $B \simeq \Sigma x{:}B_1.B_2$ for some A_1, A_2, B_1 and B_2 such that, $A_1 \succ_i B_1$ and $A_2 \succeq_i B_2$, or $A_1 \succeq_i B_1$ and $A_2 \succ_i B_2$.

For the first case, there is no infinite decreasing sequence starting from $A \succ B$ by induction hypothesis and Lemma 3.5. For the second case, by Lemma 3.4, every component of a decreasing $\succ_{i+1}$-sequence starting from $A \succ B$ is convertible to a term of Π-form. Hence, if such a sequence is infinite, there must be an infinite decreasing sequence starting from $A_2 \succ B_2$, which is impossible by induction hypothesis and Lemma 3.5. The third case for Σ can be similarly proved. Hence, every $\preceq_i$ is well-founded and so is $\preceq$ by Lemma 3.5. □

3.2 Derivable judgements and derivability

Shown in this section and the next are the basic properties of ECC. We show in this section that, if a judgement $\Gamma \vdash M : A$ is derivable, where $\Gamma \equiv x_1{:}A_1, ..., x_n{:}A_n$, then

- $\Gamma^i \equiv x_1{:}A_1, ..., x_i{:}A_i$ $(i = 1, ..., n)$ are valid contexts (by Lemma 3.11);
- A and A_i are types in contexts Γ and Γ^{i-1}, respectively (by Lemma 3.9 and Theorem 3.15);
- the variables $x_1, ..., x_n$ are distinct, the free variables in M and A are among $x_1, ..., x_n$ and those in A_i are among $x_1, ..., x_{i-1}$ (Lemma 3.10).

These give us a better understanding of the forms of derivable judgements.

We also show that the following operations on derivable judgements are admissible in the sense that they preserve the derivability of judgements:

- Context replacement by $B \preceq A$ (Lemma 3.13);
- Type-preserving substitution or Cut (Theorem 3.14);
- Subject reduction (Theorem 3.16);
- Weakening and strengthening (Lemmas 3.12 and 3.17).

These provide us important admissible rules[13] which not only enable one to obtain a better understanding of the language (derivability, in particular) but also allow one to use them in implementations of the language.

The following three lemmas (Lemmas 3.9 to 3.11) concern the context in any derivable judgement. Their proofs are straightforward by induction on derivations[14].

[13] A rule R of the form $\frac{J_1 \; \dots \; J_n}{J}$ is *admissible* if J is derivable whenever $J_1, ..., J_n$ are.

[14] We will say 'by induction on derivations (of ...)' to mean 'by induction on the lengths of derivations (of ...)'.

Lemma 3.9. *Any derivation of* $\Gamma, x{:}A, \Gamma' \vdash M : B$ *has a subderivation*[15] *of* $\Gamma \vdash A : Type_j$ *for some* j*.*

Lemma 3.10. (free variables) *Suppose* $\Gamma \vdash M : A$*. Then,*

1. $FV(M) \cup FV(A) \subseteq FV(\Gamma)$*, and*
2. Γ *has the form* $x_1{:}A_1, ..., x_n{:}A_n$ *such that* $x_1, ..., x_n$ *are distinct and* $FV(A_i) \subseteq \{x_1, ..., x_{i-1}\}$ *for* $i = 1, ..., n$*.*

Lemma 3.11. (context validity) *Any derivation of* $\Gamma, \Gamma' \vdash M : A$ *has a subderivation of* $\Gamma \vdash Prop : Type_0$*.*

The following weakening lemma expresses the monotonicity of the calculus, i.e. postulating more assumptions does not invalidate provable results.

Lemma 3.12. (weakening) *If* $\Gamma \vdash M : A$ *and* Γ' *is a valid context which contains every component of* Γ*, then* $\Gamma' \vdash M : A$*.*

Proof By induction on derivations. For the rules other than $(\Pi 1)(\lambda)$, apply induction hypothesis and the same rule. For $(\Pi 1)(\lambda)$, use Lemma 3.9 and then similar. □

The following lemma shows that replacing an assumption in the context of a judgement by a computationally equal or cumulatively stronger assumption preserves the derivability.

Lemma 3.13. (context replacement) *If* $\Gamma, x{:}A, \Gamma' \vdash M : C$ *and* $B \preceq A$ *is a* Γ*-type, then* $\Gamma, x{:}B, \Gamma' \vdash M : C$*.*

Proof By induction on derivations of $\Gamma, x{:}A, \Gamma' \vdash M : C$. The only two non-trivial cases are rule (C) and rule (var). For rule (C), we have two possibilities:

1. $\Gamma' \equiv \Gamma_1', y{:}A_1$, $M \equiv Prop$ and $C \equiv Type_0$:

$$\frac{\Gamma, x{:}A, \Gamma_1' \vdash A_1 : Type_j}{\Gamma, x{:}A, \Gamma_1', y{:}A_1 \vdash Prop : Type_0}$$

   with $y \notin FV(\Gamma, x{:}A, \Gamma_1')$. By induction hypothesis, $\Gamma, x{:}B, \Gamma_1' \vdash A_1 : Type_j$. By Lemma 3.10, $y \notin FV(\Gamma, x{:}B, \Gamma_1')$. So, applying (C) suffices.

[15] If $J_1, ..., J_n$ is a derivation, it has $J_1, ..., J_i$ $(1 \leq i \leq n)$ as its subderivation.

2. $\Gamma' \equiv \langle\rangle$:

$$\frac{\Gamma \vdash A : Type_j}{\Gamma, x{:}A \vdash Prop : Type_0}$$

with $x \notin FV(\Gamma)$. As B is a Γ-type, $\Gamma \vdash B : Type_j$ for some j. Applying (C) suffices.

For rule (var), with $M \equiv x$ and $C \equiv A$,

$$\frac{\Gamma, x{:}A, \Gamma' \vdash Prop : Type_0}{\Gamma, x{:}A, \Gamma' \vdash x : A}$$

By induction hypothesis, $\Gamma, x{:}B, \Gamma' \vdash Prop : Type_0$. By rule (var), $\Gamma, x{:}B, \Gamma' \vdash x : B$. As A is a Γ-type by Lemma 3.9, we have by Weakening (Lemma 3.12) that A is a $(\Gamma, x{:}B, \Gamma')$-type. Hence, $\Gamma, x{:}B, \Gamma' \vdash x : A$ by rule $(\preceq)$ as $B \preceq A$. □

The following theorem shows that a type-preserving substitution preserves the derivability of a judgement. As we indicated in Section 2.2.2, it is an important property based on which the meaning of hypothetical judgements is understood and explained.

Theorem 3.14. (cut) *If $\Gamma, x{:}N, \Gamma' \vdash P : A$ and $\Gamma \vdash M : N$, then $\Gamma, [M/x]\Gamma' \vdash [M/x]P : [M/x]A$.*

Proof By induction on derivations of $\Gamma, x{:}N, \Gamma' \vdash P : A$. Here, we only check the rules (var), $(\Pi 1)$ and $(pair)$. The other cases are simpler or similar. For rule (var), with $\Gamma, x{:}N, \Gamma' \equiv \Gamma_1, y{:}B, \Gamma_2$,

$$\frac{\Gamma_1, y{:}B, \Gamma_2 \vdash Prop : Type_0}{\Gamma_1, y{:}B, \Gamma_2 \vdash y : B}$$

there are two cases:

1. $x{:}N \equiv y{:}B$, $\Gamma \equiv \Gamma_1$ and $\Gamma' \equiv \Gamma_2$. By Lemma 3.10, $x \notin FV(N)$. So, we only have to show $\Gamma, [M/x]\Gamma' \vdash M : N$. This is true by induction hypothesis and Weakening (Lemma 3.12), as $\Gamma \vdash M : N$.

2. $x{:}N$ occurs in Γ_1 or Γ_2. By induction hypothesis, $\Gamma, [M/x]\Gamma' \vdash Prop : Type_0$. As $x \not\equiv y$ by Lemma 3.10, $\Gamma, [M/x]\Gamma'$ contains the component $y{:}[M/x]B$. So, an application of rule (var) yields the result.

For rule ($\Pi 1$), with $P \equiv \Pi x{:}P_1.P_2$ and $A \equiv Prop$,

$$\frac{\Gamma, x{:}N, \Gamma', y{:}P_1 \vdash P_2 : Prop}{\Gamma, x{:}N, \Gamma' \vdash \Pi x{:}P_1.P_2 : Prop}$$

As $x \not\equiv y$ by Lemma 3.10, $\Gamma, [M/x]\Gamma', y{:}[M/x]P_1 \vdash [M/x]P_2 : Prop$ by induction hypothesis. By rule ($\Pi 1$), $\Gamma, [M/x]\Gamma' \vdash \Pi y{:}[M/x]P_1.[M/x]P_2 : Prop$. Since M is a Γ-object, $y \notin FV(M)$ by Lemma 3.10. So, $\Gamma, [M/x]\Gamma' \vdash [M/x]\Pi x{:}P_1.P_2 : Prop$ as required.

For rule (*pair*), (write Γ_1 for $\Gamma, x{:}N, \Gamma'$,)

$$\frac{\Gamma_1 \vdash M_1 : A_1 \quad \Gamma_1 \vdash N_1 : [M_1/y]B_1 \quad \Gamma_1, y{:}A_1 \vdash B_1 : Type_j}{\Gamma_1 \vdash \langle M_1, N_1 \rangle_{\Sigma y:A_1.B_1} : \Sigma y{:}A_1.B_1}$$

Note that $x \not\equiv y$ and $x \notin FV(M)$ by Lemma 3.10. By induction hypothesis, we have

$$\Gamma, [M/x]\Gamma' \vdash [M/x]M_1 : [M/x]A_1$$
$$\Gamma, [M/x]\Gamma' \vdash [M/x]N_1 : [M/x][M_1/x]B_1$$
$$\Gamma, [M/x]\Gamma', y{:}[M/x]A_1 \vdash [M/x]B_1 : Type_j$$

Noticing that $[M/x][M_1/y]B_1 \equiv [[M/x]M_1/y][M/x]B_1$, we have by rule ($\Sigma$),

$$\Gamma, [M/x]\Gamma' \vdash \langle [M/x]M_1, [M/x]N_1 \rangle_{\Sigma y:[M/x]A_1.[M/x]B_1} : \Sigma y{:}[M/x]A_1.[M/x]B_1.$$

As $x \not\equiv y$, this judgement is

$$\Gamma, [M/x]\Gamma' \vdash [M/x]\langle M_1, N_1 \rangle_{\Sigma y:A_1.B_1}(M_1, N_1) : [M/x]\Sigma y{:}A_1.B_1,$$

as required. □

The theorem below shows that every inhabited term is indeed (a name of) a type which has some universe as its type.

Theorem 3.15. (type reflection) *If $\Gamma \vdash M : A$, then A is a Γ-type.*

Proof By induction on derivations of $\Gamma \vdash M : A$. For the rules except (*app*) and ($\pi 2$), it is easy. (We only remark that Lemmas 3.9 and 3.12 are used for (var), and Lemma 3.9 for (λ).) The cases for (*app*) and ($\pi 2$) are similar. We check ($\pi 2$) here. With $M \equiv \pi_2(M')$ and $A \equiv [\pi_1(M')/x]A_2$,

$$\frac{\Gamma \vdash M' : \Sigma x{:}A_1.A_2}{\Gamma \vdash \pi_2(M') : [\pi_1(M')/x]A_2}$$

By induction hypothesis, $\Gamma \vdash \Sigma x{:}A_1.A_2 : U$ for some universe U. Any derivation D of this judgement must have (Σ) or ($\preceq$) as the last rule used.

So, D must have a subderivation which is a derivation of $\Gamma \vdash \Sigma x{:}A_1.A_2 : Type_j$ with (Σ) as the last rule; i.e. we have

$$\frac{\Gamma \vdash A_1 : Type_j \quad \Gamma, x{:}A_1 \vdash A_2 : Type_j}{\Gamma \vdash \Sigma x{:}A_1.A_2 : Type_j}$$

As $\Gamma \vdash \pi_1(M') : A_1$, we have $\Gamma \vdash [\pi_1(M')/x]A_2 : Type_j$ by Cut (Theorem 3.14). So, A is a Γ-type. □

Remark The converse of the above theorem is not true in general; not every Γ-type is necessarily Γ-inhabited (see Theorem 5.4).

The following theorem of subject reduction shows that computation (reduction) preserves the typing relation. This is one of the most important properties of the type systems like ECC. Besides its importance in understanding the language of the type theory as discussed in Section 2.2.1 and its meta-theory, it also saves much work in implementation; e.g. it saves type checking when computing is performed.

Theorem 3.16. (subject reduction) *If* $\Gamma \vdash M : A$ *and* $M \rhd N$, *then* $\Gamma \vdash N : A$.

Proof We only need to show that, if $\Gamma \vdash M : A$ and $M \rhd_1 N$, then $\Gamma \vdash N : A$. This is proved by induction on derivations of $\Gamma \vdash M : A$. For the rules $(Ax)(C)(T)(var)(\preceq)$, the arguments are either trivial or straightforward. For the rules $(\Pi 1)(\Pi 2)(\lambda)(\Sigma)(pair)$, the proofs are similar in which Lemma 3.13 and (or) Lemma 3.9 and (or) Theorem 3.14 are used. For the rules $(app)(\pi 1)(\pi 2)$, the Church-Rosser theorem and Lemma 3.4 are used.

Here, we check the cases for $(pair)$ and (app) (see [Luo90a] for more details). Consider $(pair)$:

$$\frac{\Gamma \vdash M_1 : A_1 \quad \Gamma \vdash N_1 : [M_1/x]B_1 \quad \Gamma, x{:}A_1 \vdash B_1 : Type_j}{\Gamma \vdash \langle M_1, N_1\rangle_{\Sigma x:A_1.B_1} : \Sigma x{:}A_1.B_1}$$

So, $M \equiv \langle M_1, N_1\rangle_{\Sigma x:A_1.B_1} \rhd_1 \langle M_1', N_1'\rangle_{\Sigma x:A_1'.B_1'} \equiv N$. There are four cases:

1. $M_1 \rhd_1 M_1'$: By induction hypothesis, $\Gamma \vdash M_1' : A_1$; by Cut (Theorem 3.14) and applying rule $(\preceq)$, we have $\Gamma \vdash N_1 : [M_1'/x]B_1$.
2. $N_1 \rhd_1 N_1'$: By induction hypothesis, $\Gamma \vdash N_1' : [M_1/x]B_1$.
3. $A_1 \rhd_1 A_1'$: By Lemma 3.9, induction hypothesis, Context Replacement (Lemma 3.13) and rule $(\preceq)$, $\Gamma \vdash M_1 : A_1'$ and $\Gamma, x{:}A_1' \vdash B_1 : Type_j$.

4. $B_1 \rhd_1 B_1'$: By induction hypothesis, Cut (Theorem 3.14) and rule $(\preceq)$, $\Gamma, x{:}A_1 \vdash B_1' : Type_j$ and $\Gamma \vdash N_1 : [M_1/x]B_1'$.

Then applying (*pair*) suffices in every case above.

For (*app*), with $M \equiv M_1 N_1$ and $A \equiv [N_1/x]B_1$,

$$\frac{\Gamma \vdash M_1 : \Pi x{:}A_1.B_1 \quad \Gamma \vdash N_1 : A_1}{\Gamma \vdash M_1 N_1 : [N_1/x]B_1}$$

There are two cases:

1. $N \equiv M_1' N_1'$ and either $M_1 \rhd_1 M_1'$ or $N_1 \rhd_1 N_1'$. In this case, by induction hypothesis, $\Gamma \vdash M_1' : \Pi x{:}A_1.B_1$ and $\Gamma \vdash N_1' : A_1$. So, applying (*app*) yields $\Gamma \vdash N : [N_1'/x]B_1$. Since $[N_1'/x]B_1 \simeq [N_1/x]B_1$, we have $\Gamma \vdash N : [N_1/x]B_1$ by Type Reflection (Theorem 3.15) and rule $(\preceq)$.

2. $M \equiv M_1 N_1 \equiv (\lambda x{:}A_1'.M_1')N_1 \rhd_1 [N_1/x]M_1' \equiv N$. The last rule used in any derivation of $\Gamma \vdash M_1 : \Pi x{:}A_1.B_1$ must be (λ) or $(\preceq)$. If it is (λ), applying Cut (Theorem 3.14) suffices. If it ends with $(\preceq)$, we have for some $X \preceq \Pi x{:}A_1.B_1$,

$$\frac{\Gamma \vdash \lambda x{:}A_1'.M_1' : X \quad \Gamma \vdash X : Type_j}{\Gamma \vdash \lambda x{:}A_1'.M_1' : \Pi x{:}A_1.B_1}$$

We may assume that the last rule used to derive $\Gamma \vdash \lambda x{:}A_1'.M_1' : X$ is not $(\preceq)$, then it must be (λ), i.e.

$$\frac{\Gamma, x{:}A_1' \vdash M_1' : B_1'}{\Gamma \vdash \lambda x{:}A_1'.M_1' : \Pi x{:}A_1'.B_1'}$$

where $X \equiv \Pi x{:}A_1'.B_1'$. By Lemma 3.4, $X \simeq \Pi x{:}A_1''.B_1'' \preceq \Pi x{:}A_1.B_1$ for some A_1'' and B_1'' such that $A_1'' \simeq A_1$ and $B_1'' \preceq B_1$. By the Church-Rosser theorem, $X \rhd \Pi x{:}A_0.B_0$ and $\Pi x{:}A_1''.B_1'' \rhd \Pi x{:}A_0.B_0$ for some A_0 and B_0 such that $A_1' \rhd A_0$, $A_1'' \rhd A_0$, $B_1' \rhd B_0$ and $B_1'' \rhd B_0$. So, we have

$$A_1' \simeq A_0 \simeq A_1'' \simeq A_1 \quad \textit{and} \quad B_1' \simeq B_0 \simeq B_1'' \preceq B_1$$

By Type Reflection (Theorem 3.15), Context Replacement (Lemma 3.13) and rule $(\preceq)$, we have $\Gamma, x{:}A_1 \vdash M_1' : B_1$. Then, by Cut (Theorem 3.14), $\Gamma \vdash [N_1/x]M_1' : [N_1/x]B_1$, i.e. $\Gamma \vdash N : [N_1/x]B_1$. □

Remark Although subject reduction holds, the following rule is *not* admissible in ECC:

$$(**) \qquad \frac{\Gamma \vdash M{:}A \quad \Gamma \vdash N{:}B}{\Gamma \vdash M{:}B} \quad (M \rhd N)$$

For example, we have $\vdash Prop : Type_0$, but $\not\vdash (\lambda x{:}Type_1.x)Prop : Type_0$. In fact, we only have $\vdash (\lambda x{:}Type_1.x)Prop : Type_i$ for $i \geq 1$, i.e. its principal type is $Type_1$ (see Section 3.3).

The following lemma of strengthening shows that removing redundant (or unused) assumptions from a context preserves derivability, which may be viewed as a dual to weakening (Lemma 3.12). The proof of this property is quite tricky and the idea considered in the following proof can be applied to proving strengthening for other similar systems as well.

Lemma 3.17. (strengthening) *If $\Gamma, y{:}Y, \Gamma' \vdash M : A$ and $y \notin FV(M) \cup FV(A) \cup FV(\Gamma')$, then $\Gamma, \Gamma' \vdash M : A$.*

Proof Note that a straightforward induction on derivations does not work as the eliminations rules $(app)(\pi 1)(\pi 2)$ lose information of variable occurrences. To solve this problem, we notice that we only have to prove the following statement:

(∗) if $\Gamma, y{:}Y, \Gamma' \vdash M : A$ and $y \notin FV(M) \cup FV(\Gamma')$, then there exists $A' \preceq A$ such that $\Gamma, \Gamma' \vdash M : A'$.

For then, supposing $\Gamma, y{:}Y, \Gamma' \vdash M : A$ and $y \notin FV(M) \cup FV(A) \cup FV(\Gamma')$, we have by (∗) that there exists $A' \preceq A$ such that $\Gamma, \Gamma' \vdash M : A'$. We only have to show $\Gamma, \Gamma' \vdash A : U$ for some universe U in order to apply rule $(\preceq)$ to show $\Gamma, \Gamma' \vdash M : A$. By Type Reflection (Theorem 3.15), $\Gamma, y{:}Y, \Gamma' \vdash A : U$ for some universe U. As $y \notin FV(A) \cup FV(\Gamma')$, by (∗), there exists $B \preceq U$ such that $\Gamma, \Gamma' \vdash A : B$. Because universe U is a (Γ, Γ')-type (by rules (Ax), (C) and (T)), we can apply rule $(\preceq)$ to have $\Gamma, \Gamma' \vdash A : U$.

(∗) is proved by induction on derivations of $\Gamma, y{:}Y, \Gamma' \vdash M : A$. We consider the case for the rule (app) below and remark that, for the cases $(C)(T)(var)(\Pi 1)(\Pi 2)(\Sigma)(\lambda)(\preceq)$, the arguments are straightforward and use the Church-Rosser theorem; for the case $(pair)$, Theorem 3.14 is used; and the cases for $(\pi 1)(\pi 2)$ are similar to that for (app), to be given below. (For the complete proof, see [Luo90a].)

For (*app*), with $\Gamma, y{:}Y, \Gamma' \equiv \Gamma_1$, $M \equiv M_1 M_2$ and $A \equiv [M_2/x]B_1$,

$$\frac{\Gamma_1 \vdash M_1 : \Pi x{:}A_1.B_1 \quad \Gamma_1 \vdash M_2 : A_1}{\Gamma_1 \vdash M_1 M_2 : [M_2/x]B_1}$$

By induction hypothesis, there exist $C \preceq \Pi x{:}A_1.B_1$ and $D \preceq A_1$ such that $\Gamma, \Gamma' \vdash M_1 : C$ and $\Gamma, \Gamma' \vdash M_2 : D$. By Lemma 3.4, $C \simeq \Pi x{:}A_1'.B_1'$ for some $A_1' \simeq A_1$ and $B_1' \preceq B_1$. By the Church-Rosser theorem, $C \rhd \Pi x{:}A_0.B_0$ and $\Pi x{:}A_1'.B_1' \rhd \Pi x{:}A_0.B_0$ for some A_0 and B_0 such that $A_1' \rhd A_0$ and $B_1' \rhd B_0$. So, $A_0 \simeq A_1$, $B_0 \preceq B_1$. By Lemma 3.10, $y \notin FV(C) \cup FV(D)$, which implies that $y \notin FV(\Pi x{:}A_0.B_0)$. By Type Reflection (Theorem 3.15), Subject Reduction (Theorem 3.16) and rule ($\preceq$), $\Gamma, \Gamma' \vdash M_1 : \Pi x{:}A_0.B_0$ and $\Gamma, \Gamma' \vdash M_2 : A_0$. Applying rule (*app*), we have $\Gamma, \Gamma' \vdash M_1 M_2 : [M_2/x]B_0$ and $[M_2/x]B_0 \preceq [M_2/x]B_1$. □

3.3 Principal types

Because of the type inclusions induced by universes, type uniqueness up to conversion fails for ECC. However, we show that ECC has a simple notion of *principal type* which characterises the set of types of a well-typed term, and yields a simple and straightforward type inference algorithm as we shall show in Section 5.2. Based on this notion of principal type, it is possible to show the extensionality of the computational equality between inhabited types (Theorem 3.26).

First, we show that the cumulativity relation characterises the type cumulativity (or type inclusions) in the language.

Lemma 3.18. (type cumulativity) *Let A and B be Γ-types. Then, $A \preceq B$ if and only if $\Gamma, x{:}A \vdash x : B$, where $x \notin FV(\Gamma)$.*

Proof The sufficiency is by induction on derivations of $\Gamma, x{:}A \vdash x : B$. The necessity is proved by means of rules ($\preceq$)(C)(*var*) and Context Replacement (Lemma 3.13). □

Corollary 3.19. *Let A and B be Γ-types. If $A \preceq B$, then, for any term M, $\Gamma \vdash M : A$ implies $\Gamma \vdash M : B$.*

Proof By Lemma 3.18, $\Gamma, x{:}A \vdash x : B$, where $x \notin FV(\Gamma)$. By Cut (Theorem 3.14), $\Gamma \vdash M : [M/x]B$; i.e., $\Gamma \vdash M : B$, as x does not occur free in Γ-type B by Lemma 3.10. □

Remark The converse of the above corollary is *not* true in general, as A may be empty (not inhabited by any term) in Γ. For example, it will be shown (cf. Theorem 5.4) that both $\Pi X{:}Prop.X$ and $\Pi X{:}Type_0.X$ are empty in the empty context, but $\Pi X{:}Prop.X \not\preceq \Pi X{:}Type_0.X$. However, when A is Γ-inhabited, the converse of the above corollary is true (see Lemma 3.25 below).

Lemma 3.20. (diamond property of $\preceq$) *If $\Gamma \vdash M : A$ and $\Gamma \vdash M : B$, then there exists a term C such that $C \preceq A$, $C \preceq B$ and $\Gamma \vdash M : C$.*

Proof By induction on the sum of the lengths of derivations of $\Gamma \vdash M : A$ and $\Gamma \vdash M : B$. Here, we only consider the case when both derivations use (*app*) as the last rule. The other cases are easy. Suppose $M \equiv M_1M_2$, $A \equiv [M_2/x]B_1$, $B \equiv [M_2/x]B_2$ and, for $i = 1, 2$,

$$\frac{\Gamma \vdash M_1 : \Pi x{:}A_i.B_i \quad \Gamma \vdash M_2 : A_i}{\Gamma \vdash M_1M_2 : [M_2/x]B_i}$$

By induction hypothesis, there exists C such that $\Gamma \vdash M_1 : C$ and $C \preceq \Pi x{:}A_i.B_i$ $(i = 1, 2)$. By Lemma 3.4 and the Church-Rosser theorem, $C \rhd \Pi x{:}A_0.B_0$ for some $A_0 \simeq A_i$ and $B_0 \preceq B_i$ $(i = 1, 2)$. By Type Reflection and Subject Reduction (Theorems 3.15 and 3.16), $\Pi x{:}A_0.B_0$ and A_0 are Γ-types. So by rule $(\preceq)$, we have $\Gamma \vdash M_1 : \Pi x{:}A_0.B_0$ and $\Gamma \vdash M_2 : A_0$. Hence, $\Gamma \vdash M_1M_2 : [M_2/x]B_0$. Noticing that $[M_2/x]B_0 \preceq [M_2/x]B_i$ $(i = 1, 2)$, we have the required result. □

Remark The above lemma implies that, if A and B are types of M (in Γ), then $A \approx B$ (see the remark after Lemma 3.4). It is a sort of 'Church-Rosser property' for types concerning $\approx$.

An immediate consequence of the above diamond property (and the well-foundedness (Corollary 3.8)) of the cumulativity relation is that every Γ-object has a *minimum type* (in Γ) with respect to the order $\preceq$.

Lemma 3.21. (existence of minimum type) *Let M be a Γ-object and $T = \{ A \mid \Gamma \vdash M : A \}$. Then, there exists $A \in T$ such that $A \preceq A'$ for all $A' \in T$.*

Proof T is not empty as M is a Γ-object. Let A be a minimal element in T (A exists by the well-definedness of $\preceq$ (Corollary 3.8)). Then, by the diamond property of $\preceq$ (Lemma 3.20), for any $A' \in T$, there exists $B \in T$

such that $B \preceq A$ and $B \preceq A'$. Since $B \not\preceq A$, we have $A \simeq B \preceq A'$. □

The minimum type of a Γ-object is obviously unique up to conversion. We now show that the minimum type is indeed the *most general* one (principal type).

Definition 3.22. (principal type) *A is called a* principal type *of M (in Γ) if and only if*

1. $\Gamma \vdash M : A$, *and*

2. *for any* A', $\Gamma \vdash M : A'$ *if and only if* $A \preceq A'$ *and* A' *is a* Γ*-type.*

Theorem 3.23. (existence of principal type) *Every* Γ*-object* M *has a principal type (in* Γ*); it is the minimum type of* M *(in* Γ*) with respect to* $\preceq$.

Proof Let A be the minimum type of M (in Γ) with respect to $\preceq$ (A exists by Lemma 3.21). Then, $\Gamma \vdash M : A$. For any A' such that $\Gamma \vdash M : A'$, we have $A \preceq A'$ and A' is a Γ-type by Type Reflection (Theorem 3.15). Suppose A' is a Γ-type such that $A \preceq A'$. By Corollary 3.19, we have $\Gamma \vdash M : A'$. □

Notation We use $T_\Gamma(M)$ to denote the principal type (being more precise, any of the principal types) of Γ-object M in Γ.

Now, we give some examples of principal types, which will also be used below to prove the extensionality of type equality.

Example 3.24. Let Γ be a valid context and A be a Γ-type. Then, by induction of derivations, we can prove the following:[16]

1. A is the principal type of x in Γ, if $x{:}A$ occurs in Γ.

2. $A \to A$ is the principal type of $\lambda x{:}A.x$ in Γ.

3. A is the principal type of $(\lambda x{:}A.x)a$ in Γ, if $\Gamma \vdash a : A$.

[16] In an implementation of the type theory, it is the algorithm for type checking (and type inference) that automatically checks such facts. Therefore, it is not surprising that the arguments used in the proofs for these examples are similar to those in the correctness proofs of the algorithm. See Section 5.2.

The proofs for the above are similar in spirit. For example, to argue for the first, we only have to observe that, since (*var*) and ($\preceq$) are the only rules that can be used to type x in Γ (for $x{:}A$ occurs in Γ), any derivation of $\Gamma \vdash x : B$ (for any B) must have a subderivation of $\Gamma \vdash x : A$ such that $A \preceq B$.

The argument for the second is similar, but may use the first result. For the third, we have $\Gamma \vdash a : A$ and $\Gamma \vdash (\lambda x{:}A.x)a : A$. If $\Gamma \vdash (\lambda x{:}A.x)a : B$ for some $B \prec A$, there would be a subderivation of $\Gamma \vdash \lambda x{:}A.x : \Pi x{:}A'.B'[x]$ for some A' and $B'[x]$ such that $A' \simeq A$ and $B'[a] \preceq B \prec A$. But since $T_\Gamma(\lambda x{:}A.x)$ is $A \rightarrow A$ (by the second example), we would have $A \rightarrow A \preceq \Pi x{:}A'.B'[x]$, which implies $A \equiv [a/x]A \preceq B'[a] \prec A$, a contradiction. Therefore, A is the principal type of $(\lambda x{:}A.x)a$ in Γ.

Remark An immediate consequence of the third example above is that for any Γ-inhabited type A, there is an Γ-object a_A with A as its principal type in Γ.

Now, we can prove the converse of Corollary 3.19 for the inhabited types, which implies the extensionality of computational equality between inhabited types.

Lemma 3.25. *Let A and B be Γ-types. If A is Γ-inhabited and, for any a, $\Gamma \vdash a : A$ implies $\Gamma \vdash a : B$, then, $A \preceq B$.*

Proof Let a_A be a Γ-object with A as its principal type. (a_A exists by Example 3; cf., the remark above.) Therefore, since $\Gamma \vdash a_A : B$, we have $A \preceq B$. □

Theorem 3.26. (extensionality of type equality) *Let A and B be Γ-inhabited types. Then,*

$$A \simeq B \quad \textit{if and only if} \quad Obj_\Gamma(A) = Obj_\Gamma(B),$$

where $Obj_\Gamma(C) = \{\, a \mid \Gamma \vdash a : C \,\}$ is the set of objects of type C in Γ.

Proof The necessity is obvious by rule ($\preceq$). The sufficiency is by Lemma 3.25 and the antisymmetry of the cumulativity relation. □

4
Strong normalisation

In this chapter, we prove the most important meta-theoretic result for ECC—the strong normalisation theorem: *Every well-typed term in* ECC *is strongly normalisable.* That is, every computation sequence starting from a well-typed term is finite, and in particular, every object computes into a value.

The normalisation property plays a central role in understanding the language of the type theory as it guarantees the harmony between the different aspects of use of the entities in the language (cf. Section 1.2.3). It is the basis to prove many other important properties of the language, which include the basic properties of the internal logic such as logical consistency and equality reflection, and the decidability results of the type system such as the decidability of the computational equality for well-typed terms and the decidability of type inference and type checking (see Chapter 5). It therefore provides a solid basis for various applications of the language such as program specification and the implementation of the type theory in proof development systems.

The strong normalisation theorem will be proved by means of the Girard–Tait reducibility method [Gir72, GLT90, Tai75], which provides a powerful proof-theoretic technique worth investigating in its own right. We shall first give a brief introduction to the method and discuss the problems one may meet with when using the method to prove normalisation theorems for more sophisticated type systems. In particular, we explain how the presence of predicative universes in ECC causes a problem to be solved in applying the reducibility method. Our solution to the problem (by proving a *quasi-normalisation theorem*) leads to a proof-theoretic clarification of the notion of predicativity, which is itself an interesting result. Then, the proof of strong normalisation for ECC is given based on the quasi-normalisation result and Coquand's extension of the Girard–Tait method used in his proof of the normalisation theorem for the calculus of constructions [Coq86b].

4.1 The Girard–Tait reducibility method

We first discuss in general the Girard–Tait method for normalisation proofs. We explain why it is difficult to prove (strong) normalisation for type theories with more sophisticated type structures like the calculus of constructions. In particular, we discuss from a proof-theoretic point of view why the predicativity of higher universes is essential to apply the Girard–Tait method to prove strong normalisation for ECC. Consideration of Σ-types leads us to a more general definition of the key notion of saturated sets which gives a better understanding of the reducibility method.

4.1.1 The reducibility method and the notion of predicativity

The Girard–Tait reducibility method has been widely used to prove the (strong) normalisation property for various type systems including the second-order λ-calculus [Gir72, GLT90] and the calculus of constructions [Coq85, Coq86b, Pot87]. One can find a nice and rather detailed explication of the method for proving strong normalisation of the second-order λ-calculus in [Gal90].

The basic idea of the method comes from the fact that a proof of normalisation by straightforward induction on the structure of terms fails because β-reduction may result in a term with a larger size. A stronger induction method was invented by Tait [Tai67] and generalised to higher-order systems by Girard [Gir71, Gir72, Tai75]; it is very adaptable for different type systems. The general steps of the reducibility method can be analysed as follows:[17]

1. Define a notion of *saturated sets* or *candidates of reducibility.*

2. Define an interpretation of types A, $Eval_\rho A$, with respect to type variable assignment ρ.

3. Prove that $Eval_\rho A$ is a saturated set (or candidate of reducibility) for every type A.

4. Prove the soundness of the interpretation $Eval$, i.e. for any object a of type A, a is in $Eval_\rho A$.

As by the very definition of saturated sets or candidates of reducibility (see Section 4.1.3), every term in a saturated set or a candidate of reducibility

[17] We consider only the typed version of the reducibility method here. We remark that the erasing trick used in the untyped version of the reducibility method [Tai75, Mit86] does not seem to apply to the calculus of constructions or richer calculi as it is based on *separation* of type reduction and term reduction which might not be done when type-valued functions exist.

is (strongly) normalisable, one concludes from the above that every well-typed term is (strongly) normalisable.

The above outline of the reducibility method is rather informal but is enough for understanding our following discussions and also gives some guidelines to understand our proof of strong normalisation in Section 4.3.

To apply the method above, besides the careful considerations needed in the proofs of the last two steps, defining the notion of saturated set and defining the interpretation are two key steps. Here, assuming the notion of saturated set is given, we discuss informally how to define an interpretation $Eval_\rho A$ such that every type is interpreted as a saturated set. This is interesting since it is an important aspect in applying the reducibility method to type theories with rich type structures, and in particular, it leads us to consider the intuitive notion of predicativity from a proof-theoretic point of view.

For simple type systems such as the simply typed λ-calculus and the second-order λ-calculus, the interpretation of types can be defined straightforwardly by induction on the structure of types (see, for example, [Tai67] and [Gir72, Mit86]), because in those systems types are essentially separated from the other objects and there are no type-valued functional objects. However, for richer systems like the calculus of constructions, types (propositions) are mixed up with other terms and cannot be simply dealt with separately. In particular, there are *type-valued λ-terms* or intuitively functions with types as their values. For example, in the calculus of constructions, one has $\vdash \lambda X{:}Prop.X : Prop \to Prop$. Therefore, a term of the form MN may be a type (a proposition) too. Then, the problem is how to define the interpretation of types of the form MN.

Coquand [Coq86b, Coq85] gives a nice solution to this problem for the calculus of constructions: in his extension of the reducibility method, not only types are interpreted, but the other terms as well. In order to show that the interpretation defined by induction on the structure of terms is well-defined and does interpret every type as a saturated set, he makes substantial use of the fact that there is a complexity measure of the *non-propositional* types in the calculus of constructions. Any non-propositional type in the calculus of constructions is of the form $\Pi x_1{:}A_1...x_n{:}A_n.Prop$. In other words, there are no functional terms with non-propositional types as values and any type of the form MN is a proposition.[18] Therefore, similar to the simple type theory (cf. [Chu40]), there is a straightforward complexity measure β of types by assigning $\beta(P) = 0$ for any proposition P, $\beta(Prop) = 1$ and $\beta(\Pi x{:}A.B) = max\{\beta(A) + 1, \beta(B)\}$ for any non-propositional type $\Pi x{:}A.B$. Indeed, it is this complexity measure that

---

[18] Note that propositions are not lifted as higher-level types in the calculus of constructions.

enables Coquand to succeed in applying the reducibility method to prove the normalisation property of the calculus of constructions.

The existence of such a complexity measure may be seen as an explicit proof-theoretic justification that the formation of non-propositional types in the calculus of constructions is *predicative* or non-circular in the sense that the formation of any non-propositional type depends only on those types with less complexity. As noted by Coquand [Coq86b], this is essential for the logical consistency of the calculus of constructions and it is impossible to have such a measure for the inconsistent type theory with $Type : Type$ considered by Martin-Löf in [ML71]. It may also be seen as a formal explanation of the remark by Girard that 'all attempts to strengthen this system [the calculus of constructions], in particular to temper with the fourth level, should be considered very cautiously' [Gir86]. For example, adding another impredicative level to the calculus of constructions would lead to logical inconsistency [Coq86a].

The above analysis explains one aspect of why the predicativity of the non-propositional types in the type theories such as the calculus of constructions and ECC is essential. However, for ECC where there is a much richer type structure (in particular, predicative universes), the proof-theoretic justification of the predicativity of non-propositional types is not so obvious as in the calculus of constructions. That is because there are now functions which have non-propositional types as values as well. For example, we have $\vdash \lambda X{:}Type_j.X : Type_j \to Type_j$. As a consequence, terms of the form MN or $\pi_i(M)$ may also be non-propositional types and we do not have the obvious complexity measure shown above for the calculus of constructions. Furthermore, propositions in ECC are lifted to higher-level types; it allows judgements like $\vdash \Pi X{:}Type_j \Pi B{:}Type_j \to Prop.B(X) : Type_j$ to be derivable, although this is only because that $\Pi X{:}Type_j \Pi B{:}Type_j \to Prop.B(X)$ is a proposition. One may doubt the predicativity and wonder whether there is any circularity in the formation of non-propositional types. This requires a proof-theoretic clarification of the predicativity of the non-propositional type hierarchy in ECC, and more technically, calls for a complexity measure for non-propositional types so that the reducibility method can be applied to prove the strong normalisation theorem. To meet this requirement, we shall in Section 4.2 prove a quasi-normalisation theorem which allows us to define a two-dimensional complexity measure of types for such a purpose.

In the rest of this section, we first introduce a technical machinery for strong normalisation proofs of dependent type systems and then consider the definition of saturated sets (and their relationship with candidates of reducibility).

4.1.2 Environments

Because of the nature of dependent types, one needs some technical tool to deal with the variable bindings occurring in the system. In particular, in a proof of normalisation, an infinite 'universal' context is called for and proves to be very useful.[19] In their proofs of (strong) normalisation of the calculus of constructions, Coquand [Coq86b] uses a notion of environment of constants and Pottinger [Pot87] a notion of environment of infinite variable bindings.

We follow the idea of Pottinger to introduce below a notion of environment for ECC and show that the notions and results relative to valid contexts like those for principal types can all be extended to environments.

Definition 4.1. (Environment) *An* environment $\mathcal{E}$ *is an infinite sequence*

$$\mathcal{E} \equiv e_1{:}E_1, e_2{:}E_2, \ldots$$

where e_i is a variable and E_i is a term, such that, for any $i \in \omega$,

1. *$\mathcal{E}^i \equiv e_1{:}E_1, \ldots, e_i{:}E_i$ is a valid context, and*
2. *for any $\mathcal{E}^i$-type A, there are infinitely many k such that $E_k \equiv A$.*

Lemma 4.2. (existence of environment) *There exists an environment.*

Proof We construct an environment $\mathcal{E}$ as follows. Assume that we are given a canonical enumeration of variables and a canonical enumeration of derivations in ECC. Define $\mathcal{E}^n$ by induction on $n \in \omega$ and, define at the same time a diagonal enumeration $p^n = (p_1^n, p_2^n)$ with the property $p_1^n + p_2^n \leq n$ as follows:

1. $\mathcal{E}^0 =_{\mathrm{df}} \langle\rangle$ (the empty context) and $p^0 =_{\mathrm{df}} (0, 0)$.
2. Supposing that $\mathcal{E}^i$ for $i < n$ have been defined, define $\mathcal{E}^n$ and p^n as follows. Let T^i $(i < n)$ be the sub-sequence of the canonical enumeration of derivations consisting of the derivations of the judgements of the form $\mathcal{E}^i \vdash A : U$ (where U is a universe). If the kth element of T^i

[19]Recently, Coquand and Gallier [CG90] considered an alternative approach where possible context extensions are explicitly associated in the interpretation of terms. Using an extra notion of infinite context, however, makes the interpretation look simpler.

is $\mathcal{E}^i \vdash A : U$, we write $T^i_k \equiv A$. (Note that T^i is infinite.) Then, we define

$$\mathcal{E}^n =_{\mathrm{df}} \mathcal{E}^{n-1}, x{:}T^{p_1^{n-1}}_{p_2^{n-1}},$$

where x is the first variable in the canonical enumeration of variables such that $x \notin FV(\mathcal{E}^{n-1})$, and

$$p^n =_{\mathrm{df}} \begin{cases} (p_2^{n-1} + 1, 0) & \text{if } p_1^{n-1} = 0, \\ (p_1^{n-1} - 1, p_2^{n-1} + 1) & \text{if } p_1^{n-1} \neq 0. \end{cases}$$

$\mathcal{E}^n$ thus defined is a valid context.

By Weakening (Lemma 3.12), it is easy to show that every $\mathcal{E}^n$-type occurs in $\mathcal{E}$ infinitely many times. □

Remark In fact, as shown in [Pot87], one may similarly prove a stronger result which says that every valid context can be extended to an environment. However, the above lemma is enough for our purpose.

Notation From now on until the end of this chapter, if not explicitly stated otherwise, $\mathcal{E}$ will stand for a fixed arbitrary environment

$$\mathcal{E} \equiv e_1{:}E_1, e_2{:}E_2, e_3{:}E_3, \ldots ,$$

that is, $\mathcal{E}_i \equiv e_i{:}E_i$ is the ith component of $\mathcal{E}$ and $\mathcal{E}^i \equiv e_1{:}E_1, \ldots, e_i{:}E_i$ is the valid context consisting of the first i components of $\mathcal{E}$.

Most of the notions relative to valid contexts defined before can be similarly defined for environment $\mathcal{E}$. We shall write

$$\mathcal{E} \vdash M : A$$

for '$\mathcal{E}^i \vdash M : A$ for some $i \in \omega$'. A term M is called an *$\mathcal{E}$-object*, *$\mathcal{E}$-type*, *$\mathcal{E}$-proposition*, *non-propositional $\mathcal{E}$-type*, and *$\mathcal{E}$-proof* if and only if, for some $i \in \omega$, M is an $\mathcal{E}^i$-object, $\mathcal{E}^i$-type, $\mathcal{E}^i$-proposition, non-propositional $\mathcal{E}^i$-type, and $\mathcal{E}^i$-proof, respectively. It is obvious from the definition of environments and Weakening (Lemma 3.12) that, if $\mathcal{E}^i \vdash M : A$, then $\mathcal{E}^k \vdash M : A$ for all $k \geq i$; if $Qx{:}M.N$ is an $\mathcal{E}$-object, where $Q \in \{\lambda, \Pi, \Sigma\}$, then there exist $\mathcal{E}$-objects x' and N' such that $Qx{:}M.N \equiv Qx'{:}M.N'$.

The notion of principal type (Definition 3.22) and the proof of its existence (Theorem 3.23) can also be extended to environment. The notion of principal type in environment $\mathcal{E}$ is defined as in Definition 3.22 by replacing Γ by $\mathcal{E}$. The principal type of an $\mathcal{E}$-object M (in $\mathcal{E}$) is denoted as $T_{\mathcal{E}}(M)$.

4.1.3 Saturated sets and candidates of reducibility

The core notion of the reducibility method is that of saturated sets [Tai75] (or candidates of reducibility [Gir71, Gir72]) which are the denotations of types in the interpretation of terms.

Instead of giving the ordinary definition of saturated sets, where people only consider λ-terms, we give a slightly more general definition using a notion of base term (Definition 4.3) and a notion of key redex (Definition 4.4), which makes explicit the idea behind the notion of saturated set, incorporates terms for Σ-types, and can easily be extended for other data types.

Definition 4.3. (base terms) Base terms *and the* key variable *of a base term are inductively defined on the structure of terms as follows:*

- *A variable is a base term and is the key variable of itself;*
- *If M is a base term, so are MN, $\pi_1(M)$ and $\pi_2(M)$, and their key variable is that of M.*

Examples of base terms are: x, $xM_1...M_n$, $\pi_i(xM_1...M_n)$, $\pi_i(\pi_k(x)M)N$, etc. x is the key variable of the base terms in these examples.

Remark Note that base terms have the following properties, which can readily be proved by induction on the structure of base terms:

1. If M is a base term and $M \rhd M'$, then M' is a base term, too.
2. If variable y is different from the key variable of a base term M, then $[N/y]M$ is also a base term, where N is an arbitrary term.

Definition 4.4. (key redex) *The notion of* key redex *of a term M is defined as follows:*

1. *If M is a redex, then M has key redex and it is the key redex of itself.*
2. *If M has key redex, then so do MN, $\pi_1(M)$ and $\pi_2(M)$, and their key redexes are that of M.*

(Thus, a term has at most one key redex.) If M has key redex, then we write $\mathrm{red}_{\mathbf{k}}(M)$ *for the term obtained from M by contracting the key redex of M.*

For example, the redexes $(\lambda x{:}A.M)N$ and $\pi_1(\langle M, N\rangle_A)$ are the key redexes of $(\lambda x{:}A.M)NN_1...N_m$ and $\pi_1(\langle M, N\rangle_A)N_1...N_m$, respectively. The intuitive idea behind the notion of key redex is that every computation sequence, starting from a term with key redex and ending with a normal form, will necessarily contract the key redex of the term (possibly after contracting some redexes in subterms of the key redex). Furthermore, it is easy to show that the notion of key redex has the following property.

Lemma 4.5. *If M has key redex and $M \rhd M'$ without contracting any key redex, then* $\mathrm{red}_{\mathbf{k}}(M) \rhd \mathrm{red}_{\mathbf{k}}(M')$.

We are now ready to define the notion of saturated set.

Notation Let A be an $\mathcal{E}$-type. Then, $SN(A)$ is the set of strongly normalisable terms M such that $\mathcal{E} \vdash M : A$.

Definition 4.6. (saturated sets) *Let A be an $\mathcal{E}$-type. S is an A-*saturated set *if and only if*

(S1) $S \subseteq SN(A)$;

(S2) *if $M \in SN(A)$ is a base term, then $M \in S$;*

(S3) *if $M \in SN(A)$ has key redex and* $\mathrm{red}_{\mathbf{k}}(M) \in S$, *then $M \in S$.*

$Sat(A)$ is defined to be the set of A-saturated sets.

Remark $Sat(A)$ is not empty. In fact, $SN(A) \in Sat(A)$. To show the generality of the above definition, we remark that ($S2$) has the following as special cases:

- If $M \equiv xM_1...M_n \in SN(A)$, then $M \in S$.
- If $M \equiv \pi_{i_1}(...\pi_{i_j}(x)) \in SN(A)$, then $M \in S$, where $i_k \in \{1,2\}$.

And ($S3$) has the following as special cases:

- if $M \equiv (\lambda x{:}B.M')NN_1...N_m \in SN(A)$ and $([N/x]M')N_1...N_m \in S$, then $M \in S$;
- if $M \equiv \pi_{i_1}(...\pi_{i_j}(\langle M_1, M_2\rangle_B)) \in SN(A)$ and $\pi_{i_1}(...\pi_{i_{j-1}}(M_{i_j})) \in S$, then $M \in S$, where $i_k \in \{1,2\}$.

With the notions of base term and key redex, the definition of saturated sets is generic (or parametric) in that, to consider further data types, one only needs to extend the definitions of base terms and key redexes.

Saturated sets and Girard's candidates: a digression

As a digression, we would like to compare the notion of saturated sets with the notion of candidates of reducibility of Girard [Gir72, GLT90] and show that the conditions for the latter are stronger. We believe that such a result is interesting since both notions have been widely used.

Definition 4.7. (candidates of reducibility) *([GLT90]) Let A be an $\mathcal{E}$-type. S is an A-*candidate of reducibility *if and only if*

(CR1) *$S \subseteq SN(A)$;*

(CR2) *if $M \in S$ and $M \rhd_1 N$, then $N \in S$;*

(CR3) *if $\mathcal{E} \vdash M : A$, M is simple (i.e. M is of the form x, $M_1 M_2$ or $\pi_i(M')$), and $N \in S$ for every N such that $M \rhd_1 N$, then $M \in S$.*

$CR(A)$ is defined to be the set of A-candidates of reducibility.

We have the following relationship between saturated sets and Girard's candidates of reducibility.

Proposition 4.8. *$CR(A) \subseteq SAT(A)$, i.e. every A-candidate of reducibility is an A-saturated set.*

Proof Suppose that S is an A-candidate of reducibility. We show that S satisfies (S1)(S2)(S3). Notice that, for every $\mathcal{E}$-object M, M is simple if and only if M is a base term or has key redex. We use this fact below tacitly.

(S1) By definition.

(S2) We show that every base term M in $SN(A)$ is in S by induction on the height $h(M)$ of the reduction tree of M. If $h(M) = 0$, i.e. M is strongly normalisable, then $M \in S$ by (CR3). If $h(M) = n + 1$, then, for every N such that $M \rhd_1 N$, $N \in SN(A)$ is a base term and $h(N) < h(M)$; and hence $N \in S$ by induction hypothesis. Therefore, $M \in S$ by (CR3).

(S3) We show, by induction on the height $h(M)$ of the reduction tree of M, that $M \in S$ for every M in $SN(A)$ which has key redex and whose key reduct $\text{red}_{\mathbf{k}}(M)$ is in S. If $h(M) = 1$, then if $M \rhd_1 N$, we have $N \equiv \text{red}_{\mathbf{k}}(M) \in S$. So, $M \in S$ by (CR3). If $h(M) = n+1$, then if $M \rhd_1 N$, we have either $N \equiv \text{red}_{\mathbf{k}}(M) \in S$, or N has key redex and $\text{red}_{\mathbf{k}}(M) \rhd \text{red}_{\mathbf{k}}(N)$ by Lemma 4.5. In the former case, $N \in S$ by assumption. In the latter case, as $\text{red}_{\mathbf{k}}(M) \in S$, $\text{red}_{\mathbf{k}}(N) \in S$ by (CR2); and by induction hypothesis, we have $N \in S$ as $h(N) < h(M)$. Therefore, $M \in S$ by (CR3). □

Remark The condition (CR2) is necessary to prove the above proposition. The converse of the proposition is not true; some saturated sets are not candidates of reducibility because they do not satisfy (CR2). The above relationship between saturated sets and candidates of reducibility has also been noticed by Gallier [Gal90].

4.2 Quasi-normalisation

This section is devoted to a proof-theoretic understanding of the predicativity of the type universes $Type_j$ in ECC, that is, the formation of non-propositional types is essentially non-circular. We prove a *quasi-normalisation* theorem (Theorem 4.13) which shows that any well-typed term can be reduced to a *quasi-normal form*. Besides gaining a better understanding of the language, this result implies that every type can be reduced to certain head normal form (Corollary 4.14) and allows us to assign a two-dimensional complexity measure (Definition 4.17) to the types, which makes explicit the predicativity (non-circularity) of formations of the non-propositional types (Lemma 4.19). This complexity measure then provides us with an important basis to apply the reducibility method to prove the strong normalisation theorem.

Since the proof of the quasi-normalisation theorem is sophisticated, we shall first concentrate on the explanation of the complexity measure and the quasi-normalisation results, and then present the proof at the end of this section (Section 4.2.4).

4.2.1 Levels of types

We first define the notion of levels of $\mathcal{E}$-types, which will be the first dimension of our complexity measure to be defined in Section 4.2.3. Intuitively, that the level of $\mathcal{E}$-type A is j means that $Type_j$ ($Prop$ when $j = -1$) is the lowest universe in which A resides up to the computational equality.

Definition 4.9. (levels of $\mathcal{E}$-types) *The* level *of an $\mathcal{E}$-type A, $\mathcal{L}(A)$, is defined as follows:*

- *If A is an $\mathcal{E}$-proposition, then $\mathcal{L}(A) =_{\mathrm{df}} -1$.*
- *If A is not an $\mathcal{E}$-proposition, then $\mathcal{L}(A)$ is defined to be the minimum $j \in \omega$ such that $\mathcal{E} \vdash B : Type_j$ for some $B \simeq A$.*

Remark We have that $\mathcal{L}(A) \geq 0$ ($\mathcal{L}(A) = -1$) if and only if A is a non-propositional $\mathcal{E}$-type ($\mathcal{E}$-proposition).

Lemma 4.10. *The levels of $\mathcal{E}$-types have the following properties.*

1. *If $A \simeq B$ are $\mathcal{E}$-types, then $\mathcal{L}(A) = \mathcal{L}(B)$.*
2. *If $A \preceq B$ are $\mathcal{E}$-types, then $\mathcal{L}(A) \leq \mathcal{L}(B)$.*
3. *Let $A \equiv Qx{:}A_1.A_2$ ($Q \in \{\Pi, \Sigma\}$) be a non-propositional $\mathcal{E}$-type. Then, $\mathcal{L}(A) = j \in \omega$ if and only if*
   (a) *$\mathcal{L}(A_1) \leq j$ and $\mathcal{L}(A_2) \leq j$ (for $Q \equiv \Pi$, also $\mathcal{L}(A_2) \geq 0$); and*
   (b) *either $\mathcal{L}(A_1) = j$ or $\mathcal{L}(A_2) = j$.*
4. *If $\mathcal{E}^k \vdash N : E_{k+1}$ and B is an $\mathcal{E}^{k+1}$-type, then $\mathcal{L}([N/e_{k+1}]B) \leq \mathcal{L}(B)$.*
5. *If $\mathcal{E}$-object R is of the form MN or $\pi_i(M)$ ($i = 1, 2$), then $\mathcal{L}(T_{\mathcal{E}}(R)) \leq \mathcal{L}(T_{\mathcal{E}}(M))$.*

Proof The first three lemmas can readily be proved (see [Luo90a] for details). We give the proofs of the last two here. For the fourth lemma, suppose $\mathcal{L}(B) < \mathcal{L}([N/e_{k+1}]B) = j$. Then, there is B' convertible to B such that $\mathcal{E} \vdash B' : U$ for some universe $U \prec Type_j$. By the Church-Rosser theorem, Subject Reduction (Theorem 3.16), and Strengthening (Lemma 3.17), we may assume $\mathcal{E}^{k+1} \vdash B' : U$. But then, by Cut (Theorem 3.14), $\mathcal{E} \vdash [N/e_{k+1}]B' : U$, which implies $\mathcal{L}([N/e_{k+1}]B) < j$ as $[N/e_{k+1}]B \simeq [N/e_{k+1}]B'$, contradicting the assumption. So, $\mathcal{L}([N/e_{k+1}]B) \leq \mathcal{L}(B)$.

For the fifth lemma, we prove the case when $R \equiv MN$. The other two cases are similar. As $R \equiv MN$ is an $\mathcal{E}$-object, one of the principal types of M has the form $\Pi x{:}A.B$. Then, we have $\mathcal{E} \vdash R : [N/x]B$. By Lemma 4.10(2) and Lemma 4.10(4), $\mathcal{L}(T_{\mathcal{E}}(R)) \leq \mathcal{L}([N/x]B) \leq \mathcal{L}(B) \leq \mathcal{L}(\Pi x{:}A.B) = \mathcal{L}(T_{\mathcal{E}}M)$. □

Remarks Here are some explanations of the above properties of levels.

1. As computationally equal $\mathcal{E}$-types have the same level (Lemma 4.10(1)), we use $\mathcal{L}(T_{\mathcal{E}}(M))$ to denote the level of the principal type of M in $\mathcal{E}$.
2. Lemma 4.10(4) shows that type-preserving substitutions do not increase the level of an $\mathcal{E}$-type. In particular, for any $\mathcal{E}$-type of the form $\Pi x{:}A.B$ or $\Sigma x{:}A.B$, if $\mathcal{E} \vdash N : A$, then $\mathcal{L}([N/x]B) \leq \mathcal{L}(B)$, for we can always choose x to be e_{k+1} for some k such that $E_{k+1} \equiv A$, $\mathcal{E}^k \vdash N : A$ and B is an $\mathcal{E}^{k+1}$-type.
3. As a consequence of Lemma 4.10(5), the level of the principal type of the major term of a redex is not less than that of the principal type of the redex.

4.2.2 Quasi-normalisation and degrees of types

Now we consider the quasi-normalisation results, and define the second dimension of our complexity measure—the degrees of types. The basic idea to obtain an explicit justification of the predicativity of universes $Type_j$ by defining the notion of degrees of types (and their levels) is to proceed as follows:

1. Define a notion of quasi-normal form.
2. Prove the quasi-normalisation theorem—every $\mathcal{E}$-object can be reduced to a quasi-normal form.
3. Show that, by the quasi-normalisation theorem and the notion of quasi-normal form, every $\mathcal{E}$-type can be reduced to certain head-normal form.
4. Then, it is possible to define the degrees of $\mathcal{E}$-types which serve as the second dimension of the complexity measure to be defined.

However, it turns out that the proof of the quasi-normalisation theorem requires some notion of degrees of types and is quite sophisticated. In the following, we shall first give a summary of the quasi-normalisation results and present the proof of the theorem in Section 4.2.4.

Definition 4.11. (quasi-normal forms) *An $\mathcal{E}$-object is* quasi-normal *(or* in quasi-normal form*) if and only if it does not contain any σ-redex or any β-redex whose major term has a non-propositional principal type.*

Remark Equivalently, an $\mathcal{E}$-object is quasi-normal if and only if, for any redex in the $\mathcal{E}$-object with major term M (i.e. the redex is of the form MN or $\pi_i(M)$), $\mathcal{L}(T_{\mathcal{E}}(M)) = -1$. An $\mathcal{E}$-object may have (i.e. be reduced to) different quasi-normal forms. Furthermore, arbitrary reduction does not in general preserve quasi-normalness. In particular, contracting a β-redex which is an $\mathcal{E}$-proof may create a new redex so that the resulting term is not in quasi-normal form. For example, consider the following $\mathcal{E}$-object

$$M_0 \equiv (\lambda g{:}A \to A.f(g(a)))Id_A,$$

where A is a non-propositional $\mathcal{E}$-type, f a variable of type $\forall x{:}A.P$ which is an $\mathcal{E}$-proposition, a an $\mathcal{E}$-object of type A, and $Id_A \equiv \lambda x{:}A.x$, all being assumed to be in normal form. Then, M_0 is in quasi-normal form, as the major term of its only redex has $\mathcal{E}$-proposition $\forall g{:}A \to A.P$ as its principal type. However, contracting that redex we obtain the $\mathcal{E}$-object $f(Id_A(a))$ which is not in quasi-normal form, since $T_{\mathcal{E}}(Id_A) \equiv A \to A$ is a non-propositional type.

Every $\mathcal{E}$-type in quasi-normal form must be in certain head-normal form, as the following lemma shows.

Lemma 4.12. (forms of quasi-normal $\mathcal{E}$-types) *Every $\mathcal{E}$-type in quasi-normal form has one of the following forms:*

a universe U, a base term, $\Pi x{:}A.B$, or $\Sigma x{:}A.B$.

Therefore, it is indeed of the form

$$(*) \qquad Q_1 x_1{:}A_1 ... Q_n x_n{:}A_n.B,$$

where $n \in \omega$, $Q_i \in \{\Pi, \Sigma\}$, B is either a universe or a base term, and each A_i is also of form $(*)$ above.

Proof By induction on the structure of quasi-normal $\mathcal{E}$-type A. We only remark that when A is of the form $A_1 A_2$ or $\pi_i(A_1)$ $(i = 1, 2)$, A must be a base term. Otherwise, by Lemma 4.10(5), there would be a redex in A whose major term has a non-propositional principal type, contradicting the assumption that A is quasi-normal. □

Theorem 4.13. (quasi-normalisation of* ECC*) *Every $\mathcal{E}$-object can be reduced to some quasi-normal form.*

Proof See Section 4.2.4. □

Corollary 4.14. *Every $\mathcal{E}$-type can be reduced to a quasi-normal form as described in Lemma 4.12.*

Proof By Theorem 4.13 and Lemma 4.12. □

Now, we can define the second dimension of the complexity measure of types—the degrees of types. The idea is that we first define the degrees for the types in quasi-normal form by induction on their structures as made explicit by Lemma 4.12, and then define the degree for any type which is not in quasi-normal form as the same as that of its quasi-normal form, which exists by the quasi-normalisation theorem.

Definition 4.15. (j-degree $\mathcal{D}_j$) *Let A be an $\mathcal{E}$-type. Define the* j-degree *of A for $j \in \omega$, $\mathcal{D}_j A$, as follows.*

- *If A is in quasi-normal form, then $\mathcal{D}_j A$ is defined by induction on its structure:*

  1. *If $\mathcal{L}(A) \neq j$, then $\mathcal{D}_j A =_{\mathrm{df}} 0$;*
  2. *If $A \equiv Type_{j-1}$ (Prop when $j = 0$), then $\mathcal{D}_j A =_{\mathrm{df}} 1$;*
  3. *If A is a base term and $\mathcal{L}(A) = j$, then $\mathcal{D}_j A =_{\mathrm{df}} 1$;*
  4. *If $A \equiv \Pi x{:}A_1.A_2$ or $A \equiv \Sigma x{:}A_1.A_2$, and $\mathcal{L}(A) = j$, then $\mathcal{D}_j A =_{\mathrm{df}} max\{\mathcal{D}_j A_1, \mathcal{D}_j A_2\} + 1$.*

- *If A is not in quasi-normal form, then, let A° be a quasi-normal $\mathcal{E}$-type such that $A \rhd A^\circ$ (A° exists by the quasi-normalisation theorem), and define $\mathcal{D}_j A =_{\mathrm{df}} \mathcal{D}_j A^\circ$.*

We also define $\mathcal{D}_{-1} A =_{\mathrm{df}} 0$ for every $\mathcal{E}$-type A.

Remark Note that the above definition is given in two steps. The degrees of the $\mathcal{E}$-types in quasi-normal form are well-defined by Lemma 4.12. But, since quasi-normal forms are in general not unique, we must show that the degrees for non-quasi-normal types are well defined, that is, the arbitrary choice of A° in the second part of the definition gives a unique degree value. This well-definedness can be proved by Theorem 4.13, Lemma 4.12, and the Church-Rosser theorem, as the first of the following lemmas shows.

Lemma 4.16. *The degrees of types have the following properties.*

1. *$\mathcal{D}_j$ is a function from $\mathcal{E}$-types to natural numbers and respects the computational equality, i.e. $\mathcal{D}_j A = \mathcal{D}_j B$ for any $\mathcal{E}$-types $A \simeq B$.*
2. *For $j \in \omega$, $\mathcal{L}(A) = j$ if and only if $\mathcal{D}_j A \geq 1$.*
3. *For $\mathcal{E}$-types $A \preceq B$, either $\mathcal{L}(A) < \mathcal{L}(B)$ or $\mathcal{L}(A) = \mathcal{L}(B)$ and $\mathcal{D}_j A \leq \mathcal{D}_j B$.*
4. *Suppose $\mathcal{E}^k \vdash N : E_{k+1}$ and B is an $\mathcal{E}^{k+1}$-type. If $\mathcal{L}(E_{k+1}) \leq j$ and $\mathcal{L}(B) \leq j$, then $\mathcal{D}_j([N/e_{k+1}]B) \leq \mathcal{D}_j(B)$.*

Proof The proofs of the above are given as follows.

1. By Lemma 4.12 and the quasi-normalisation theorem, we only have to show that, for $j \in \omega$ and for $\mathcal{E}$-types A and B in quasi-normal form, $A \simeq B$ implies $\mathcal{D}_j A = \mathcal{D}_j B$. As $A \simeq B$, $\mathcal{L}(A) = \mathcal{L}(B) = k$, by Lemma 4.10(1). If $\mathcal{L}(A) \neq j$, then $\mathcal{D}_j(A) = \mathcal{D}_j(B) = 0$. If $\mathcal{L}(A) = j$, $\mathcal{D}_j(A) = \mathcal{D}_j(B)$ can be proved by induction on the structure of A and B using Lemma 4.12, and the Church-Rosser theorem.

2. Obvious from the definition of degrees, Lemma 4.10(1) and Lemma 4.16(1).

3. By Lemma 4.10(2), Lemma 4.16(1) and the quasi-normalisation theorem, we only have to show $\mathcal{D}_j A \leq \mathcal{D}_j B$ for A and B in quasi-normal form such that $A \preceq B$ and $\mathcal{L}(A) = \mathcal{L}(B) = j$. This can be proved by induction on the structure of A and B using Lemma 4.12, Lemma 3.4 and the Church-Rosser theorem.

4. By the quasi-normalisation theorem and Lemma 4.16(1), we only have to show $\mathcal{D}_j[N/e_{k+1}]B \leq \mathcal{D}_j B$ for B in quasi-normal form. We prove this by induction on the structure of B. By Lemma 4.12 and Lemma 4.10(4), we only have to consider the following cases assuming $\mathcal{L}([N/e_{k+1}]B) = \mathcal{L}(B) = j$:

   (a) $B \equiv Type_{j-1}$. Obvious.

   (b) B is a base term. Let y be the key variable of B. If $y \not\equiv e_{k+1}$, then $[N/e_{k+1}]B$ is also a base term and, by definition $\mathcal{D}_j[N/e_{k+1}]B = \mathcal{D}_j B = 1$. If $y \equiv e_{k+1}$, then by Lemma 4.10(5), $\mathcal{L}(T_\mathcal{E}(e_{k+1})) \geq \mathcal{L}(T_\mathcal{E} B) = j + 1$, contradicting the assumption that $\mathcal{L}(E_{k+1}) \leq j$.

   (c) B has the form $\Pi x{:}B_1.B_2$ or $\Sigma x{:}B_1.B_2$. Then, by induction hypothesis, $\mathcal{D}_j[N/e_{k+1}]B = max\{\mathcal{D}_j[N/e_{k+1}]B_1, \mathcal{D}_j[N/e_{k+1}]B_2\} + 1 \leq max\{\mathcal{D}_j B_1, \mathcal{D}_j B_2\} + 1 = \mathcal{D}_j B$. □

Remark Since computationally equal $\mathcal{E}$-types have the same j-degree (Lemma 4.16(1)), we use $\mathcal{D}_j(T_\mathcal{E}(M))$ to denote the j-degree of the principal type of an $\mathcal{E}$-object M.

Lemma 4.16(4) shows that type-preserving substitution does not increase the j-degree of an $\mathcal{E}$-type B if the levels of B and the principal type of the substituted variable are not bigger than j (cf. Remark 2 after Lemma 4.10). Note that the condition $\mathcal{L}(E_{k+1}) \leq j$ is necessary and important (cf. the proof of Lemma 4.19 below).

4.2.3 The complexity measure of types

We are now ready to define the complexity measure of types that makes explicit the predicativity of the formation of non-propositional types.

Definition 4.17. ***(complexity of $\mathcal{E}$-types, β)*** *Let A be an $\mathcal{E}$-type. Then define the complexity of A, βA, as follows:*

$$\beta A \ =_{\mathrm{df}} \ (\mathcal{L}(A)+1,\ \mathcal{D}_{\mathcal{L}(A)}A)$$

where $\mathcal{L}(A)$ is the level of A and $\mathcal{D}_j A$ is the j-degree of A. β-values of $\mathcal{E}$-types are ordered by the lexicographic ordering, denoted by $\leq$.

Lemma 4.18. *Let A and B be $\mathcal{E}$-types.*

1. *If $A \simeq B$, then $\beta(A) = \beta(B)$.*
2. *If $A \preceq B$, then $\beta(A) \leq \beta(B)$.*

Proof By Lemmas 4.10(1)(2) and Lemma 4.16(2). □

The following lemma shows that the complexity measure β makes explicit the predicativity or non-circularity of the formation of *non-propositional* types in the sense that they can be ranked in such a way (by β) that the existence of any non-propositional type depends essentially only on those types with lower ranks. This is one of the key properties used to prove strong normalisation for ECC.

Lemma 4.19. *Let A be a non-propositional $\mathcal{E}$-type. Then, if A reduces to a quasi-normal $\mathcal{E}$-type of the form $\Pi x{:}A_1.A_2$ or $\Sigma x{:}A_1.A_2$, we have*

1. *$\beta(A_1) < \beta(A)$, and*
2. *$\beta([N/x]A_2) < \beta(A)$ for every N such that $\mathcal{E} \vdash N : A_1$.*

Proof As $\mathcal{L}(A_1) \leq \mathcal{L}(A)$ and $\mathcal{L}(A) \geq 0$, either $\mathcal{L}(A_1) < \mathcal{L}(A)$ or $\mathcal{L}(A_1) = \mathcal{L}(A)$ and $\mathcal{D}_{\mathcal{L}(A_1)}A_1 < \mathcal{D}_{\mathcal{L}(A)}A$. So, by definition, $\beta(A_1) < \beta(A)$.

Suppose $\mathcal{E} \vdash N : A_1$. If $\mathcal{L}([N/x]A_2) = -1$, then $\beta([N/x]A_2) = (0,0) < (1,0) \leq \beta A$. If $\mathcal{L}([N/x]A_2) = j \geq 0$, then $\mathcal{L}(A_2) \geq \mathcal{L}([N/x]A_2) = j$ by Lemma 4.10(5). There are two cases to consider:

1. $\mathcal{L}(A_2) > \mathcal{L}([N/x]A_2) = j$. Then, $\beta([N/x]A_2) = (j{+}1, \mathcal{D}_j([N/x]A_2)) < (\mathcal{L}(A_2)+1, \mathcal{D}_{\mathcal{L}(A_2)}A_2) \leq (\mathcal{L}(A)+1, \mathcal{D}_{\mathcal{L}(A)}A) = \beta A$.
2. $\mathcal{L}(A_2) = \mathcal{L}([N/x]A_2) = j$. Then, by Lemma 4.16(4), either $\mathcal{L}(A_1) > j$ or $\mathcal{L}(A_1) \leq j$ and $\mathcal{D}_j([N/x]A_2) \leq \mathcal{D}_j A_2$. For the former case, $\beta([N/x]A_2) = (j+1, \mathcal{D}_j([N/x]A_2)) < \beta A_1 < \beta A$; for the latter case, by Lemma 4.16(4), and the fact $\mathcal{L}(A) = \mathcal{L}(A_2) = j \geq \mathcal{L}(A_1)$, $\beta([N/x]A_2) = (j+1, \mathcal{D}_j([N/x]A_2)) \leq (\mathcal{L}(A_2)+1, \mathcal{D}_j A_2) = \beta A_2 < \beta A$.

This completes the proof of the lemma. □

Remark Note that only *non-propositional* types can be stratified to have the above property. For propositions, there is no complexity measure to stratify them in such a way because the formation of propositions is impredicative (circular). For example, we might have defined $\mathcal{D}_{-1}$ in the same way as $\mathcal{D}_j$ for $j \geq 0$. Then, we would have $\mathcal{D}_{-1}(\Pi X{:}Prop.X) = 2$ but $\mathcal{D}_{-1}([N/X]X) = 3$ for $N \equiv \Pi X{:}Prop.X \to X$.

4.2.4 An inductive proof of the quasi-normalisation theorem

In this section, we prove the quasi-normalisation theorem (Theorem 4.13). As we have seen in Section 4.2.2, the theorem is used to define the degrees of types. However, as we have mentioned there, the quasi-normalisation theorem can not be proved directly without the help of some notion of degrees of types.

The idea to solve this problem is to consider the subsystems ECC^n of ECC. Roughly speaking, ECC^n is the type system obtained from ECC by 'cutting off' the infinite universes at the nth level. It can be readily proved that the non-propositional types at the highest level (i.e. the nth level) of ECC^n have head-normal forms (Lemma 4.20); and therefore their degrees can be defined. Based on this, we can prove the quasi-normalisation result for ECC^n by induction from n to 0, as shown below. Then, the quasi-normalisation theorem for ECC, that is, Theorem 4.13, follows by induction on $n \in \omega$.

The subsystems ECC^n

The subsystems ECC^n ($n \in \omega$) are obtained from ECC via the following changes:

1. The constants $Type_{n+k+1}$ ($k \in \omega$) are removed from the definition of terms.
2. The following side conditions are added to inference rules:
   - $0 \leq j \leq n$ for rules $(C)(\Pi 2)(\Sigma)(pair)(\preceq)$,
   - $0 \leq j < n$ for rule (T), and
   - $B \not\equiv Type_n$ for rule (λ).
3. The following new inference rule is added:

$$\frac{\Gamma \vdash M : U}{\Gamma \vdash M : Type_n} \quad (U \prec Type_n \textit{ is a universe})$$

Informally, we can describe the relationship of ECC^n with ECC as follows:

$$\mathrm{ECC} = \bigcup_{n \in \omega} \mathrm{ECC}^n.$$

As any derivation is finite, it can easily be proved by induction on derivations that a sequence of judgements is a derivation in ECC if and only if it is a derivation in ECC^n for some $n \in \omega$.

Remark All of the notions we have defined for ECC before are defined in the same way for ECC^n, except that the notion of principal type for ECC^n is defined by changing the second clause of Definition 3.22 to the following:

- for any term A', $\Gamma \vdash M : A'$ if and only if $A \preceq A'$ and either A' is a Γ-type or $A' \equiv Type_n$.

All of the theorems and lemmas in Chapter 3 and Section 4.2.1 can be similarly proved except that Theorem 3.15 for ECC^n has an assumption that $A \not\equiv Type_n$. Note that $Type_n$ is not a Γ-type or $\mathcal{E}$-type in ECC^n.

The following lemma shows that the top-level $\mathcal{E}$-types in ECC^n are in head-normal form, which will enable us to establish the basis of the inductive proof of quasi-normalisation for ECC^n.

Lemma 4.20. *Let A be an $\mathcal{E}$-type in* ECC^n *and $\mathcal{L}(A) = n$. Then, either $A \equiv Type_{n-1}$ (Prop when $n = 0$) or A has the form of $\Pi x{:}A_1.A_2$ or $\Sigma x{:}A_1.A_2$.*

Proof By induction on derivations of $\mathcal{E}^i \vdash A : Type_n$ in ECC^n. □

An inductive proof of quasi-normalisation

To prove the quasi-normalisation theorem for ECC, we only have to prove the quasi-normalisation theorem of $\mathrm{ECC}^{\mathbf{n}}$ for an arbitrary $\mathbf{n} \in \omega$. In the rest of this section, $\mathbf{n}$ stands for a fixed (arbitrary) natural number for which $\mathrm{ECC}^{\mathbf{n}}$ is under consideration.

Definition 4.21. ***(j-quasi-normal $\mathcal{E}$-objects)*** *Let $0 \leq j \leq \mathbf{n}$. An $\mathcal{E}$-object in* $\mathrm{ECC}^{\mathbf{n}}$ *is j-*quasi-normal *if and only if for any redex occurring in the $\mathcal{E}$-object with major term M, $\mathcal{L}(T_{\mathcal{E}}(M)) \neq j$.*

Lemma 4.22. *Let $0 \leq j \leq \mathbf{n}$ and $\mathcal{E}$-type A be i-quasi-normal for every i such that $j \leq i \leq \mathbf{n}$ and $\mathcal{L}(A) = j - 1$. Then, A has the form of*

$Type_{j-2}$ (Prop when $j = 1$), a base term, $\Pi x{:}A_1.A_2$ or $\Sigma x{:}A_1.A_2$.

Proof By induction on the structure of A. We only remark that when A is of the form A_1A_2 or $\pi_i(A_1)$ $(i = 1, 2)$, A must be a base term. Otherwise, by Lemma 4.10(5), there would be a redex in A whose major term has a principal type with level $i \geq j$, contradicting the assumption that A is i-quasi-normal. □

The quasi-normalisation theorem for $\mathrm{ECC}^{\mathbf{n}}$ is proved by induction on $\mathbf{j}$ from $\mathbf{n}$ and downwards showing that at each step, every $\mathcal{E}$-object can be reduced to an object in i-quasi-normal form for $i \geq \mathbf{j}$. The proof consists of the following definitions, lemmas, and theorems in the rest of this section which are inductively defined and proved for $\mathbf{j} = \mathbf{n}, \mathbf{n} - 1, ..., 0$. We first summarise and explain the inductive proof steps as follows:

1. Define the notion of $\mathbf{j}$-degree $\mathcal{D}_{\mathbf{j}}$ of $\mathcal{E}$-types (Definition 4.23) and prove its properties (Lemma 4.24).

   For the base case $\mathbf{j} = \mathbf{n}$, $\mathcal{D}_{\mathbf{n}}$ is well-defined by Lemma 4.20. For the induction case $\mathbf{j} = k < \mathbf{n}$, $\mathcal{D}_k$ is well-defined by Lemma 4.22, and Theorem 4.27 for $\mathbf{j} = k + 1$, which holds by induction hypothesis.

2. Define two auxiliary complexity measures $\delta_{\mathbf{j}}$ and $\gamma_{\mathbf{j}}$ and prove their properties (Lemma 4.26).

3. Prove the quasi-normalisation theorem for the $\mathbf{j}$th level (Theorem 4.27 and Corollary 4.28).

Also, we remark that the following proofs do not depend on any results proved in Section 4.2.2 and Section 4.2.3.

***Definition 4.23.* (j-degree $\mathcal{D}_{\mathbf{j}}$ of $\mathcal{E}$-types in $\mathrm{ECC}^{\mathbf{n}}$)** *The* $\mathbf{j}$-degree *$\mathcal{D}_{\mathbf{j}}(A)$ of an $\mathcal{E}$-type A in $\mathrm{ECC}^{\mathbf{n}}$ is defined as follows.*

- *$\mathcal{D}_{\mathbf{j}}$ for the $\mathcal{E}$-types A, which are i-quasi-normal for $\mathbf{j} < i \leq \mathbf{n}$, is defined as follows:*

  1. *If $\mathcal{L}(A) \neq \mathbf{j}$, then $\mathcal{D}_{\mathbf{j}}(A) =_{\mathrm{df}} 0$;*
  2. *If $A \equiv Type_{\mathbf{j}-1}$ (Prop when $\mathbf{j} = 0$), then $\mathcal{D}_{\mathbf{j}}(A) =_{\mathrm{df}} 1$;*
  3. *If $\mathcal{L}(A) = \mathbf{j}$ and A is a base term, then $\mathcal{D}_{\mathbf{j}}(A) =_{\mathrm{df}} 1$;*
  4. *If $\mathcal{L}(A) = \mathbf{j}$, and $A \equiv Qx{:}A_1.A_2$, where $Q \in \{\Pi, \Sigma\}$, then $\mathcal{D}_{\mathbf{j}}(A) =_{\mathrm{df}} max\{\mathcal{D}_{\mathbf{j}}(A_1), \mathcal{D}_{\mathbf{j}}(A_2)\} + 1$.*

- *If the $\mathcal{E}$-type A is not k-quasi-normal for some $k > \mathbf{j}$, then, let A° be an i-quasi-normal term for $i > \mathbf{j}$ such that $A \rhd A^\circ$ (A° exists by Theorem 4.27 for $\mathbf{j}+1$) and define $\mathcal{D}_{\mathbf{j}}(A) =_{\mathrm{df}} \mathcal{D}_{\mathbf{j}}(A^\circ)$.*

Remark The reader may have noticed the similarity of the above definition to Definition 4.15. When $\mathbf{j} = \mathbf{n}$, the above definition is well-defined by Lemma 4.20. For $\mathbf{j} < \mathbf{n}$, it is well-defined by Lemma 4.22 and Theorem 4.27, the latter of which holds for $\mathbf{j}+1$ by induction hypothesis.

Lemma 4.24. *The $\mathbf{j}$-degrees of $\mathcal{E}$-types in $\mathrm{ECC}^{\mathbf{n}}$ have the following properties.*

1. *$\mathcal{D}_{\mathbf{j}}$ is a function from the $\mathcal{E}$-types of $\mathrm{ECC}^{\mathbf{n}}$ to natural numbers and respects conversion, i.e. $\mathcal{D}_{\mathbf{j}}A = \mathcal{D}_{\mathbf{j}}B$ if $A \simeq B$ are $\mathcal{E}$-types of $\mathrm{ECC}^{\mathbf{n}}$.*
2. *$\mathcal{L}(A) = \mathbf{j}$ if and only if $\mathcal{D}_{\mathbf{j}}A \geq 1$.*
3. *If $A \preceq B$, then either $\mathcal{L}(A) < \mathcal{L}(B)$, or $\mathcal{L}(A) = \mathcal{L}(B)$ and $\mathcal{D}_{\mathbf{j}}A \leq D_{\mathbf{j}}B$.*
4. *Suppose $\mathcal{E}^k \vdash N : E_{k+1}$ and B is an $\mathcal{E}^{k+1}$-type. If $\mathcal{L}(E_{k+1}) \leq \mathbf{j}$ and $\mathcal{L}(B) \leq \mathbf{j}$, then $\mathcal{D}_{\mathbf{j}}([N/e_{k+1}]B) \leq \mathcal{D}_{\mathbf{j}}(B)$.*

Proof The proofs for the above are very similar to those given for Lemma 4.16, except that instead of Lemma 4.12 and Theorem 4.13, we use Lemma 4.20 (when considering $\mathbf{j} = \mathbf{n}$), Lemma 4.22 and Theorem 4.27 (when considering $\mathbf{j} < \mathbf{n}$), the last of which holds for $\mathbf{j}+1$ by induction hypothesis. See [Luo90a] for details. □

The aim of quasi-normalisation at the $\mathbf{j}$th level is to show that every $\mathcal{E}$-object can be reduced to a term which is i-quasi-normal for every i such that $\mathbf{j} \leq i \leq \mathbf{n}$. We first define two auxiliary measures and prove some of their properties, which will be used in the proof of the theorem of quasi-normalisation below.

Definition 4.25. *Let $\mathcal{E}$-object R be a redex. We define $\delta_{\mathbf{j}}R$ to be the $\mathbf{j}$-degree of the principal type of the major term of R; that is, if M is the major term of redex R,*

$$\delta_{\mathbf{j}}R =_{\mathrm{df}} \mathcal{D}_{\mathbf{j}}(T_{\mathcal{E}}M).$$

For any $\mathcal{E}$-object M, we define $\gamma_{\mathbf{j}}M$ to be the largest $\delta_{\mathbf{j}}$-value of the redexes occurring in M; that is,

$$\gamma_{\mathbf{j}}M =_{\mathrm{df}} max\{\, \delta_{\mathbf{j}}(R) \mid R \text{ is a redex occurring in } M \,\}.$$

Remark Note that, by Lemma 4.24(2), an $\mathcal{E}$-type in ECC$^{\mathbf{n}}$ is $\mathbf{j}$-quasi-normal if and only if $\gamma_{\mathbf{j}}M = 0$. The above measures are extensions of those considered by Pottinger and Seldin [Pot87].

Lemma 4.26. *The above measures have the following properties.*

1. *Suppose* $\mathcal{E}^k \vdash N : E_{k+1}$, $\mathcal{E}^{k+1} \vdash M : B$ *and* M *is* i*-quasi-normal for* $i > \mathbf{j}$. *Then,* $\gamma_{\mathbf{j}}([N/e_{k+1}]M) \leq max\{\gamma_{\mathbf{j}}M, \gamma_{\mathbf{j}}N, \mathcal{D}_{\mathbf{j}}(T_{\mathcal{E}}N)\}$.

2. *Let* $\mathcal{E}$*-object* M *be a redex and* M' *be its contractum. If* M *is* i*-quasi-normal for* $\mathbf{j} < i \leq \mathbf{n}$ *and* M *is the only redex in* M *whose* $\delta_{\mathbf{j}}$*-value equals* $\gamma_{\mathbf{j}}M > 0$*, then*

   (a) $\gamma_{\mathbf{j}}M' < \gamma_{\mathbf{j}}M$, *and*

   (b) $\mathcal{D}_{\mathbf{j}}(T_{\mathcal{E}}M') < \gamma_{\mathbf{j}}M$, *if* M' *is of* λ*-form or pair-form.*

Proof (1) The first lemma is proved by induction on the structure of M. The only interesting cases are when M is of the form M_1M_2 or $\pi_i(M_1)$; the other cases are either obvious or straightforward by induction hypothesis. Here, we consider the case for $M \equiv M_1M_2$. If $[N/e_{k+1}]M$ is not a β-redex such that $\delta_{\mathbf{j}}([N/e_{k+1}]M) > 0$, then by induction hypothesis,

$$\gamma_{\mathbf{j}}([N/e_{k+1}]M) \leq max\{\gamma_{\mathbf{j}}M, \gamma_{\mathbf{j}}N, \mathcal{D}_{\mathbf{j}}(T_{\mathcal{E}}N)\}.$$

If $[N/e_{k+1}]M$ is a β-redex such that $\delta_{\mathbf{j}}([N/e_{k+1}]M) > 0$, then by induction hypothesis we only have to show

$$\delta_{\mathbf{j}}[N/e_{k+1}]M = \mathcal{D}_{\mathbf{j}}(T_{\mathcal{E}}[N/e_{k+1}]M_1) \leq max\{\gamma_{\mathbf{j}}M, \gamma_{\mathbf{j}}N, \mathcal{D}_{\mathbf{j}}(T_{\mathcal{E}}N)\}.$$

As $[N/e_{k+1}]M$ is a β-redex, there are two cases to consider:

1. $M_1 \equiv e_{k+1}$ and N is of λ-form. Then, $\mathcal{D}_{\mathbf{j}}(T_{\mathcal{E}}[N/e_{k+1}]M_1) = \mathcal{D}_{\mathbf{j}}(T_{\mathcal{E}}N)$.

2. M_1 is of λ-form. We only have to show $\mathcal{D}_{\mathbf{j}}(T_{\mathcal{E}}[N/e_{k+1}]M_1) \leq \mathcal{D}_{\mathbf{j}}(T_{\mathcal{E}}M_1)$, as $\mathcal{D}_{\mathbf{j}}(T_{\mathcal{E}}M_1) = \delta_{\mathbf{j}}M \leq \gamma_{\mathbf{j}}M$. By Cut (Theorem 3.14), $\mathcal{E}^k \vdash [N/e_{k+1}]M_1 : [N/e_{k+1}]T_{\mathcal{E}}M_1$. So, $T_{\mathcal{E}}[N/e_{k+1}]M_1 \preceq [N/e_{k+1}]T_{\mathcal{E}}M_1$. Furthermore, by the assumption that $\mathcal{D}_{\mathbf{j}}(T_{\mathcal{E}}[N/e_{k+1}]M_1) > 0$, Lemmas 4.10(2)(4) and the assumption that M is i-quasi-normal for $i > \mathbf{j}$,

   $$\mathbf{j} = \mathcal{L}(T_{\mathcal{E}}[N/e_{k+1}]M_1) \leq \mathcal{L}([N/e_{k+1}]T_{\mathcal{E}}M_1) \leq \mathcal{L}(T_{\mathcal{E}}M_1) \leq \mathbf{j},$$

   which implies that $\mathcal{L}(T_{\mathcal{E}}[N/e_{k+1}]M_1) = \mathcal{L}([N/e_{k+1}]T_{\mathcal{E}}M_1)$. Hence, by Lemma 4.16(3) and induction hypothesis, $\mathcal{D}_{\mathbf{j}}(T_{\mathcal{E}}[N/e_{k+1}]M_1) \leq \mathcal{D}_{\mathbf{j}}([N/e_{k+1}]T_{\mathcal{E}}M_1) \leq \mathcal{D}_{\mathbf{j}}(T_{\mathcal{E}}M_1)$.

(2) Now, we prove the second lemma, which has two conclusions. For conclusion (*a*), if M is a σ-redex, it is obvious. If $M \equiv (\lambda x{:}A.M_1)N \rhd_1 [N/x]M_1 \equiv M'$, we have by the assumptions, $\gamma_{\mathbf{j}} M_1 < \gamma_{\mathbf{j}} M$, $\gamma_{\mathbf{j}} N < \gamma_{\mathbf{j}} M$, and $\mathcal{D}_{\mathbf{j}} A < \mathcal{D}_{\mathbf{j}}(T_{\mathcal{E}}(\lambda x{:}A.M_1)) = \gamma_{\mathbf{j}} M$. By Lemma 4.10(2) and the assumption that M is i-quasi-normal for $i > \mathbf{j}$ and $\gamma_{\mathbf{j}} M > 0$, $\mathcal{L}(T_{\mathcal{E}} N) \leq \mathcal{L}(A) \leq \mathbf{j}$. So, $\mathcal{D}_{\mathbf{j}}(T_{\mathcal{E}} N) \leq \mathcal{D}_{\mathbf{j}} A$. So, by Lemma 4.26(1) proved above, $\gamma_{\mathbf{j}} M' < \gamma_{\mathbf{j}} M$.

For conclusion (*b*), if $M \equiv \pi_i(\langle M_1, M_2 \rangle_C)$ is a σ-redex, then, $\mathcal{D}_{\mathbf{j}}(T_{\mathcal{E}} M') = \mathcal{D}_{\mathbf{j}}(T_{\mathcal{E}} M_i) < \mathcal{D}_{\mathbf{j}} C = \gamma_{\mathbf{j}} M$. If $M \equiv (\lambda x{:}A.M_1)N$ is a β-redex and M' is of λ-form (or pair-form), we have two possibilities:

1. $M_1 \equiv x$. Then $\mathcal{D}_{\mathbf{j}}(T_{\mathcal{E}} M') = \mathcal{D}_{\mathbf{j}}(T_{\mathcal{E}} N) \leq \mathcal{D}_{\mathbf{j}} A < \mathcal{D}_{\mathbf{j}}(T_{\mathcal{E}}(\lambda x{:}A.M_1)) = \gamma_{\mathbf{j}} M$.

2. M_1 is of λ-form (or pair-form). Then, by Lemma 4.16(2), Lemma 4.24(4) and the assumption that $\gamma_{\mathbf{j}} M > 0$, $\mathcal{D}_{\mathbf{j}}(T_{\mathcal{E}} M') = \mathcal{D}_{\mathbf{j}}(T_{\mathcal{E}}[N/x]M_1) \leq \mathcal{D}_{\mathbf{j}}([N/x]T_{\mathcal{E}} M_1) \leq \mathcal{D}_{\mathbf{j}}(T_{\mathcal{E}} M_1) < \mathcal{D}_{\mathbf{j}}(T_{\mathcal{E}}(\lambda x{:}A.M_1)) = \gamma_{\mathbf{j}} M$.

This completes the proof of the lemma. □

We are now ready to prove the quasi-normalisation theorem at the $\mathbf{j}$th level for $\mathrm{ECC}^{\mathbf{n}}$.

Theorem 4.27. *Every $\mathcal{E}$-object in* $\mathrm{ECC}^{\mathbf{n}}$ *can be reduced to some $\mathcal{E}$-object which is i-quasi-normal for every i such that* $\mathbf{j} \leq i \leq \mathbf{n}$.

Proof By our global induction hypothesis (on $\mathbf{j}$), we only have to show that if $\mathcal{E}$-object M is i-quasi-normal for all i such that $\mathbf{j} < i \leq \mathbf{n}$, then $M \rhd N$ for some N which is i-quasi-normal for all i such that $\mathbf{j} \leq i \leq \mathbf{n}$. So, it is enough to prove the following two points:

1. Any $\mathcal{E}$-object M can be reduced to a $\mathbf{j}$-quasi-normal term by contracting σ-redexes and β-redexes which are not $\mathcal{E}$-proofs.

2. Reducing σ-redexes and β-redexes which are not $\mathcal{E}$-proofs preserves i-quasi-normalness for $i > \mathbf{j}$.

The first can be proved by double induction on $\gamma_{\mathbf{j}} M$ and the number of redexes occurring in M whose $\delta_{\mathbf{j}}$-values are equal to $\gamma_{\mathbf{j}} M > 0$. Given an $\mathcal{E}$-object M, take any redex in the term whose $\delta_{\mathbf{j}}$-value is $\gamma_{\mathbf{j}} M > 0$ and whose proper subterms do not contain any redex whose $\delta_{\mathbf{j}}$-value is $\gamma_{\mathbf{j}} M$. (Note that such a redex is not an $\mathcal{E}$-proof if it is a β-redex.) By Lemma 4.26(2) above, reducing M by contracting the redex thus selected decreases by one the number of redexes whose $\delta_{\mathbf{j}}$-values are equal to $\gamma_{\mathbf{j}}M > 0$ and, if it is the only redex whose $\delta_{\mathbf{j}}$-value is $\gamma_{\mathbf{j}}M$, $\gamma_{\mathbf{j}}M$ is decreased by one or more.

For the second point, when $\mathbf{j} = \mathbf{n}$, it is trivial. We now prove it for $\mathbf{j} < \mathbf{n}$. By our global induction on $\mathbf{j}$, we only have to show that, if M is i-quasi-normal for $i > \mathbf{j}$ and $M \rhd_1 N$ by contracting a σ-redex or a β-redex which is not an $\mathcal{E}$-proof, then N is $(\mathbf{j}+1)$-quasi-normal. We prove this by induction on the structure of M.

1. M is not a variable or a universe.
2. M is of the form $\Pi x{:}A.B$, $\lambda x{:}A.B$, $\Sigma x{:}A.B$ or $\langle B, C\rangle_A$. By induction hypothesis.
3. $M \equiv M_1M_2$. Consider the following three subcases:
   (a) $M \equiv M_1M_2 \rhd_1 M_1N_2 \equiv N$. By induction hypothesis.
   (b) $M \equiv M_1M_2 \rhd_1 N_1M_2 \equiv N$. By induction hypothesis, if N is not $(\mathbf{j}+1)$-quasi-normal, N must be a β-redex ($N_1 \equiv \lambda x{:}X.Y$) such that $\delta_{\mathbf{j}+1}N > 0$. This is impossible as the following shows:
      - $M_1 \equiv \lambda x{:}X_1.Y_1 \rhd_1 \lambda x{:}X.Y \equiv N_1$. But then, as $T_{\mathcal{E}}N_1 \preceq T_{\mathcal{E}}M_1$, by Lemma 4.16(3), either $\mathcal{L}(T_{\mathcal{E}}N_1) \le \mathcal{L}(T_{\mathcal{E}}M_1) < \mathbf{j}+1$ or $\mathcal{D}_{\mathbf{j}+1}(T_{\mathcal{E}}N_1) \le \mathcal{D}_{\mathbf{j}+1}(T_{\mathcal{E}}M_1) = 0$.
      - $M_1 \equiv (\lambda x{:}X_1.Y_1)Z_1 \rhd_1 [Z_1/x]Y_1 \equiv N_1$. Then, either $Y_1 \equiv x$ and $Z_1 \equiv N_1$, or $Y_1 \equiv \lambda y{:}Y_1'.Y_1''$. In either case, by Lemma 4.16(2,3), $\delta_i M_1 > 0$ for some $i \ge \mathbf{j}+1$, which is impossible.
      - $M_1 \equiv \pi_i(\langle X_1, X_2\rangle_A) \rhd_1 X_i \equiv N_1$. Then, either $\mathcal{L}(T_{\mathcal{E}}N_1) < \mathcal{L}(A)$ or $\mathcal{D}_{\mathbf{j}+1}(T_{\mathcal{E}}N_1) \le \mathcal{D}_{\mathbf{j}+1}A = 0$.
   (c) $M \equiv M_1M_2 \equiv (\lambda x{:}X.Y)M_2 \rhd_1 [M_2/x]Y \equiv N$. By Lemma 4.26(1), $\gamma_{\mathbf{j}+1}N \le max\{\gamma_{\mathbf{j}+1}Y, \gamma_{\mathbf{j}+1}M_2, \mathcal{D}_{\mathbf{j}+1}(T_{\mathcal{E}}M_2)\}$. By induction hypothesis, if N is not $(\mathbf{j}+1)$-quasi-normal, M_2 must be the major term of a new-created redex in N such that $\mathcal{D}_{\mathbf{j}+1}(T_{\mathcal{E}}M_2) > 0$. However, as $T_{\mathcal{E}}M_2 \preceq X$ and M is not an $\mathcal{E}$-proof , we would have $\delta_i M = \mathcal{D}_i(T_{\mathcal{E}}M_1) \ge \mathcal{D}_i X > 0$ for some $i \ge \mathbf{j}+1$.
4. $M \equiv \pi_i(M')$. Consider the following two subcases:
   (a) $M \equiv \pi_i(M') \equiv \pi_i(\langle X_1, X_2\rangle_A) \rhd_1 X_i \equiv N$. Obvious.
   (b) $M \equiv \pi_i(M') \rhd_1 \pi_i(N') \equiv N$. By induction hypothesis, if N is not $(\mathbf{j}+1)$-quasi-normal, it must be the case that $N' \equiv \langle X, Y\rangle_A$ and $\delta_{\mathbf{j}+1}N = \mathcal{D}_{\mathbf{j}+1}A > 0$. There are only three possibilities:

- $M' \equiv \langle X_1, Y_1\rangle_{A_1}$. Then, $\delta_{\mathbf{j}+1}N = \mathcal{D}_{\mathbf{j}+1}A = \mathcal{D}_{\mathbf{j}+1}A_1 = \delta_{\mathbf{j}+1}M = 0$.
- $M' \equiv M_0 \equiv (\lambda x{:}X_0.Y_0)Z_0 \triangleright_1 [Z_0/x]Y_0 \equiv N'$. Then either (1) $Y_0 \equiv x$ and $Z_0 \equiv N_0$, or (2) $Y_0 \equiv \langle X_1, Y_1\rangle_{A_1}$. In either case, we have $\delta_i M_0 > 0$ for some $i \geq \mathbf{j} + 1$, which is impossible.
- $M' \equiv M_0 \equiv \pi_i(\langle X_1, Y_1\rangle_{A_1}) \triangleright_1 X_i \equiv N'$. Then, either $\mathcal{L}(A) \leq \mathcal{L}(A_1) < \mathbf{j}+1$ or $\delta_{\mathbf{j}+1}M' = \mathcal{D}_{\mathbf{j}+1}(A) \leq \mathcal{D}_{\mathbf{j}+1}(A_1) = 0$.

This completes the proof of the theorem. □

Remark In the above proof, the condition that a β-redex to be reduced is not an $\mathcal{E}$-proof is important. Reducing a proof β-redex may create a new redex, destroying the i-quasi-normalness of a term. For example, in the example given in the remark after Definition 4.11, it may be the case that $\mathcal{L}(A \to A) \geq \mathbf{j}$.

Corollary 4.28. *If $\mathcal{E}$-type A in* ECC$^{\mathbf{n}}$ *is i-quasi-normal for every i such that $\mathbf{j} \leq i \leq \mathbf{n}$ and $\mathcal{L}(A) = \mathbf{j} - 1$, then A can be reduced to a term of the form given in Lemma 4.22 with $j = \mathbf{j}$.*

Proof By Theorem 4.27 and Lemma 4.22. □

4.3 Strong normalisation

We now apply the reducibility method to prove strong normalisation for ECC. The central theme is to define an interpretation of $\mathcal{E}$-objects in which types are interpreted as saturated sets (see Definition 4.6 in Section 4.1.3), and then prove the soundness of the interpretation, which implies the strong normalisation theorem. The outline of the reducibility method in Section 4.1.1 may be used by the reader as a guidance to understanding the following development, though it is more sophisticated.

4.3.1 Possible denotations of objects

We first define a notion of *denotation-sets* which indicates the possible denotations of an $\mathcal{E}$-object in the interpretation (subject to some variable assignment). In particular, the possible denotations of an $\mathcal{E}$-type A are the A-saturated sets.

Definition 4.29. (denotation-sets of $\mathcal{E}$-objects) *The* set of (possible) denotations *of an $\mathcal{E}$-object M, $V(M)$, is defined by considering the form of its principal type $T_{\mathcal{E}}(M)$, which is assumed to be in quasi-normal form, and by induction on the complexity measure $\beta(T_{\mathcal{E}}(M))$:*

1. *If $T_{\mathcal{E}}(M)$ is a universe (i.e. M is an $\mathcal{E}$-type), then $V(M) =_{\mathrm{df}} Sat(M)$.*
2. *If $T_{\mathcal{E}}(M)$ is an $\mathcal{E}$-proposition (i.e. M is an $\mathcal{E}$-proof), then $V(M) =_{\mathrm{df}} \{\theta\}$, where θ is a fixed arbitrary symbol.*
3. *If $T_{\mathcal{E}}(M)$ is a base term, then $V(M) =_{\mathrm{df}} \{\theta\}$.*
4. *If $T_{\mathcal{E}}(M) \equiv \Pi x{:}A_1.A_2$ is a non-propositional $\mathcal{E}$-type, then define $V(M)$ as the set consisting of the functions f such that*
   - *(a) the domain of f, $dom(f) = \{\, (N, v) \mid \mathcal{E} \vdash N : A_1, v \in V(N) \,\}$,*
   - *(b) $f(N, v) \in V(MN)$ for $(N, v) \in dom(f)$, and*
   - *(c) $f(N, v) = f(N', v)$ for $(N, v), (N', v) \in dom(f)$ such that $N \simeq N'$.*
5. *If $T_{\mathcal{E}}(M) \equiv \Sigma x{:}A_1.A_2$, then*

$$V(M) =_{\mathrm{df}} \{\, (v_1, v_2) \mid v_1 \in V(\pi_1(M)), v_2 \in V(\pi_2(M)) \,\}.$$

Remark The above definition is well-defined by the quasi-normalisation theorem (Theorem 4.13), Lemma 4.12, Lemma 4.18, Lemma 4.19, and the Church-Rosser theorem. Note that the quasi-normalisation results are essential for the definition to work and the properties of the complexity measure β are also important. For example, when non-propositional $\mathcal{E}$-type $\Pi x{:}A_1.A_2$ is the principal type of M, we know that, for $\mathcal{E} \vdash N : A_1$, $V(N)$ and $V(MN)$ are already defined because $\beta(T_{\mathcal{E}}(N)) \leq \beta(A_1) < \beta(\Pi x{:}A_1.A_2)$ and $\beta(T_{\mathcal{E}}(MN)) \leq \beta([N/x]A_2) < \beta(\Pi x{:}A_1.A_2)$ by Lemma 4.18 and Lemma 4.19.

Computationally equal objects have the same possible denotations, as the following lemma shows.

Lemma 4.30. *Let M and N be $\mathcal{E}$-objects. If $M \simeq N$, then $V(M) = V(N)$.*

Proof By the same induction principle used in Definition 4.29. □

Every $\mathcal{E}$-object has at least one possible denotation. In fact, the proof of the following lemma defines a 'canonical denotation' for each $\mathcal{E}$-object.

Lemma 4.31. (canonical denotation of $\mathcal{E}$-objects) *For every $\mathcal{E}$-object M, $V(M)$ is not empty.*

Proof The following definition gives every $\mathcal{E}$-object M a 'canonical' denotation $v_M \in V(M)$, by the same induction as used in Definition 4.29.

1. If M is an $\mathcal{E}$-type, then $v_M =_{\text{df}} SN(M)$.
2. If M is an $\mathcal{E}$-proof, then $v_M =_{\text{df}} \theta$.
3. If $T_{\mathcal{E}}(M)$ reduces to a quasi-normal base term, then $v_M =_{\text{df}} \theta$.
4. If $T_{\mathcal{E}}(M)$ reduces to a quasi-normal non-propositional $\mathcal{E}$-type $\Pi x{:}A_1.A_2$, then v_M is defined to be the function $f \in V(M)$ such that $f(N, v) = v_{MN}$ for all $(N, v) \in dom(f)$.
5. If $T_{\mathcal{E}}(M)$ reduces to $\Sigma x{:}A_1.A_2$ in quasi-normal form, then $v_M =_{\text{df}} (v_{\pi_1(M)}, v_{\pi_2(M)})$. □

4.3.2 Assignments and valuations

In this section, variable assignments and valuations are defined and studied. We first introduce a notation for simultaneous substitution.

Notation (simultaneous substitution) We write $[N_1, ..., N_n/x_1, ..., x_n]M$ for (the resulting term by) the *simultaneous substitution* of terms N_i for the free occurrences of variables x_i $(i = 1, ..., n)$ in M.

Lemma 4.32. (simultaneous substitution) *If $\mathcal{E}^k \vdash M : A$ and, for all $i \le k$, $\mathcal{E} \vdash N_i : [N_1, ..., N_{i-1}/e_1, ..., e_{i-1}]E_i$, then*

$$\mathcal{E} \vdash [N_1, ..., N_k/e_1, ..., e_k]M : [N_1, ..., N_k/e_1, ..., e_k]A.$$

Proof As $\mathcal{E}^k \vdash M : A$, we have, by repeated applications of rule (λ),

$$\mathcal{E} \vdash \lambda e_1{:}E_1 ... \lambda e_k{:}E_k.M : \Pi e_1{:}E_1 ... \Pi e_k{:}E_k.A.$$

Then, by repeated applications of rule (app) and assuming that the bound variables e_i above are not in $\bigcup_{1 \le i \le k} FV(N_i)$, we have

$$\mathcal{E} \vdash (\lambda e_1{:}E_1 ... \lambda e_k{:}E_k.M)N_1 ... N_k : [N_1, ..., N_k/e_1, ..., e_k]A.$$

The result then follows from Subject Reduction (Theorem 3.16). □

We now introduce the notions of assignment and valuation.

Definition 4.33. ***($\mathcal{E}$-assignment and $\mathcal{E}$-valuation)*** *An* $\mathcal{E}$-assignment *is a function $\phi : FV(\mathcal{E}^k) \to \mathcal{T}$ for some $k \in \omega$ such that $\mathcal{E} \vdash \phi(e_i) : \phi(E_i)$ for each $1 \leq i \leq k$, where $\mathcal{E}_i \equiv e_i{:}E_i$. (We also write ϕ for the simultaneous substitution determined by ϕ, i.e. $[\phi(e_1), ..., \phi(e_k)/e_1, ..., e_k]$.)*

An $\mathcal{E}$-valuation *is a pair of functions $\rho = (\phi, val)$ such that ϕ is an $\mathcal{E}$-assignment and val is a function with $dom(\phi)$ as its domain such that, for each $e_i \in dom(\phi)$, $val(e_i) \in V(\phi(e_i))$. The domain of ρ is the domain of ϕ.*

An $\mathcal{E}$-valuation ρ with domain $FV(\mathcal{E}^k)$ covers *an $\mathcal{E}$-object M if and only if $\mathcal{E}^k \vdash M : A$ for some A.*

Lemma 4.34. ***(extensibility of $\mathcal{E}$-valuations)*** *Let $A \equiv E_m$ be an $\mathcal{E}^k$-type, where $m \geq k$. If $\mathcal{E} \vdash N_j : [N_1, ..., N_{j-1}/e_1, ..., e_{j-1}]E_j$ for $1 \leq j \leq k$ and $\mathcal{E} \vdash N : [N_1, ..., N_k/e_1, ..., e_k]A$, then there exist variables $y_{k+1}, ..., y_{m-1}$ such that*

$$\mathcal{E} \vdash y_{k+i} : [N_1, ..., N_k, y_{k+1}, ..., y_{k+i-1}/e_1, ..., e_{k+i-1}]E_{k+i},$$

for $i = 1, ..., m-k-1$, and

$$\mathcal{E} \vdash N : [N_1, ..., N_k, y_{k+1}, ..., y_{m-1}/e_1, ..., e_{m-1}]A.$$

Proof For $i = 1, ..., m-k-1$, E_{k+i} are $\mathcal{E}^{k+i-1}$-types, and so $\Pi e_1{:}E_1 ... \Pi e_{k+i-1}{:}E_{k+i-1}.E_{k+i}$ are $\mathcal{E}$-types and there exist variables z_i such that $\mathcal{E} \vdash z_i : \Pi e_1{:}E_1 ... \Pi e_{k+i-1}{:}E_{k+i-1}.E_{k+i}$. Hence, by induction on $i = 1, ..., m-k-1$, we have

$$\begin{aligned} \mathcal{E} &\vdash z_i N_1 ... N_k y_{k+1} ... y_{k+i-1} \\ &: [N_1, ..., N_k, y_{k+1}, ..., y_{k+i-1}/e_1, ..., e_{k+i-1}]E_{k+i}. \end{aligned}$$

So, $[N_1, ..., N_k, y_{k+1}, ..., y_{k+i-1}/e_1, ..., e_{k+i-1}]E_{k+i}$ is an $\mathcal{E}$-type, by Type Reflection (Theorem 3.15). Hence, there exists y_{k+i} satisfying the requirement. Noticing that $[N_1, ..., N_k, y_{k+1}, ..., y_{m-1}/e_1, ..., e_{m-1}]A \equiv [N_1, ..., N_k/e_1, ..., e_k]A$ as $FV(A) \subseteq \{e_1, ..., e_k\}$, we have

$$\mathcal{E} \vdash N : [N_1, ..., N_k, y_{k+1}, ..., y_{m-1}/e_1, ..., e_{m-1}]A.$$

□

Remark The above lemma shows that, if $\mathcal{E}$-valuation $\rho = (\phi, val)$ covers N and A, and $\mathcal{E} \vdash N : \phi(A)$, then ρ can be extended to an $\mathcal{E}$-valuation $\rho' = (\phi', val')$ such that $\phi'(x) = N$ for some variable $x \notin dom(\rho)$.

4.3.3 The interpretation

We now define the interpretation of $\mathcal{E}$-objects. Every $\mathcal{E}$-object is given a unique denotation in its denotation-set, subject to an $\mathcal{E}$-valuation.

***Definition 4.35. (Evaluation** $Eval_\rho$) *Let $\rho = (\phi, val)$ be an $\mathcal{E}$-valuation. The* evaluation function *$Eval_\rho$ of $\mathcal{E}$-objects which are covered by ρ are defined as follows:*

1. *If M is an $\mathcal{E}$-proof, then $Eval_\rho(M) =_{\mathrm{df}} \theta$.*
2. *If M is not an $\mathcal{E}$-proof, $Eval_\rho(M)$ is defined by induction on the structure of M:*
   (a) *M is a universe. Then $Eval_\rho(M) =_{\mathrm{df}} SN(M)$.*
   (b) *M is a variable. Then $Eval_\rho(M) =_{\mathrm{df}} val(M)$.*
   (c) *$M \equiv \Pi x{:}M_1.M_2$. We may assume that $x \notin dom(\rho)$. Then, $Eval_\rho(M)$ is defined to be the set of the terms F such that*
      i. *$\mathcal{E} \vdash F : \phi(M)$, and*
      ii. *$FN \in Eval_{\rho'}(M_2)$ for every $\mathcal{E}$-valuation $\rho' = (\phi', val')$ which extends ρ such that $\phi'(x) = N \in Eval_\rho(M_1)$.*
   (d) *$M \equiv \lambda x{:}M_1.M_2$. We may assume that $x \notin dom(\rho)$. Then, $Eval_\rho(M)$ is defined to be the function f such that*
      i. *$dom(f) = \{\, (N, v) \mid \mathcal{E} \vdash N : \phi(M_1), v \in V(N) \,\}$, and*
      ii. *$f(N, v) = Eval_{\rho'}(M_2)$ for $(N, v) \in dom(f)$, where ρ' extends ρ such that $\rho'(x) = (N, v)$.*
   (e) *$M \equiv M_1 M_2$. $Eval_\rho(M) =_{\mathrm{df}} Eval_\rho(M_1)(\phi(M_2), Eval_\rho(M_2))$.*
   (f) *$M \equiv \Sigma x{:}M_1.M_2$. We may assume that $x \notin dom(\rho)$. Then, $Eval_\rho(M)$ is defined to be the set of the terms P such that*
      i. *$\mathcal{E} \vdash P : \phi(M)$, and*
      ii. *$\pi_1(P) \in Eval_\rho(M_1)$ and $\pi_2(P) \in Eval_{\rho'}(M_2)$ for every $\mathcal{E}$-valuation $\rho' = (\phi', val')$ which extends ρ such that $\phi'(x) = \pi_1(P)$.*
   (g) *$M \equiv \langle M_1, M_2 \rangle_A$. $Eval_\rho(M) =_{\mathrm{df}} (Eval_\rho(M_1), Eval_\rho(M_2))$.*
   (h) *$M \equiv \pi_i(M')$. Then, $Eval_\rho(M) =_{\mathrm{df}} v_i$, if $Eval_\rho(M') = (v_1, v_2)$, where $i \in \{1, 2\}$.*

The following lemma guarantees the well-definedness of the interpretation. In particular, it implies that every $\mathcal{E}$-type is interpreted as a saturated set.

Lemma 4.36. (well definedness of Eval) *Let $\rho = (\phi, val)$ be an $\mathcal{E}$-valuation which covers $\mathcal{E}$-object M.*

1. *If $\mathcal{E}$-valuation $\rho' = (\phi', val')$ covers M, and $\phi(x) \simeq \phi'(x)$ and $val(x) = val'(x)$ for every $x \in FV(M)$, then $Eval_\rho M = Eval_{\rho'} M$.*

2. *$Eval_\rho(M) \in V(\phi(M))$.*

Proof If M is an $\mathcal{E}$-proof, then so are $\phi(M)$ and $\phi'(M)$, and we have

$$Eval_\rho M = Eval_{\rho'} M = \theta \in \{\theta\} = V(\phi(M)) = V(\phi'(M))$$

If M is not an $\mathcal{E}$-proof, we prove the two statements of the lemma by mutual induction on the structure of M.[20] The proof of the first statement is given as follows.

1. M is a universe. $Eval_\rho M = SN(M) = Eval_{\rho'} M$.

2. M is a variable. $Eval_\rho M = val(M) = val'(M) = Eval_{\rho'} M$.

3. $M \equiv \Pi x{:}M_1.M_2$. We show $Eval_\rho M \subseteq Eval_{\rho'} M$ and the other direction is the same. Suppose $F \in Eval_\rho M$. Then, $\mathcal{E} \vdash F : \phi'(M)$ as $\phi(M) \simeq \phi'(M)$. For any extension $\rho'_1 = (\phi'_1, val'_1)$ of ρ' such that $\phi'_1(x) = N \in Eval_{\rho'} M_1$, by Lemma 4.34 we can find an extension $\rho_1 = (\phi_1, val_1)$ of ρ such that $\phi_1(x) = N \in Eval_\rho M_1$ as $Eval_\rho M_1 = Eval_{\rho'} M_1$ by induction hypothesis. Hence, $FN \in Eval_{\rho_1} M_2 = Eval_{\rho'_1} M_2$ by induction hypothesis.

4. $M \equiv \lambda x{:}M_1.M_2$. We have $dom(Eval_\rho M) = dom(Eval_{\rho'} M)$ as $\phi(M_1) \simeq \phi'(M_1)$, and $Eval_\rho M(N, v) = Eval_{\rho_1} M_2 = Eval_{\rho'_1} M_2 = Eval_{\rho'_1} M$ by induction hypothesis, where ρ_1 and ρ'_1 extend ρ and ρ' respectively as in the definition of $Eval$.

5. $M \equiv M_1 M_2$. As $\phi(M_2) \simeq \phi'(M_2)$ and $Eval_{\rho'} M_1 \in V(\phi'(M_1))$ by (mutual) induction hypothesis, we have by induction hypothesis

$$\begin{aligned} Eval_\rho M &= Eval_\rho M_1(\phi(M_2), Eval_\rho M_2) \\ &= Eval_{\rho'} M_1(\phi(M_2), Eval_{\rho'} M_2) \\ &= Eval_{\rho'} M_1(\phi'(M_2), Eval_{\rho'} M_2) \\ &= Eval_{\rho'} M. \end{aligned}$$

[20] By mutual induction, we mean to prove the two statements *simultaneously* but just write the proofs separately.

6. The case for $M \equiv \Sigma x{:}M_1.M_2$ is similar to the Π-case, and for $M \equiv \langle M_1, M_2\rangle_A$ and $M \equiv \pi_i(M')$, applying the induction hypothesis suffices.

The proof of the second statement is given as follows.

1. M is a universe. $Eval_\rho M = SN(M) \in Sat(M) = V(M) = V(\phi(M))$.

2. M is a variable. $Eval_\rho M = val(M) \in V(\phi(M))$.

3. $M \equiv \Pi x{:}M_1.M_2$. We have to show that $Eval_\rho M$ is a $\phi(M)$-saturated set.

    (S1) Suppose $F \in Eval_\rho M$. We only have to show that F is strongly normalisable. Take a variable y such that $\mathcal{E} \vdash y : \phi(M_1)$. As $Eval_\rho M_1 \in V(\phi(M_1)) = Sat(\phi(M_1))$ is a saturated set by induction hypothesis, $y \in Eval_\rho M_1$. Let ρ' be an extension of ρ such that $\rho'(x) = (y, v_y)$, where v_y is the canonical denotation of y. Then, by induction hypothesis, $Eval_{\rho'} M_2 \in V(\phi'(M_2)) = Sat(\phi'(M_2))$ is a saturated set. So, $Fy \in Eval_{\rho'} M_2$ is strongly normalisable, which implies that F is strongly normalisable.

    (S2) Suppose $M_0 \in SN(\phi(M))$ is a base term. We only have to show $M_0 N \in Eval_{\rho'} M_2$ for any extension $\rho' = (\phi', val')$ of ρ such that $\phi'(x) = N \in Eval_\rho M_1$. This follows from that $Eval_{\rho'} M_2$ is a $\phi'(M_2)$-saturated set (by induction hypothesis), $M_0 N$ is a base term and $\mathcal{E} \vdash M_0 N : \phi'(M_2)$ (as $\phi'(M_2) \equiv [N/x]\phi(M_2)$).

    (S3) Suppose $M_0 \in SN(\phi(M))$ has key redex and $\text{red}_{\mathbf{k}}(M_0) \in Eval_\rho M$. We only have to show $M_0 N \in Eval_{\rho'} M_2$ for any extension $\rho' = (\phi', val')$ of ρ such that $\phi'(x) = N \in Eval_\rho M_1$. By induction hypothesis, $Eval_{\rho'} M_2 \in Sat(\phi'(M_2))$ is a saturated set. As $\text{red}_{\mathbf{k}}(M_0) \in Eval_\rho M$, $\text{red}_{\mathbf{k}}(M_0)N \in Eval_{\rho'} M_2$ is strongly normalisable which by Lemma 4.5 and the assumption that M_0 is strongly normalisable, implies that $M_0 N$ is strongly normalisable. Noticing that $\mathcal{E} \vdash M_0 N : \phi'(M_2)$ and $M_0 N$ has the same key redex as M_0, we have $M_0 N \in Eval_{\rho'} M_2$.

4. $M \equiv \lambda x{:}M_1.M_2$. For any extension $\rho' = (\phi', val')$ of ρ such that $\rho'(x) = (N, v) \in dom(Eval_\rho M)$, we have by induction hypothesis,

$$Eval_\rho M(N, v) = Eval_{\rho'}(M_2)$$

$$\in \quad V(\phi'(M_2)) = V([N/x]\phi(M_2)) = V(\phi(M)N).$$

If $\mathcal{E} \vdash N' : \phi(M_1)$ and $N' \simeq N$, we have, by (mutual) induction hypothesis,

$$Eval_\rho(M)(N, v) = Eval_{\rho'}(M_2) = Eval_{\rho'_{N'}}(M_2) = Eval_\rho(M)(N', v),$$

where $\rho'_{N'}$ extends ρ such that $\rho'_{N'}(x) = (N', v)$.

5. $M \equiv M_1 M_2$. As $T_\mathcal{E}(\phi(M_1))$ has the form $\Pi x{:}A_1.A_2$, $Eval_\rho M_1 \in V(\phi(M_1))$ is a function f such that $f(N, v) \in V(\phi(M_1)N)$ for any N such that $\mathcal{E} \vdash N : A_1$ and any $v \in V(N)$. Noticing that $\mathcal{E} \vdash \phi(M_2) : A_1$ (as $M_1 M_2$ is an $\mathcal{E}$-object) and $Eval_\rho M_2 \in V(\phi(M_2))$, we have $Eval_\rho M = Eval_\rho M_1(\phi(M_2), Eval_\rho M_2) \in V(\phi(M_1)\phi(M_2)) = V(\phi(M))$.

6. $M \equiv \Sigma x{:}M_1.M_2$. We have to show that $Eval_\rho M$ is a $\phi(M)$-saturated set.

   (S1) Suppose $P \in Eval_\rho M$. We only have to show that P is strongly normalisable. By induction hypothesis, $\pi_1(P) \in Eval_\rho M_1 \in V(\phi(M_1)) = Sat(\phi(M_1))$ is strongly normalisable, so is P.

   (S2) Suppose $M_0 \in SN(\phi(M))$ is a base term. Then, $\pi_1(M_0) \in SN(\phi(M_1))$ is also a base term, so $\pi_1(M_0)$ is in $\phi(M_1)$-saturated set $Eval_\rho M_1$. For any $\mathcal{E}$-valuation $\rho' = (\phi', val')$ which extends ρ such that $\phi'(x) = \pi_1(P)$ (assuming $x \notin dom(\rho)$), $\pi_2(M_0) \in SN([\pi_1(M_0)/x]\phi(M_2)) = SN(\phi'(M_2))$ is also a base term, and so $\pi_2(M_0)$ is in $\phi'(M_2)$-saturated set $Eval_{\rho'} M_2$. Hence, $M_0 \in Eval_\rho M$.

   (S3) Suppose $M_0 \in SN(\phi(M))$ has key redex and $\mathrm{red}_\mathbf{k}(M_0) \in Eval_\rho M$. Then, $\pi_1(M_0) \in SN(\phi(M_1))$ has the same key redex and $\pi_1(\mathrm{red}_\mathbf{k}(M_0)) \in Eval_\rho M_1$, so $\pi_1(M_0)$ is in the $\phi(M_1)$-saturated set $Eval_\rho M_1$. For any $\mathcal{E}$-valuation $\rho' = (\phi', val')$ which extends ρ such that $\phi'(x) = \pi_1(P)$ (assuming $x \notin dom(\rho)$), $\pi_2(M_0) \in SN([\pi_1(M_0)/x]\phi(M_2)) = SN(\phi'(M_2))$ has the same key redex and $\pi_2(\mathrm{red}_\mathbf{k}(M_0)) \in Eval_{\rho'} M_2$, so $\pi_2(M_0)$ is in the $\phi'(M_2)$-saturated set $Eval_{\rho'} M_2$. Hence, $M_0 \in Eval_\rho M$.

7. $M \equiv \langle M_1, M_2 \rangle_A$. By induction hypothesis and Lemma 4.30.

8. $M \equiv \pi_i(M')$. As $T_\mathcal{E}(M')$ has Σ-form, $Eval_\rho M' = (v_1, v_2) \in V(\phi(M'))$ such that $v_i \in V(\pi_i(\phi(M')))$, where $i = 1, 2$. So, $Eval_\rho M = v_i \in V(\pi_i(\phi(M'))) = V(\phi(M))$. □

Corollary 4.37. *If A is an $\mathcal{E}$-type and $\rho = (\phi, val)$ is an $\mathcal{E}$-valuation which covers A, then $Eval_\rho A$ is a $\phi(A)$-saturated set.*

Proof By Lemma 4.36 and the definition of denotation-sets. □

4.3.4 Soundness of the interpretation

We prove that the interpretation $Eval_\rho$ is sound in the following sense:

1. It respects the computational equality and the cumulativity relation (Lemma 4.39);
2. If M is of type A, then, under a suitable variable assignment, M is an element of the interpretation of A (Theorem 4.40).

To prove these results, the following substitution property has to be proved first.

Lemma 4.38. (substitution property) *Suppose $\rho = (\phi, val)$ is an $\mathcal{E}$-valuation which covers N and $[N/x]M$, where $x \notin dom(\rho)$, and $\rho' = (\phi', val')$ is an extension of ρ which covers M such that $\rho'(x) = (\phi(N), Eval_\rho(N))$. Then, $Eval_\rho([N/x]M) = Eval_{\rho'}(M)$.*

Proof If M is an $\mathcal{E}$-proof, so is $[N/x]M$; then $Eval_\rho([N/x]M) = Eval_\rho(M) = \theta$. If neither M nor $[N/x]M$ is an $\mathcal{E}$-proof, we prove the lemma by induction on the structure of M.

1. M is a universe. $Eval_\rho([N/x]M) = Eval_\rho(M) = SN(M) = Eval_{\rho'}(M)$.
2. M is a variable. If $M \not\equiv x$, then $Eval_\rho([N/x]M) = Eval_\rho(M) = val(M) = val'(M) = Eval_{\rho'}(M)$. If $M \equiv x$, then $Eval_\rho([N/x]M) = Eval_\rho(N) = val'(M) = Eval_{\rho'}(M)$.
3. $M \equiv \Pi y{:}M_1.M_2$. We may assume $y \notin dom(\rho')$. We have
   - $\phi([N/x]M) \equiv [\phi(N)/z]\phi([z/x]M) \equiv \phi'(M)$, by suitably choosing variable z;
   - $Eval_\rho([N/x]M_1) = Eval_{\rho'}(M_1)$, by induction hypothesis; and
   - by Lemma 4.34, for any $\mathcal{E}$-valuation $\rho_1 = (\phi_1, val_1)$ which extends ρ such that $\phi_1(y) = N_1 \in Eval_\rho M_1$, we can find an $\mathcal{E}$-valuation $\rho_1' = (\phi_1', val_1')$ which extends ρ' such that $\phi_1'(y) = N_1 \in Eval_\rho M_1$, (and vice versa); furthermore, by Lemma 4.36, $Eval_{\rho_1} M_2 = Eval_{\rho_1'} M_2$.

   From these, by the definition of $Eval$, $Eval_\rho([N/x]M) = Eval_{\rho'}(M)$.

4. $M \equiv \lambda y{:}M_1.M_2$. We may assume $y \notin dom(\rho')$. We have

   - $dom(Eval_\rho[N/x]M) = dom(Eval_{\rho'}M)$, as $\phi([N/x]M_1) \equiv [\phi(N)/z]\phi([z/x]M_1) \equiv \phi'(M_1)$, by suitably choosing variable z;
   - for any $(N_1, v_1) \in dom(Eval_\rho[N/x]M)$, by induction hypothesis, $(Eval_\rho[N/x]M)(N_1, v_1) = Eval_{\rho_1}M_2 = Eval_{\rho'_1}[N/x]M_2 = (Eval_{\rho'}M)(N_1, v_1)$, where ρ_1 and ρ'_1 extend ρ and ρ' such that $\rho_1(y) = \rho'_1(y) = (N_1, v_1)$.

   Hence, by the definition of *Eval*, $Eval_\rho([N/x]M) = Eval_{\rho'}(M)$.

5. $M \equiv M_1M_2$. As $\phi([N/x]M_2) \equiv [\phi(N)/z]\phi([z/x]M_2) \equiv \phi'(M_2)$ (by suitably choosing variable z), we have by induction hypothesis

$$\begin{aligned} Eval_\rho([N/x]M) &= Eval_\rho([N/x]M_1)(\phi([N/x]M_2), Eval_\rho([N/x]M_2)) \\ &= Eval_{\rho'}(M_1)(\phi'(M_2), Eval_{\rho'}(M_2)) \\ &= Eval_{\rho'}(M). \end{aligned}$$

6. $M \equiv \Sigma y{:}M_1.M_2$. Similar to the Π-case.
7. $M \equiv \langle M_1, M_2\rangle_A$. By induction hypothesis.
8. $M \equiv \pi_i(M')$, $i = 1, 2$. By induction hypothesis, $Eval_\rho[N/x]M' = Eval_{\rho'}M' = (v_1, v_2)$. So, $Eval_\rho[N/x]M = Eval_\rho\pi_i([N/x]M') = v_i = Eval_{\rho'}M$. □

Lemma 4.39. *Let $\rho = (\phi, val)$ be an $\mathcal{E}$-valuation.*

1. *If M and N are $\mathcal{E}$-objects covered by ρ and $M \simeq N$, then $Eval_\rho(M) = Eval_\rho(N)$.*
2. *If M and N are $\mathcal{E}$-types covered by ρ and $M \preceq N$, then $Eval_\rho(M) \subseteq Eval_\rho(N)$.*

Proof By induction on the structure of M.

Proof of the first statement. By the Church-Rosser theorem and Subject Reduction (Theorem 3.16), we only have to prove the statement for $M \rhd_1 N$. Then, M can not be a universe or variable. For the cases M is of Π-form, λ-form, Σ-form or pair-form, it is true by induction hypothesis. The cases that $M \equiv \pi_i(M')$ can readily be verified by induction hypothesis and the definition of $Eval_\rho$. We consider the case when $M \equiv M_1M_2$. There are two subcases.

1. $M \equiv M_1M_2 \rhd_1 N_1N_2 \equiv N$ with $M_1 \rhd_1 N_1$ or $M_2 \rhd_1 N_2$. Then, $Eval_\rho(M_1) = Eval_\rho(N_1) \in V(\phi(N_1))$, by induction hypothesis and Lemma 4.36. As $\phi(M_2) \simeq \phi(N_2)$ and $\mathcal{E} \vdash \phi(N_2) : T_\mathcal{E}(\phi(M_2))$ by Subject Reduction (Theorem 3.16), and noticing that $T_\mathcal{E}(\phi(N_1))$ is of Π-form, we have by induction hypothesis and the definition of denotation-sets,

$$\begin{aligned} Eval_\rho(N) &= Eval_\rho(N_1)(\phi(N_2), Eval_\rho(N_2)) \\ &= Eval_\rho(M_1)(\phi(N_2), Eval_\rho(M_2)) \\ &= Eval_\rho(M_1)(\phi(M_2), Eval_\rho(M_2)) \\ &= Eval_\rho(M). \end{aligned}$$

2. $M \equiv M_1M_2 \equiv (\lambda x{:}X.Y)M_2 \rhd_1 [M_2/x]Y \equiv N$. By Lemma 4.34, there exists an $\mathcal{E}$-valuation ρ' which extends ρ such that $\rho'(x) = (\phi(M_2), Eval_\rho M_2)$. By Lemma 4.38,

$$\begin{aligned} Eval_\rho M &= Eval_\rho(\lambda x{:}X.Y)(\phi(M_2), Eval_\rho M_2) \\ &= Eval_{\rho'} Y = Eval_\rho[M_2/x]Y = Eval_\rho N. \end{aligned}$$

Proof of the second statement. By the first statement just proved and Lemma 3.4, we only have to consider the following cases.

1. $M \preceq N$ are universes. Then, $Eval_\rho M = SN(M) \subseteq SN(N) = Eval_\rho N$.
2. $M \equiv Qx{:}M_1.M_2 \preceq Qx{:}N_1.N_2 \equiv N$, where $Q \in \{\Pi, \Sigma\}$, and, $M_1 \begin{cases} \simeq N_1 & \text{if } Q \equiv \Pi \\ \preceq N_1 & \text{if } Q \equiv \Sigma \end{cases}$ and $M_2 \preceq N_2$. The result then follows from induction hypothesis.

This completes the proof of the lemma. □

We now prove the soundness theorem of the interpretation.

Theorem 4.40. (soundness) *Let $\rho = (\phi, val)$ be an $\mathcal{E}$-valuation with $FV(\mathcal{E}^k)$ as domain such that $\phi(e_i) \in Eval_\rho(E_i)$ for $e_i \in dom(\rho)$. If $\mathcal{E}^k \vdash M : A$, then $\phi(M) \in Eval_\rho A$.*

Proof By induction on the structure of M.

1. M is a universe. Then, $T_\mathcal{E}(M) \preceq A$ is convertible to a universe. By Lemma 4.39, $\phi(M) = M \in SN(T_\mathcal{E}(M)) = Eval_\rho T_\mathcal{E}(M) \subseteq Eval_\rho A$.

2. $M \equiv e_i$ is a variable. Then, E_i is the principal type of M. By assumption and Lemma 4.39, $\phi(M) \in Eval_\rho E_i \subseteq Eval_\rho A$.

3. $M \equiv \Pi x{:}M_1.M_2$. Then $A \simeq U$ for some universe U and $Eval_\rho A = Eval_\rho U = SN(U)$ by Lemma 4.39. We only have to show that $\mathcal{E} \vdash \phi(M) : U$ and $\phi(M)$ is strongly normalisable. As $\mathcal{E} \vdash M : U$ and ϕ is an $\mathcal{E}$-assignment, $\mathcal{E} \vdash \phi(M) : U$ by Lemma 4.32. Since $\mathcal{E}^k \vdash M_1 : U_1$ for some universe U_1, we have by induction hypothesis that $\phi(M_1) \in Eval_\rho U_1 = SN(U_1)$ is strongly normalisable. We may assume that $x \equiv e_j$ with $E_j \equiv M_1$ for some $j > k$ such that $\mathcal{E}^j \vdash M_2 : U_2$ for some universe U_2. Let $\rho' = (\phi', val')$ be an extension of ρ such that $\phi'(e_{k+i})$ is an variable y_{k+i} such that $\mathcal{E} \vdash y_{k+i} : [\phi(e_1), ..., \phi(e_k), y_{k+1}, ..., y_{k+i-1}/e_1, ..., e_{k+i-1}]E_{k+i}$ and $val'(e_{k+i})$ is any denotation in $V(y_{k+i})$, where $1 \leq i \leq j-k$. Then, ρ' is an $\mathcal{E}$-valuation and, by induction hypothesis, $\phi'(M_2) \in Eval_{\rho'} U_2 = SN(U_2)$ is strongly normalisable, which implies that $\phi(M_2)$ is strongly normalisable. Therefore, $\phi(M) \equiv \Pi x{:}\phi(M_1).\phi(M_2)$ is strongly normalisable.

4. $M \equiv \lambda x{:}M_1.M_2$. Then, by the Church-Rosser theorem and Lemma 3.20, $A \simeq \Pi x{:}M_1.A_2$ for some $\mathcal{E}$-type A_2.

   (a) $\mathcal{E} \vdash \phi(M) : \phi(\Pi x{:}M_1.A_2)$ by Lemma 4.32, as $\mathcal{E} \vdash M : \Pi x{:}M_1.A_2$,

   (b) $\phi(M)N \in Eval_{\rho_1} A_2$ for any $\mathcal{E}$-valuation $\rho_1 = (\phi_1, val_1)$ which extends ρ and covers x such that $\phi_1(x) = N \in Eval_\rho M_1$. To show this, we may assume that $x \equiv e_j$ for some $j > k$ such that $E_j \equiv x{:}M_1$ and $\mathcal{E}^j \vdash M_2 : A_2$. Then, we can find another $\mathcal{E}$-valuation ρ' with $FV(\mathcal{E}^j)$ as domain which extends ρ in the similar way as in the above case except that $\rho'(x) = \rho_1(x)$; ρ' satisfies the condition required by the theorem. . By induction hypothesis and Lemma 4.36, $\phi_1(M_2) = \phi'(M_2) \in Eval_{\rho'} A_2 = Eval_{\rho_1} A_2$, and $Eval_{\rho_1} A_2$ is a saturated set. Therefore, since $\mathrm{red}_{\mathbf{k}}(\phi(M)N) \equiv [\phi_1(x)/x]\phi(M_2) \equiv \phi_1(M_2) \in Eval_{\rho_1} A_2$ (and hence $\phi(M)N$ is strongly normalisable because $\phi(M)$ and N are strongly normalisable by induction hypothesis and $N \in Eval_\rho M_1$), we have $\phi(M)N \in Eval_{\rho_1} A_2$.

   So, we have $\phi(M) \in Eval_\rho(\Pi x{:}M_1.A_2)$; hence, $\phi(M) \in Eval_\rho A$, by Lemma 4.39.

5. $M \equiv M_1 M_2$. Then, $\mathcal{E} \vdash M_1 : \Pi x{:}B_1.B_2$, $\mathcal{E} \vdash M_2 : B_1$ and $[M_2/x]B_2 \preceq A$ for some B_1 and B_2. Let $\rho' = (\phi', val')$ be an $\mathcal{E}$-valuation extending ρ such that $\rho'(x) = (\phi(M_2), Eval_\rho M_2)$. By induction hypothesis, Lemmas 4.38 and 4.39, $\phi(M) \equiv \phi(M_1)\phi'(x) \in Eval_{\rho'} B_2 =$

$Eval_\rho[M_2/x]B_2 \subseteq Eval_\rho A$.

6. $M \equiv \Sigma x{:}M_1.M_2$. Similar to the Π-case.

7. $M \equiv \langle M_1, M_2\rangle_B$. Then, by the Church-Rosser theorem and Lemma 3.20, $A \rhd \Sigma x{:}A_1.A_2$ for some A_1 and A_2.

   (a) As $\mathcal{E} \vdash M : \Sigma x{:}A_1.A_2$, $\mathcal{E} \vdash \phi(M) : \phi(\Sigma x{:}A_1.A_2)$ by Lemma 4.32.

   (b) Noticing that $Eval_\rho A_1$ is a saturated set, we have $\pi_1(\phi(M)) \in Eval_\rho A_1$, because it is a redex (and hence is the key redex of itself) and its contractum is in $Eval_\rho A_1$ by induction hypothesis. We may assume that $x \equiv e_j$ for some $j > k$. Suppose $\rho_1 = (\phi_1, val_1)$ is an $\mathcal{E}$-valuation extending ρ such that $\phi_1(x) = \pi_1(M)$. Similar to the λ-case, we can find a ρ' which satisfies the condition required in the theorem and $\rho'(x) = \rho_1(x)$. Noticing that $Eval_{\rho'} A_2$ is a saturated set, we have $\pi_1(\phi(M)) \in Eval_\rho A_1$ and $\pi_2(\phi(M)) \in Eval_{\rho'} A_2$, because its contractum is in $Eval_\rho A_1$ by induction hypothesis.

   Hence, $\phi(M) \in Eval_\rho \Sigma x{:}A_1.A_2 = Eval_\rho A$.

8. $M \equiv \pi_i(M')$, $i = 1, 2$. Then, $\mathcal{E} \vdash M' : \Sigma x{:}B_1.B_2$ for some B_1 and B_2. By induction hypothesis, $\phi(M') \in Eval_\rho \Sigma x{:}B_1.B_2$.

   (a) $i = 1$. Then $B_1 \preceq A$. We have $\phi(M) \equiv \pi_1(\phi(M')) \in Eval_\rho B_1 \subseteq Eval_\rho A$, by the definition of *Eval* and Lemma 4.39.

   (b) $i = 2$. Then $[\pi_1(M')/x]B_2 \preceq A$. We may assume $x \equiv e_j$ for some $j > k$ such that $E_j \equiv B_1$ and let ρ' be an $\mathcal{E}$-valuation extending ρ such that $\rho'(x) = (\pi_1(\phi(M')), Eval_\rho \phi(M'))$. Then, by the definition of *Eval*, Lemma 4.38 and Lemma 4.39, $\phi(M) \equiv \pi_2(\phi(M')) \in Eval_{\rho'} B_2 = Eval_\rho[\pi_1(M')/x]B_2 \subseteq Eval_\rho A$.

This completes the proof of the theorem. □

4.3.5 The strong normalisation theorem

The strong normalisation theorem is now a corollary of the above results.

Theorem 4.41. (strong normalisation) *If* $\Gamma \vdash M : A$, *then* M *is strongly normalisable.*

Proof We first show that $\vdash M : A$ implies that M is strongly normalisable. Let $\rho = (\phi, val)$ be any $\mathcal{E}$-valuation. If $\vdash M : A$, then

1. $FV(M) = FV(A) = \emptyset$, by Lemma 3.10;

2. $\phi(M) \in Eval_\rho(A)$, by the soundness theorem (Theorem 4.40);

3. A is an $\mathcal{E}$-type, by Type Reflection (Theorem 3.15); and

4. $Eval_\rho(A) \in V(\phi(A))$, by Lemma 4.36.

So, we have $M \equiv \phi(M) \in Eval_\rho(A) \in V(\phi(A)) = V(A) = Sat(A)$. By the definition of saturated sets, $M \in Eval_\rho(A) \subseteq SN(A)$ is strongly normalisable.

For the arbitrary case, if $\Gamma \vdash M : A$, $\Gamma \equiv x_1{:}A_1, ..., x_m{:}A_m$ by Lemma 3.10. Applying rule (λ), we have

$$\vdash \lambda x_1{:}A_1 ... \lambda x_m{:}A_m.M : \Pi x_1{:}A_1 ... \Pi x_m{:}A_m.A.$$

So, $\lambda x_1{:}A_1 ... \lambda x_m{:}A_m.M$ is strongly normalisable; and this implies that M is strongly normalisable. □

Corollary 4.42. *If $x_1{:}A_1, ..., x_n{:}A_n \vdash M : A$, then $A_1, ..., A_n, A$ and M are all strongly normalisable.*

Proof By the above strong normalisation theorem, Type Reflection (Theorem 3.15) and Lemma 3.9. □

By the strong normalisation theorem, every object in the type theory computes to a value in canonical form. For example, (in the empty context) every object of a Π-type computes into a value of λ-form, every object of a Σ-type computes into a pair, and (in ECC) every type computes to a universe, a Π-type or a Σ-type. Therefore, the normalisation theorem provides a proof-theoretic justification of the harmony between the different uses of the entities in the type theory, as considered in a verificationistic operational semantics (cf. Section 1.2.3).

5
The internal logic and decidability

In this chapter, we study the internal higher-order logic in the language and the decidability of the type theory. The understanding of the logic provides a sound basis of using the type theory in various applications such as program specification and theorem proving. The decidability results provide a direct basis for computer implementations of the language for development of programs and proofs. The normalisation property proved in the previous chapter is a key basis for understanding the internal logic and for the decidability results.

5.1 The internal higher-order logic

As we have informally explained in Section 2.2.6, based on the principle of propositions-as-types, there is an internal higher-order logic in ECC. In this section, we describe the internal logic in more details, prove its logical consistency and the property that the Leibniz equality reflects the computational equality, and explain the meanings of the logical operators.

5.1.1 The internal logic and its consistency

Viewing logical formulas as types, the notion of formula in the internal logic is essentially given by the notion of proposition and a formula is provable if and only if it is inhabited by some proof.

Definition 5.1. (formulas, proofs, and provability) *Let Γ be a valid context.*

1. *A term P is called a* Γ-formula *if $\Gamma \vdash P : Prop$.*
2. *A term p is called a* proof *of Γ-formula P (in Γ) if $\Gamma \vdash p : P$.*
3. *A Γ-formula is* provable in Γ *if and only if it is Γ-inhabited.*

Remark Because of the subtyping induced by the universe inclusions, the notion of formula is slightly different from that of proposition. A formula is always a proposition but not vice versa. For instance, for any formula P, $(\lambda X{:}Type_0.X)P$ is a proposition, but not of type *Prop*. However, every proposition has a formula as its value under computation. Therefore, these two notions are essentially equivalent.

Since logical formulas form a totality (*Prop*) in the type theory, there is an internal notion of predicates or relations (as propositional functions).

Definition 5.2. (predicates and relations) *A* Γ*-object* F *is called an* (n-ary) Γ-predicate (over A_1, ..., A_n) *if* $\Gamma \vdash F : \Pi x_1{:}A_1 ... \Pi x_n{:}A_n.Prop.$

When $n \geq 2$ *and* $A_i \equiv A$ $(i = 1, ..., n)$ *are the same type, an* n*-ary predicate over* A_1, ..., A_n *is also called an* n-ary relation over A.

As mentioned in Section 2.2.6, the ordinary logical operators can be defined using the type constructor Π for impredicative dependent products. We repeat the definitions below. (Propositional equality will be discussed in Section 5.1.3.)

Definition 5.3. (logical operators) *Let* Γ *be a valid context,* P_1 *and* P_2 Γ*-formulas,* A *a* Γ*-type, and* $P[x]$ *a* $(\Gamma, x{:}A)$*-formula. Then,*

$$
\begin{array}{rcl}
\forall x{:}A.P[x] & =_{\mathrm{df}} & \Pi x{:}A.P[x] \\
P_1 \supset P_2 & =_{\mathrm{df}} & \forall x{:}P_1.P_2 \\
\mathbf{true} & =_{\mathrm{df}} & \forall X{:}Prop.\ X \supset X \\
\mathbf{false} & =_{\mathrm{df}} & \forall X{:}Prop.X \\
P_1\ \&\ P_2 & =_{\mathrm{df}} & \forall X{:}Prop.\ (P_1 \supset P_2 \supset X) \supset X \\
P_1 \vee P_2 & =_{\mathrm{df}} & \forall X{:}Prop.\ (P_1 \supset X) \supset (P_2 \supset X) \supset X \\
\neg P_1 & =_{\mathrm{df}} & P_1 \supset \mathbf{false} \\
\exists x{:}A.P[x] & =_{\mathrm{df}} & \forall X{:}Prop.\ (\forall x{:}A.(P[x] \supset X)) \supset X.
\end{array}
$$

Remark The idea of defining logical operators as above goes back to the study of traditional second-order logic (see, e.g. [Pra65]). Most of the definitions above (except those for $\forall$, $\supset$ and **true**) are codings of the usual elimination rule of the corresponding operator. This may be seen as defining (or giving meanings to) a logical operator by its use in deducing further logical consequences (as expressed by its elimination rule). However, as we shall explain in Section 5.1.2 below, it is also possible to understand the meanings of these logical operators by considering how they can be proved (by canonical proofs).

By the strong normalisation theorem, the internal higher-order logic is logically consistent in the sense that there exist unprovable formulas.

Theorem 5.4. (consistency) ECC *is logically consistent in the sense that there exist unprovable formulas; in particular,* **false** *is not provable in the empty context, i.e.* $\nvdash M : \forall X{:}Prop.X$ *for any term* M.

Proof Suppose $\vdash M : \forall X{:}Prop.X$. By the strong normalisation theorem and Subject Reduction (Theorem 3.16), we may assume that M is in normal form. So, by an easy induction on derivations and Lemma 3.10, M must be of the form $\lambda X{:}Prop.M'$ and $X{:}Prop \vdash M' : X$, where M' is a base term whose key variable is X. We show that this is impossible by induction on the structure of base terms. If $M' \equiv X$, we would have $X{:}Prop \vdash X : X$. By Lemma 3.20, Lemma 3.4, and the Church-Rosser theorem, we would have $Prop \simeq X$, which is impossible. If $M' \equiv M_1'M_2'$ or $\pi_i(M_1')$, then it must be the case that $X{:}Prop \vdash X : Qy{:}A.B$ for some A and B, where $Q \in \{\Pi, \Sigma\}$. This would imply, by Lemma 3.20, Lemma 3.4, and the Church-Rosser theorem, that $Prop \simeq Qy{:}A.B$ which is impossible, either. So, we conclude that $\nvdash M : \forall X{:}Prop.X$. □

Remark In fact, the above argument can be used to show that for any universe U, $\Pi X{:}U.X$ is not inhabited in the empty context.

Note that the above theorem says that **false** is not provable in the empty context, while it can be proved in certain (inconsistent) contexts, for example, context x:**false**. This induces a notion of *consistent context*. If one views valid contexts as theories (in the sense of ordinary logics) a consistent context corresponds to a consistent theory in the traditional sense.

Definition 5.5. (consistent contexts) *A valid context* Γ *is* consistent *if and only if not every* Γ*-formula is provable in* Γ*, or equivalently, if and only if* **false** *is not provable in* Γ.

We have the following corollary of the consistency theorem which gives us a way to prove the consistency of certain contexts.

Corollary 5.6. *Let* $\Gamma \equiv x_1{:}A_1, ..., x_n{:}A_n$ *be a valid context. If there exist* $a_1, ..., a_n$ *such that* $\vdash a_i : [a_1, ..., a_{i-1}/x_1, ..., x_{i-1}]A_i$ *for* $i = 1, ..., n$*, then* Γ *is a consistent context.*

Proof Suppose Γ is not consistent, i.e. $\Gamma \vdash M[x_1, ..., x_n] : \mathbf{false}$ for some M. Then, by Cut (Theorem 3.14), $\vdash M[a_1, ..., a_n] : \mathbf{false}$, contradicting the consistency theorem 5.4. So, Γ is consistent. □

Example 5.7. The following context, which assumes that there is an arbitrary equivalence relation over a type A,

$$\begin{array}{rcl} A & : & Type_j, \\ Q & : & A \to A \to Prop, \\ reflex & : & \forall x{:}A.\ Q(x,x), \\ sym & : & \forall x{:}A \forall y{:}A.\ Q(x,y) \supset Q(y,x), \\ trans & : & \forall x{:}A \forall y{:}A \forall z{:}A.\ Q(x,y) \supset Q(y,z) \supset Q(x,z) \end{array}$$

is consistent, since we can apply the above corollary by taking, for example, A and Q to be $Prop$ and $=_{Prop}$, respectively.

Remark Proving the consistency of a valid context is certainly non-trivial, except for some simple classes of contexts, as the above corollary and example show. Sometimes, one may use the normalisation theorem to prove the consistency of some more subtle contexts.

5.1.2 Understanding the logical operators

The internal logic is an intuitionistic higher-order logic. An advantage of an intuitionistic logic over the classical logic is that the former allows a simple understanding of the logical machinery (the logical operators, in particular) based on an operational meaning theory. We now explain in more details the logical operators defined above with the aim of obtaining a better understanding of the logical operators—how they may be used in reasoning and how their meanings can be understood.

To grasp how a logical operator may be used in reasoning, we first explain that the ordinary logical inference rules for the logical operator are sound according to the above definition, as the following shows. The introduction rules reflect how to prove a logical formula with the operator concerned as the main connective, and the elimination rules reflect how to use such a formula to deduce other logical consequences.

1. Truth: **true** *is provable in every valid context.*

$$id =_{\mathrm{df}} \lambda X{:}Prop \lambda x{:}X.x$$

   is a proof of **true**. (The elimination rule for **true** is trivial.)

2. Absurdity: **false** *has no proof in the empty context (Theorem 5.4), and it implies every formula.* Suppose f is a proof of **false** in Γ. Then, for any Γ-formula R, $f(R)$ is a proof of R.

3. $\supset$-introduction: *If Γ-formula P_2 is provable under the extra assumption that Γ-formula P_1 is provable (i.e. $\Gamma, p_1{:}P_1 \vdash p_2 : P_2$ for some p_2), then $P_1 \supset P_2$ is a provable Γ-formula.* This is reflected by rule (λ).

4. $\supset$-elimination (Modus Ponens): *If $P_1 \supset P_2$ and P_1 are provable Γ-formulas, then so is P_2.* By rule (*app*), $p'p$ is a proof of P_2, if p and p' are proofs of P_1 and $P_1 \supset P_2$, respectively.

5. &-introduction: *If Γ-formula P_1 and P_2 are provable, so is P_1 & P_2.* If p_i is a proof of P_i $(i = 1, 2)$, then

$$pair(p_1, p_2) =_{\mathrm{df}} \lambda X{:}Prop\lambda h{:}P_1 \to P_2 \to X.\ h(p_1, p_2)$$

is a proof of P_1 & P_2.

6. &-elimination: *If Γ-formula P_1 & P_2 is provable, so are P_1 and P_2.* If h is a proof of P_1 & P_2, then $h(P_i, \lambda p_1{:}P_1\lambda p_2{:}P_2.p_i)$ is a proof of P_i $(i = 1, 2)$.

7. $\vee$-introduction: *If Γ-formula P_1 (or P_2) is provable, so is $P_1 \vee P_2$.* Suppose p_i is a proof of P_i, where $i \in \{1, 2\}$. Then,

$$in_i(p_i) =_{\mathrm{df}} \lambda X{:}Prop\lambda h_1{:}P_1 \to X\lambda h_2{:}P_2 \to X.\ h_i(p_i)$$

is a proof of $P_1 \vee P_2$.

8. $\vee$-elimination: *If Γ-formula $P_1 \vee P_2$ is provable, and for $i = 1, 2$, Γ-formula R is provable under the extra assumption that P_i is provable, then R is provable in Γ.* Suppose h is a proof of $P_1 \vee P_2$ and r_i is a proof of R in $\Gamma, p_i{:}P_i$ $(i = 1, 2)$. Then, $h(R, \lambda p_1{:}P_1.r_1, \lambda p_2{:}P_2.r_2)$ is a proof of R in Γ.

9. $\forall$-introduction: *If $P[x]$ is provable in $\Gamma, x{:}A$, then $\forall x{:}A.P[x]$ is provable in Γ.* By rule (λ).

10. $\forall$-elimination: *If Γ-formula $\forall x{:}A.P[x]$ is provable and a is an object of type A in Γ, then $P[a]$ is provable in Γ.* By rule (*app*).

11. $\exists$-introduction: *If $P[a]$ is provable for some object a of type A, then $\exists x{:}A.P[x]$ is provable.* Suppose p is a proof of $P[a]$, where a is an object of type A. Then

$$ex\_intro(a, p) =_{\mathrm{df}} \lambda X{:}Prop\lambda h{:}(\Pi x{:}A.P[x] \to X).\ h(a, p)$$

is a proof of $\exists x{:}A.P[x]$.

12. $\exists$-elimination: *If* Γ*-formula* $\exists x{:}A.P[x]$ *is provable in* Γ *and* Γ*-formula* R *is provable in* $\Gamma, x{:}A, p{:}P[x]$*, then* R *is provable in* Γ. If h is a proof of $\exists x{:}A.P[x]$ in Γ and r is a proof of R in $\Gamma, x{:}A, p{:}P[x]$, then, $h(R, \lambda x{:}A\lambda p{:}P[x].r)$ is a proof of R in Γ.

13. $\neg$-introduction: *If* **false** *is provable in* $\Gamma, x{:}P$*, where* P *is a* Γ*-formula, then* $\neg P$ *is provable in* Γ. By rule (λ).

14. $\neg$-elimination:[21] *If both* P *and* $\neg P$ *are provable, so is any formula.* By rule (*app*).

As we have remarked above, most of the logical operators are defined by coding their elimination rules using the higher-order logical machinery in our type theory. Then, the meaning of such a logical operator seems to be determined by its elimination rule which indicates how a formula with the operator as the main connective can be used to deduce other logical consequences, and that seems to amount to a pragmatist meaning explanation.

It is our view that the meaning of a logical formula is determined by its use in the sense that one should grasp *both* how the formula can be proved and how it can be used to deduce further consequences. Therefore, it would be desirable to understand the meaning of a logical operator by grasping the former aspect as well as the latter. As we explain below, based on the operational meaning explanation of the type theory, it is possible to explain the meaning of a logical operator by considering 'canonical proofs'. This does not simply mean that, since the logical formulas are all of the form of universal quantification, their canonical proofs are λ-terms in certain form. We want to show that the usual Heying semantics for the defined operators is essentially the same as well. In fact, in the above detailed explanation of the validity of the introduction rules of the logical operators, we have indicated the canonical ways to prove a formula with the operator as the main connective.

The Heyting-style meaning explanation via canonical proofs for the logical operators is given as follows. We explain the notion of canonical proof of a formula in the empty context, and without loss of generality, we assume that the formulas considered be in normal form.

1. The canonical proof of **true** is $id =_{\mathrm{df}} \lambda X{:}Prop\lambda x{:}X.x$ and the value of any proof of **true** has the form *id*.[22]

---

[21]Note that the classical law of double negation is not provable. This can be proved by using the strong normalisation theorem and the consistency theorem (Theorem 5.4) to conclude that there is no proof in normal form of type $\forall P{:}Prop.(\neg\neg P) \supset P$ in the empty context.

[22]This can be proved by using the strong normalisation theorem to observe that *id* is

2. **false** has no proof.

3. A canonical proof of P_1 & P_2 is of the form $pair(p_1, p_2)$, where p_i is a canonical proof of P_i $(i = 1, 2)$.

4. A canonical proof of $P_1 \vee P_2$ is of the form $in_i(p_i)$, where p_i is a canonical proof of P_i $(i \in \{1, 2\})$.

5. A canonical proof of $\exists x{:}A.P[x]$ is of the form $ex\_intro(a, p)$, where a is a canonical object of type A and p is a canonical proof of $P[a]$.

6. For the logical operators $\forall$, $\supset$, and $\neg$, the canonical proofs are just the canonical proofs in λ-form (as in the usual Heyting semantics).

This recovery of a notion of canonical proof for the defined logical operators is possible because the normalisation theorem guarantees the intrinsic harmony between the two aspects of use of the logical formulas.

5.1.3 The Leibniz equality and equality reflection

The higher-order logical machinery allows us to define a propositional equality based on the Leibniz principle that two objects of the same type are equal if and only if they cannot be distinguished by any property (expressed by a predicate over the type of the objects). The idea of using Leibniz's principle to define propositional equality goes back to [WR25].

Definition 5.8. (Leibniz equality) *Let A be a Γ-type. The* Leibniz equality over A, *notation $=_A$, is the binary relation over A defined as follows:*

$$=_A \quad =_{\mathrm{df}} \lambda x{:}A\lambda y{:}A.\ \forall F{:}A \to Prop.\ F(x) \supset F(y).$$

We shall write $a =_A b$ for $=_A (a, b)$.

In the following, we study the properties of the Leibniz equality, starting from the simple and well-known ones. First, the Leibniz equality is indeed an equivalence relation and satisfies the substitution law. For example, the reflexivity law, $x =_A x$, is inhabited in context $x{:}A$ by the following proof:

$$refl_A(x) =_{\mathrm{df}} \lambda P{:}A \to Prop\lambda p{:}P(x).p.$$

The substitution rule, stating that *for any predicate P over a type A, if formulas $P(a)$ and $a =_A b$ are provable, then so is $P(b)$*, is valid by the very definition of $=_A$; for any proof p of $P(a)$ and h of $a =_A b$, $h(P, p)$

---

the only possible proof in normal form of type **true** in the empty context. For the other cases, we do not repeat this fact or its similar argument.

is a proof of $P(b)$. One can show that $=_A$ also satisfies the symmetry and transitivity laws. In fact, the Leibniz equality is the finest reflexive relation in the sense that for any binary reflexive relation R over type A, it is provable that $\forall x, y{:}A.\ (x =_A y) \supset R(x, y)$.

An important property of the Leibniz equality is that it reflects the computational equality in the sense that every two objects are provably Leibniz-equal (in the empty context) if and only if they are computationally equal.

Theorem 5.9. (equality reflection) *Suppose* $\vdash a_1 : A$ *and* $\vdash a_2 : A$. *Then,* $a_1 \simeq a_2$ *if and only if* $\vdash M : a_1 =_A a_2$ *for some term* M.

Proof Necessity. If $a_1 \simeq a_2$, we have by rule $(\preceq)$, $refl_A(a_1)$ as defined above is a proof of $a_1 =_A a_2$ in the empty context.

Sufficiency. Suppose $\vdash M : (a_1 =_A a_2)$. By the strong normalisation theorem and Subject Reduction (Theorem 3.16), we may assume that M, A, a_1 and a_2 are all in normal form. So, M must be of the form $\lambda P{:}A \to Prop.\lambda x{:}P(a_1).M'$ such that $P{:}A \to Prop, x{:}P(a_1) \vdash M' : P(a_2)$. Since M' is in normal form, it must be a base term. Let y be the key variable of M'. Since y can not be P (for otherwise, $Prop \preceq P(a_2)$ which is impossible), we have $y \equiv x$. Therefore, it must be the case that $M' \equiv x$, for otherwise, $Qz{:}A_1.B_1 \preceq P(a_2)$ for some A_1 and B_1, where $Q \in \{\Pi, \Sigma\}$, which is impossible. Noticing that the only rule which can be used to derive $P{:}A \to Prop, x{:}P(a_1) \vdash x : P(a_2)$ is the rule of type equality (the special case of rule $(\preceq)$), we have $P(a_1) \simeq P(a_2)$, which by the Church-Rosser theorem, implies $a_1 \simeq a_2$. □

Remark The above result of equality reflection gives a justification of the adequacy of using the Leibniz equality in, e.g. program specification to characterise the computational equality (see Section 8.2).[23]

Considering the above equality reflection result, there are several related issues worth being discussed about the Leibniz equality. First, although the Leibniz equality is defined by coding an elimination rule (the law of substitution), by the equality reflection theorem its meaning may also be understood by grasping the canonical proofs of it in the similar way as we have explained for the logical operators in Section 5.1.2. If $\vdash M : (a_1 =_A a_2)$, then $M \simeq refl_A(a_1)$. The canonical proof of $a_1 =_A a_2$ in the empty

[23] The reflection result was realised and proved by the author when considering the adequacy problem of using the Leibniz equality to reflect computational equality. Martin-Löf has a similar proof of this fact for the first version of his type theory with a type of all types [ML71]. Although the system Martin-Löf considered is inconsistent, his proof is essentially the same as what we give.

context is of the form $refl_{A'}(a')$, where A' and a' are the values of A and a_1, respectively.

The reflection result has the following obvious corollary, that is, if the Leibniz *in*equality of two objects is provable, then they are not computationally equal.

Corollary 5.10. *If* $\vdash M : \neg(a =_A b)$ *for some* M, *then* $a \not\simeq b$.

Proof By the equality reflection theorem (Theorem 5.9) and the consistency theorem (Theorem 5.4). □

However, the converse of the above corollary is not true. In other words, the provability of the Leibniz inequality is incomplete with respect to the computational inequality in the sense that there is type A with objects a and b such that $a \not\simeq b$ but $\neg(a =_A b)$ is *not* provable. For example, consider the following proposition Nat (the impredicative coding of natural numbers, cf. [GLT90]):

$$Nat \ =_{\text{df}} \Pi X{:}Prop.\ X \to (X \to X) \to X,$$

and its objects

$$zero =_{\text{df}} \lambda X{:}Prop \lambda x{:}X \lambda f{:}X \to X.x,$$

$$one =_{\text{df}} \lambda X{:}Prop \lambda x{:}X \lambda f{:}X \to X.f(x).$$

Obviously, $zero \not\simeq one$. However, it is not possible to prove the Leibniz inequality $\neg(zero =_{Nat} one)$ in the type theory. This is one of the reasons that such impredicative codings of data types are too weak and inadequate, as we have mentioned in the Introduction.

We remark that the Leibniz equality is an *intensional* equality in the sense that two functions f and g of type $A \to B$ in Γ may not be Leibniz-equal even if $f(x)$ and $g(x)$ are Leibniz-equal in $\Gamma, x{:}A$. This can be explained by consulting the equality reflection theorem above. As we have explained in Section 2.3.3, the computational equality is intensional. For example, when the inductive data type N is introduced (see Section 7.1.1), the numerical functions $add_1 =_{\text{df}} \lambda x, y{:}N.x + y$ and $add_2 =_{\text{df}} \lambda x, y{:}N.y + x$ are not computationally equal, and hence not Leibniz-equal either, although the logical proposition $\forall x, y{:}N.(x + y) =_N (y + x)$ is provable.

In ECC, the Leibniz equality is not even weakly extensional in the sense that the corresponding η-rules do not hold for the Leibniz equality.

For example, the following logical formula corresponding to the rule of surjective pairing for type $Z \equiv \Sigma x{:}A.B[x]$ is not provable in ECC:

$$\forall z{:}Z.\ \langle \pi_1(z), \pi_2(z)\rangle_Z =_Z z.$$

However, the failure for such logical η-rules to be provable is due to a quite different reason, that is, the weakness of the elimination rules we have chosen for the corresponding data types (Σ-types in the above case). It is possible to strengthen the elimination rules so that the Leibniz η-rules become provable, as we shall show in Chapter 9.

5.2 Decidability of the type theory

By the strong normalisation theorem, ECC is decidable in the sense that the computational equality and the cumulativity relation are both decidable for well-typed terms and there is a simple algorithm for type inference and type checking.

5.2.1 Decidability of conversion and cumulativity

Lemma 5.11. (decidability of $\simeq$ and $\preceq$) *It is decidable whether $M \simeq N$ or $M \preceq N$ for arbitrary well-typed terms M and N.*

Proof By the Church-Rosser theorem, the normal form of a term is unique (Corollary 3.2). Therefore, conversion $\simeq$ is decidable for well-typed terms by the strong normalisation theorem. The decidability of the cumulativity relation $\preceq$ for well-typed terms follows from that of conversion. □

5.2.2 Decidability of type inference and type checking

We now give an algorithm of type inference for ECC, i.e. if a term is well-typed in a given context, the algorithm computes its principal type in the context, and otherwise, it returns a symbol indicating that the term is not well-typed in the context. Then, we shall prove that the algorithm is correct, which establishes the decidability of type inference.

Definition 5.12. (algorithm of type inference) *The algorithm of type inference $\mathcal{C}(\_;\ \_)$: when given a context $\Gamma \equiv x_1{:}A_1, ..., x_n{:}A_n$ and a term M, it checks whether M is a Γ-object, and if so, $\mathcal{C}(\Gamma;\ M) = T_\Gamma(M)$, the principal type of M in Γ; otherwise, it returns $\bot$. (For the correctness of the algorithm, see the theorem below.)*

$\mathcal{C}(\_;\ \_)$ is defined as follows by induction on the sum of the lengths of the terms A_i's and M and by considering the structure of M. In the following, we use '$\rhd_{nf}$ ...' to mean 'reduces to normal form ...', $max_{\preceq}$ to denote the maximum of the terms subject to relation $\preceq$, and $\mathcal{U}$ the set of universes.

1. *Validity of contexts: To see whether* Γ *is valid (i.e.* $\Gamma \vdash Prop : Type_0$*), check whether* $\mathcal{C}(x_1{:}A_1, ..., x_{n-1}{:}A_{n-1};\ A_n) \rhd_{\text{nf}} U \in \mathcal{U}$.

   If Γ *is not valid,* $\mathcal{C}(\Gamma;\ M) = \perp$ *for every* M*. In the following, we assume that the considered contexts are valid.*

2. M *is a universe. Then,* $\mathcal{C}(\Gamma;\ M) = \begin{cases} Type_0 & \text{if } M \equiv Prop, \\ Type_{j+1} & \text{if } M \equiv Type_j. \end{cases}$

3. M *is a variable. Then,* $\mathcal{C}(\Gamma;\ M) = \begin{cases} A_i & \text{if } M \equiv x_i, \\ \perp & \text{if } M \notin \{x_1, ..., x_n\}. \end{cases}$

4. $M \equiv \Pi x{:}M_1.M_2$. *Check whether* $\mathcal{C}(\Gamma;\ M_1) \rhd_{\text{nf}} U \in \mathcal{U}$ *and* $\mathcal{C}(\Gamma, x{:}M_1;\ M_2) \rhd_{\text{nf}} U' \in \mathcal{U}$*, and if so,*

$$\mathcal{C}(\Gamma;\ M) = \begin{cases} Prop & \text{if } U' \equiv Prop, \\ max_{\preceq}\{U, U'\} & \text{if } U' \not\equiv Prop; \end{cases}$$

   otherwise, $\mathcal{C}(\Gamma;\ M) = \perp$.

5. $M \equiv \lambda x{:}M_1.M_2$. *Check whether* $\mathcal{C}(\Gamma;\ M_1) \rhd_{\text{nf}} U \in \mathcal{U}$ *and* $\mathcal{C}(\Gamma, x{:}M_1;\ M_2) = B$ *for some* $B \neq \perp$*, and if so,* $\mathcal{C}(\Gamma;\ M) = \Pi x{:}M_1.B$*; otherwise,* $\mathcal{C}(\Gamma;\ M) = \perp$.

6. $M \equiv M_1 M_2$. *Check whether* $\mathcal{C}(\Gamma;\ M_1) \rhd_{\text{nf}} \Pi x{:}A.B$ *for some* A *and* B*, and* $\mathcal{C}(\Gamma;\ M_2) \preceq A$*, and if so,* $\mathcal{C}(\Gamma;\ M) = [M_2/x]B$*; otherwise,* $\mathcal{C}(\Gamma;\ M) = \perp$.

7. $M \equiv \Sigma x{:}M_1.M_2$. *Check whether* $\mathcal{C}(\Gamma;\ M_1) \rhd_{\text{nf}} U \in \mathcal{U}$ *and* $\mathcal{C}(\Gamma, x{:}M_1;\ M_2) \rhd_{\text{nf}} U' \in \mathcal{U}$*, and if so,* $\mathcal{C}(\Gamma;\ M) = max_{\preceq}\{U, U', Type_0\}$*; otherwise,* $\mathcal{C}(\Gamma;\ M) = \perp$.

8. $M \equiv \langle M_1, M_2 \rangle_C$. *Check whether* $C \equiv \Sigma x{:}A.B$ *for some* A *and* B*,* $\mathcal{C}(\Gamma;\ C) \rhd_{\text{nf}} U \in \mathcal{U}$*,* $\mathcal{C}(\Gamma;\ M_1) \preceq A$ *and* $\mathcal{C}(\Gamma;\ M_2) \preceq [M_1/x]B$*, and if so,* $\mathcal{C}(\Gamma;\ M) = C$*; otherwise,* $\mathcal{C}(\Gamma;\ M) = \perp$.

9. $M \equiv \pi_i(M')$. *Check whether* $\mathcal{C}(\Gamma;\ M') \rhd_{\text{nf}} \Sigma x{:}A.B$ *for some* A *and* B*, and if so,*

$$\mathcal{C}(\Gamma;\ M) = \begin{cases} A & \text{if } i = 1, \\ [\pi_1(M')/x]B & \text{if } i = 2; \end{cases}$$

   otherwise, $\mathcal{C}(\Gamma;\ M) = \perp$.

This completes the definition of the algorithm.

Remark The type inference algorithm is simple and easy to implement. This simplicity is due to the full cumulativity of the type hierarchy of ECC. For the systems with universes lacking full cumulativity like that in [Coq86a], although strong normalisation theorem holds [Luo88a], its notion of principal type becomes more complex and the algorithm for type inference is quite complicated (cf. [HP91]).

Theorem 5.13. (correctness of type inference) *The algorithm of type inference* $\mathcal{C}(\_;\ \_)$ *is correct, i.e. given a context* $\Gamma \equiv x_1{:}A_1, ..., x_n{:}A_n$ *and a term* M,

$$\mathcal{C}(\Gamma;\ M) = \begin{cases} T_\Gamma(M) & \textit{if } M \textit{ is a } \Gamma\textit{-object,} \\ \bot & \textit{otherwise.} \end{cases}$$

Proof By the same induction used in the definition above. The termination of the algorithm is guaranteed by the strong normalisation theorem. The only cases worth mentioning about this proof are when $M \equiv M_1M_2$ or $\pi_2(M')$. We discuss the former case and the latter is similar.

$M \equiv M_1M_2$. If either the normal form of $\mathcal{C}(\Gamma;\ M_1)$ is not of the form $\Pi x{:}A.B$ or it is but $\mathcal{C}(\Gamma;\ M_2) \not\preceq A$, then we certainly have by induction hypothesis that M is not a Γ-object. Otherwise, we have $\Gamma \vdash M : [M_2/x]B$ by rules (*app*) and ($\preceq$). We only have to show that $[M_2/x]B$ is the minimum type of M subject to $\preceq$. Suppose $\Gamma \vdash M : B'$ for some $B' \prec [M_2/x]B$. We may assume that the last rule used to derive $\Gamma \vdash M : B'$ is not ($\preceq$), and hence it is (*app*):

$$\frac{\Gamma \vdash M_1 : \Pi x{:}A_1.B_1 \quad \Gamma \vdash M_2 : A_1}{\Gamma \vdash M : [M_2/x]B_1}$$

where $[M_2/x]B_1 \equiv B' \prec [M_2/x]B$. Note that, by induction hypothesis, $\Pi x{:}A.B \simeq \mathcal{C}(\Gamma;\ M_1) \preceq \Pi x{:}A_1.B_1$. So, $B \preceq B_1$, which implies that $[M_2/x]B \preceq [M_2/x]B_1$, a contradiction. So, $[M_2/x]B$ is the principal type of M in Γ. □

Remark The above proof is very similar to what we have given in Example 3.24 in Section 3.3 for the specific examples of principal types. The strong normalisation theorem is used to guarantee the termination of the algorithm.

The decidability of type inference and that of the cumulativity relation implies that the problem of type checking—deciding whether an arbitrary judgement is derivable—is decidable.

Corollary 5.14. (decidability of type checking) ECC *is decidable, i.e. it is decidable whether* $\Gamma \vdash M : A$ *for arbitrary* Γ, M *and* A.

Proof By the definition of principal type, to see whether $\Gamma \vdash M : A$, just check whether $\mathcal{C}(\Gamma;\ M) \preceq A$. By Theorem 5.13 and Lemma 5.11, this is decidable. $\square$

Remark For a type theory with dependent types, the problem of type checking is no simpler than that of type inference, since the process of type checking essentially requires type inference.

6
A set-theoretic model

We explain in this chapter how the intuitive meanings of the main constructs in ECC may be understood set-theoretically. In the above chapters, we have been mainly concerned with the operational semantics of the language, which is regarded as the fundamental basis in understanding the type theory. However, a set-theoretic model may give us a semantic view from another angle and therefore enhances our understanding of the language.[24]

Intuitively, types in a type theory may be thought of as representing sets and the judgemental colon relation ($M : A$) the membership relation ($\in$). Then, Π-types stand for dependent products (function spaces) with functions expressed by λ-expressions as their elements, and Σ-types for dependent sums with pairs as their elements. However, the type theory is a very rich language. As well-known by the work of Reynolds [Rey84, RP88], the impredicative polymorphism in the second-order λ-calculus F [Gir72, Rey74] does not have non-trivial classical set-theoretic semantics. To be more precise, the standard interpretation of the simply typed λ-calculus can not be extended to a model of the second-order λ-calculus. Since F is a subsystem of ECC, we certainly can not expect any non-trivial classical set-theoretic model of our language. This calls for a more elaborate and more careful effort to understand such an impredicative calculus set-theoretically. Furthermore, the question of how type universes can be understood set-theoretically must also be answered in order to model the whole language.

As discussed and shown by many authors (e.g. [Gir72, Mog85, LM88a, See86, Pit87, CGW87, Mes88]), the impredicative polymorphism in F can be given constructive set-theoretic interpretations. In particular, the idea of interpreting types as partial equivalence relations [Gir72, Tro73] provides us a nice framework of ω-sets and modest sets in which impredicative polymorphism can be modelled in a satisfactory way. In particular, Hyland [Hyl82] studied the general properties of ω-sets (called separate objects)

[24] However, we would like to emphasize that the operational semantics or meaning theory is more basic and may be regarded as a standard semantics of the type theory.

and modest sets (called effective objects). Moggi [Mog85] showed that there is a small internal complete category in the category of ω-sets, and therefore the second-order λ-calculus can be modelled in such a framework. Later, Hyland defined a stronger notion of completeness which can be used to model complex type theories like the calculus of constructions [Hyl88, Str88, Ehr88, Luo88b].

We show in this chapter how the above intuitive meanings of the constructions in ECC can be captured set-theoretically in the constructive framework of ω-sets and modest sets. In particular, we explain how non-propositional Π-types can be understood as set-theoretic products, propositions as 'small products' isomorphic to partial equivalence relations, Σ-types as sets of dependent pairs, and the predicative universes as corresponding to large set universes. However, we shall not give the set-theoretic model in full detail, but only give a brief sketch of the basic and crucial ideas. A more detailed description can be found in [Luo91a].

6.1 Understanding ECC in the ω-Set framework

We first give the definitions of ω-sets and modest sets and then discuss the basic ideas to interpret the main type constructors in the type theory.

Definition 6.1. ***(ω-sets)*** *An ω-*set *A is a pair $A = (|A|, \Vdash_A)$ that consists of a set $|A|$ and a relation $\Vdash_A \subseteq \omega \times |A|$ which is surjective in the sense that for any $a \in |A|$, there exists $n \in \omega$ such that $n \Vdash_A a$. $|A|$ is called the* carrier set *of A and $\Vdash_A$ the* realisability relation *of A.*

A morphism *f between two ω-sets A and B is a function $f : |A| \to |B|$ realised by some partial recursive function, i.e. there exists $n \in \omega$ such that for any $a \in |A|$ and any $m \in \omega$, $m \Vdash_A a$ implies $nm \Vdash_B f(a)$, where nm denotes the result of Kleene application of n to m.*

The ω-sets and the morphisms between them form the category of ω-sets, *denoted as ω-**Set**.*

Definition 6.2. ***(modest sets)*** *A* modest set *A is an ω-set whose realisability relation is a function, i.e. for any $n \in \omega$ and $a, b \in |A|$, $n \Vdash_A a$ and $n \Vdash_A b$ imply $a = b$. The* category of modest sets, *denoted as* $\mathbf{M}$, *is the full subcategory of ω-***Set** *with the modest sets as its objects.*

Remark The morphisms between ω-sets are 'computable' in the sense that they are realised by partial recursive functions. The categories ω-**Set** and $\mathbf{M}$ are concrete (but large) locally cartesian closed category [Hyl82]. Hence, they provide us structures richer than those needed to interpret the second-order λ-calculus. An important property is that the category of modest sets is closed for arbitrary products and equivalent to the (small) category of partial equivalence relations (see Lemma 6.9 and Lemma 6.11); that provides the basis to model impredicative polymorphism.

We now discuss how the main constructs in ECC can and should be understood set-theoretically. The main question is how to interpret the type universes and the type formation operators Π and Σ so that, intuitively,

1. $Prop \in Type_0 \in Type_1 \in ...;$
2. $Prop \subseteq Type_0 \subseteq Type_1 \subseteq ...;$
3. $Type_j$ is closed under Π and Σ (predicatively);
4. $Prop$ is closed under Π (impredicatively for arbitrary products).

Notice that the universe *Prop* is impredicative and required to be closed under arbitrary dependent product formation. As we remarked above, this prevents us from working in the classical set theory to gain a non-trivial model of the language. Furthermore, there are predicative universes which must be understood set-theoretically to satisfy the above requirements.

We explain below how a model-theoretic understanding of the main constructions can be given in the framework of ω-sets and modest sets to satisfy these requirements.

- A valid context is interpreted as an ω-set which consists of 'tuples' of its components.
- Γ-types are interpreted as families of ω-sets indexed by the interpretation of context Γ; in particular, Γ-propositions are interpreted as families of objects of a full subcategory **PROP** of the category of ω-sets which is isomorphic to the category of partial equivalence relations.
- The impredicative universe *Prop* corresponds to the category **PROP**.
- The predicative universes $Type_j$ correspond to the full subcategories ω-**Set**(j) of ω-**Set** the carrier sets of whose objects belong to the corresponding large set universes.

In general, a well-typed term of type A in context Γ is interpreted as a morphism in ω-**Set** corresponding to an element of the interpretation of A indexed by the interpretation of Γ.

6.2 Valid contexts and objects

A valid context intuitively stands for a sequence of assumptions. It is interpreted as an ω-set which consists of the 'tuples' of the components of the context. To specify the interpretation of contexts, we define an ω-set constructor.

Definition 6.3. *(σ) Suppose that Γ is an ω-set and $A : |\Gamma| \to \omega\text{-}\mathbf{Set}$ is a $|\Gamma|$-indexed family of ω-sets. Then, the ω-set $\sigma(\Gamma, A)$ is defined as:*

$$|\sigma(\Gamma, A)| =_{\mathrm{df}} \{\, (\gamma, a) \mid \gamma \in |\Gamma|, a \in |A(\gamma)| \,\},$$

$$\langle m, n\rangle \Vdash_{\sigma(\Gamma,A)} (\gamma, a) \;\Leftrightarrow_{\mathrm{df}}\; m \Vdash_{\Gamma} \gamma \text{ and } n \Vdash_{A(\gamma)} a,$$

where $\langle \_, \_\rangle$ is the index for the recursive function of pairing.

The empty context is interpreted as the terminal object of ω-**Set**:

$$[\![\langle\rangle]\!] =_{\mathrm{df}} (1, \omega \times 1).$$

Suppose that A is a Γ-type interpreted as a $[\![\Gamma]\!]$-indexed family of ω-sets $[\![\Gamma \vdash A : Type_j]\!]$. Then, the valid context $\Gamma, x{:}A$ is interpreted as the following ω-set:

$$[\![\Gamma, x{:}A]\!] =_{\mathrm{df}} \sigma([\![\Gamma]\!], [\![\Gamma \vdash A : Type_j]\!]).$$

Intuitively, an object is interpreted as an 'element' of the interpretation of its type. A Γ-object of type A is interpreted as a $[\![\Gamma]\!]$-indexed element of the interpretation of A in context Γ, which in the categorical language is expressed by a morphism satisfying the following first projection property.

Definition 6.4. *(FPP-morphisms) Let Γ be an ω-set and $A : |\Gamma| \to \omega\text{-}\mathbf{Set}$ a $|\Gamma|$-indexed family of ω-sets. A morphism $f : \Gamma \to \sigma(\Gamma, A)$ in ω-**Set** is called a FPP-*morphism, *notation*

$$f : \Gamma \to_{FPP} \sigma(\Gamma, A),$$

if it satisfies the first projection property $p(\Gamma, A) \circ f = id_\Gamma$, where $p(\Gamma, A) : \sigma(\Gamma, A) \to \Gamma$ is the morphism defined by $p(\Gamma, A)(\gamma, a) =_{\mathrm{df}} \gamma$, and id_Γ is the identity morphism from Γ to Γ. Intuitively, $f : \Gamma \to_{FPP} \sigma(\Gamma, A)$ is a 'Γ-indexed element of A'.

Since in ECC we do not distinguish types with their names, a type also has a 'double identity' in a model-theoretic interpretation. This is reflected by the correspondence between constant functions to ω-**Set** and a special kind of morphisms in ω-**Set**.

Lemma 6.5. *Suppose $\Gamma \in \omega$-**Set** and $U : |\Gamma| \to \omega$-**Set** is a constant function such that, for some set X, $U(\gamma) = (X, \omega \times X)$ for all $\gamma \in |\Gamma|$. Then, there is a one-one correspondence between the FPP-morphisms $f : \Gamma \to_{FPP} \sigma(\Gamma, U)$ and the functions g from $|\Gamma|$ to X.*

Proof The correspondence is given as follows:

- Given $f : \Gamma \to_{FPP} \sigma(\Gamma, U)$, the corresponding function $f^\star : |\Gamma| \to X$ is defined by $f^\star(\gamma) =_{\mathrm{df}} x$, where $\gamma \in |\Gamma|$ and $f(\gamma) = (\gamma, x)$;
- Given $g : |\Gamma| \to X$, the corresponding morphism $g^\circ : \Gamma \to_{FPP} \sigma(\Gamma, U)$ is defined by $g^\circ(\gamma) =_{\mathrm{df}} (\gamma, x)$, where $\gamma \in |\Gamma|$ and $g(\gamma) = x$.

We have, $f^{\star\circ} = f$ and $g^{\circ\star} = g$. □

Remark By the above lemma, the interpretation of a Γ-type which is an FPP-morphism, corresponds to a $[\![\Gamma]\!]$-indexed family of ω-sets, as universes in Γ are interpreted as constant functions from $[\![\Gamma]\!]$ to ω-**Set** of the form required in the above lemma (see below).

6.3 Predicative universes and non-propositional types

Non-propositional types in a context Γ can be interpreted as $[\![\Gamma]\!]$-indexed families of ω-sets. The intuition is that Σ-types correspond to sets of dependent pairs and Π-types to set-theoretic products, which are given by the following two ω-set constructors.

Definition 6.6. *(**σ_Γ and π_Γ**) Let Γ be an ω-set, $A : |\Gamma| \to \omega$-**Set** a $|\Gamma|$-indexed family of ω-sets, and $B : |\sigma(\Gamma, A)| \to \omega$-**Set** a $|\sigma(\Gamma, A)|$-indexed family of ω-sets.*

1. *The $|\Gamma|$-indexed family of ω-sets $\sigma_\Gamma(A, B) : |\Gamma| \to \omega$-**Set** is defined as, for $\gamma \in |\Gamma|$,*

$$|\sigma_\Gamma(A,B)(\gamma)| =_{\mathrm{df}} \{\, (a,b) \mid a \in |A(\gamma)|, b \in |B(\gamma,a)| \,\},$$

$$\langle m,n\rangle \Vdash_{\sigma_\Gamma(A,B)(\gamma)} (a,b) \Leftrightarrow_{\mathrm{df}} m \Vdash_{A(\gamma)} a \text{ and } n \Vdash_{B(\gamma,a)} b.$$

2. *The $|\Gamma|$-indexed family of ω-sets $\pi_\Gamma(A, B) : |\Gamma| \to \omega$-**Set** is defined as, for $\gamma \in |\Gamma|$,*

$$|\pi_\Gamma(A,B)(\gamma)| =_{\mathrm{df}} \{\, f \in F(A,B)(\gamma) \mid \exists n \in \omega.\ n \Vdash_{\pi_\Gamma(A,B)(\gamma)} f \,\},$$

where $F(A,B)(\gamma) = \prod_{a \in |A(\gamma)|} |B(\gamma, a)|$ denotes the product of the $|A(\gamma)|$-indexed family of sets $|B(\gamma, a)|$, and $n \Vdash_{\pi_\Gamma(A,B)(\gamma)} f$ if and *only if for any* $a \in |A(\gamma)|$ *and* $m \in \omega$, $m \Vdash_{A(\gamma)} a$ *implies* $nm \Vdash_{B(\gamma,a)} f(a)$.

The interpretations of a Σ-type and a Π-type whose principal type is $Type_j$ can then be given as:

$$[\![\Gamma \vdash \Sigma x{:}A.B{:}Type_j]\!] =_{\mathrm{df}} \sigma_{[\![\Gamma]\!]}([\![\Gamma \vdash A{:}Type_j]\!], [\![\Gamma, x{:}A \vdash B{:}Type_j]\!]),$$

$$[\![\Gamma \vdash \Pi x{:}A.B{:}Type_j]\!] =_{\mathrm{df}} \pi_{[\![\Gamma]\!]}([\![\Gamma \vdash A{:}Type_j]\!], [\![\Gamma, x{:}A \vdash B{:}Type_j]\!]),$$

where $[\![\Gamma \vdash A{:}Type_j]\!]$ and $[\![\Gamma, x{:}A \vdash B{:}Type_j]\!]$ are the interpretations of A in Γ and B in $\Gamma, x{:}A$, respectively.

We now explain how the predicative universes $Type_j$ should be interpreted so that the requirements we gave in Section 6.1 can be satisfied. In other words, we interpret the predicative universes in such a way that they satisfy the membership relation $Type_j \in Type_{j+1}$, the inclusion relation $Type_j \subseteq Type_{j+1}$, and the closedness requirement for Π and Σ.

First, large set universes are used to interpret the predicative universes so that the closedness requirement is satisfied.[25] A basic insight here is that the notions of ω-sets and modest sets have nothing to do with *sizes* of the sets under consideration. Consider the ZFC set theory with infinite inaccessible cardinals[26] $\kappa_0 < \kappa_1 < \kappa_2 < \ldots$ and let V_α be the cumulative hierarchy of sets. Then $Type_j$ corresponds to the following category ω-**Set**(j).

Definition 6.7. *(ω-**Set**(j)) Let j be a natural number. ω-**Set**(j) is the full subcategory of ω-**Set** whose objects are those ω-sets whose carrier sets are in the set universe V_{κ_j}.*

The categories ω-**Set**(j) are locally cartesian closed. More importantly, they are closed under the ω-set constructors σ_Γ and π_Γ, because the set universes V_{κ_j} are models of the ZFC set theory.

Lemma 6.8. *ω-**Set**(j) is closed under the ω-set constructors σ_Γ and π_Γ, that is, if $A : |\Gamma| \to \omega$-**Set**(j) and $B : \sigma(\Gamma, A) \to \omega$-**Set**$(j)$, then we have $\sigma_\Gamma(A, B), \pi_\Gamma(A, B) : |\Gamma| \to \omega$-**Set**$(j)$.*

---

[25] The idea of interpreting $Type_j$ as large set universes was suggested to the author by Hayashi, Moggi and Coquand.

[26] A cardinal κ is (strongly) inaccessible if it is uncountable and regular, and $2^\lambda < \kappa$ for all $\lambda < \kappa$. See, e.g. [Lev79, Dev79].

The lemma above meets the closedness requirement 3 in Section 6.1. Furthermore, as $V_{\kappa_i} \subseteq V_{\kappa_{i+1}}$, ω-**Set**(j) is a full subcategory of ω-**Set**$(j+1)$. This satisfies the inclusion requirement 2 between the $Type_j$. Note that ω-**Set**(j) are *small* categories. Therefore, they can be naturally viewed as ω-sets through the embedding functor Δ from the category of sets **Set** to ω-**Set** defined as $\Delta(X) =_{\mathrm{df}} (X, \omega \times X)$ for $X \in \mathrm{Obj}(\mathbf{Set})$, and $\Delta(f) =_{\mathrm{df}} f$ for $f : X \to Y$ in **Set**. As $V_{\kappa_j} \in V_{\kappa_{j+1}}$, we have $\Delta(\mathrm{Obj}(\omega\text{-}\mathbf{Set}(j))) \in \mathrm{Obj}(\omega\text{-}\mathbf{Set}(j+1))$. This satisfies the membership requirement 1 between the predicative universes.

Based on these, we interpret the universe $Type_j$ as the following $|\,[\![\Gamma]\!]\,|$-indexed family of ω-sets, for $\gamma \in |\,[\![\Gamma]\!]\,|$,

$$[\![\Gamma \vdash Type_j : Type_{j+1}]\!](\gamma) =_{\mathrm{df}} \Delta(\mathrm{Obj}(\omega\text{-}\mathbf{Set}(j))).$$

6.4 The impredicative universe and propositions

Propositions are interpreted as a special class of ω-sets which are isomorphic to partial equivalence relations. Here, the notion of modest set [Hyl82, Hyl88, Mog85] is essential. The important point is that the category of modest sets is closed for arbitrary products and equivalent to the (small) category of partial equivalence relations.

Lemma 6.9. *The category of modest sets* $\mathbf{M}$ *is closed under the* ω*-set constructor* π_Γ *in the sense that, for any* $|\Gamma|$*-indexed family of* ω*-sets* $A : |\Gamma| \to \omega\text{-}\mathbf{Set}$ *and any* $|\sigma(\Gamma, A)|$*-indexed family of modest sets* $B : |\sigma(\Gamma, A)| \to \mathbf{M}$, $\pi_\Gamma(A, B)$ *is a* $|\Gamma|$*-indexed family of modest sets, i.e.* $\pi_\Gamma(A, B) : |\Gamma| \to \mathbf{M}$.

Proof We follow [LM88b, Hyl88] to prove the lemma. We only have to show that, for $\gamma \in |\Gamma|$, $\Vdash_{\pi_\Gamma(A,B)(\gamma)}$ is a function, i.e. $n \Vdash_{\pi_\Gamma(A,B)(\gamma)} f$ and $n \Vdash_{\pi_\Gamma(A,B)(\gamma)} g$ imply $f = g$. For any $a \in |A(\gamma)|$, let $m \in \omega$ such that $m \Vdash_{A(\gamma)} a$ (m exists as $A(\gamma)$ is an ω-set). Then we have $nm \Vdash_{B(\gamma,a)} f(a)$ and $nm \Vdash_{B(\gamma,a)} g(a)$. As $B(\gamma, a)$ is a modest set, $f(a) = g(a)$. So, $f = g$ since a is arbitrary. □

Although $\mathbf{M}$ is closed for arbitrary products as the above lemma shows, it can not be directly used to interpret the impredicative universe *Prop*. The reason is that $\mathbf{M}$ itself is *not* a small category. If *Prop* were interpreted as $\mathbf{M}$, there would be no way to justify $Prop \in Type_0$. Fortunately, $\mathbf{M}$ is an *essentially small complete* category in the sense that it is equivalent to the following small category **PROP**, which is isomorphic to the category of partial equivalence relations. (Recall that R is a partial equivalence relation (per for short) if R is symmetric and transitive.)

Definition 6.10. *(**PROP**) The category **PROP** is the full subcategory of **M** (hence, of ω-**Set**) with the following object set:*

$$\mathsf{Obj}(\mathbf{PROP}) =_{\mathrm{df}} \{ (Q(R), \in) \mid R \subseteq \omega \times \omega \text{ is a per} \}$$

where $Q(R) = \{ [n]_R \mid (n,n) \in R \}$ is the quotient set with respect to R and $\in \subseteq \omega \times Q(R)$ is the membership relation.

Lemma 6.11. *There is an equivalence of categories* **back** $: \mathbf{M} \to \mathbf{PROP}$ *such that* $\mathbf{back}(A) \cong A$ *for* $A \in \mathsf{Obj}(\mathbf{M})$*, and* $\mathbf{back}(P) = P$ *for* $P \in \mathsf{Obj}(\mathbf{PROP})$.

Proof Define the functor **back** $: \mathbf{M} \to \mathbf{PROP}$ as follows: for $A \in \mathsf{Obj}(\mathbf{M})$,

$$\mathbf{back}(A) =_{\mathrm{df}} (Q(R_A), \in),$$

where $R_A = \{ (n,m) \mid \exists a \in A.\ n \Vdash_A a \text{ and } m \Vdash_A a \}$ is the partial equivalence relation induced by A, and, for any morphism $f : A \to B$ in $\mathbf{M}$,

$$\mathbf{back}(f)([p]_{R_A}) =_{\mathrm{df}} [np]_{R_B}, \quad \text{where } n \Vdash_{A,B} f.$$

back is a category equivalence with the inclusion functor **inc** $: \mathbf{PROP} \to \mathbf{M}$ as its inverse. In fact, we have the identity natural transformation $id : id_{\mathbf{PROP}} \to \mathbf{back} \circ \mathbf{inc}$ and a natural transformation

$$\eta : id_{\mathbf{M}} \to \mathbf{inc} \circ \mathbf{back}$$

defined as follows: for $A \in \mathsf{Obj}(\mathbf{M})$ and $a \in |A|$, $\eta_A(a) =_{\mathrm{df}} [n]_{R_A}$, where $n \Vdash_A a$. Hence, for all $A \in \mathsf{Obj}(\mathbf{M})$, $\mathbf{back}(A) = \mathbf{inc} \circ \mathbf{back}(A) \cong A$. Furthermore, for $P = (Q(R), \in) \in \mathsf{Obj}(\mathbf{PROP})$, we have

$$\begin{aligned} R_P &= \{ (n,m) \mid \exists [a]_R.m \Vdash_P [a]_R \text{ and } n \Vdash_P [a]_R \} \\ &= \{ (n,m) \mid \exists a \in \omega.(m,n \in [a]_R) \} \\ &= R \end{aligned}$$

and therefore $\mathbf{back}(P) = (Q(R_P), \in) = (Q(R), \in) = P$. □

A proposition $\Pi x{:}A.P$ in context Γ is interpreted as a $|\,[\![\Gamma]\!]\,|$-indexed family of objects of **PROP**. The basic idea is that, when $\Pi x{:}A.P$ is a proposition, we first form the product by the ω-set constructor $\pi_{[\![\Gamma]\!]}$ to obtain a $|\,[\![\Gamma]\!]\,|$-indexed family of modest sets and then use **back** to 'take it back' into a family of objects in **PROP**. That is, $[\![\Gamma \vdash \Pi x{:}A.P : Prop]\!]$ is defined as

$$\mathbf{back} \circ \pi_{[\![\Gamma]\!]}([\![\Gamma \vdash A : T_\Gamma(A)]\!], [\![\Gamma, x{:}A \vdash P : Prop]\!]).$$

The impredicative universe *Prop* corresponds to the category **PROP**. By Lemma 6.9 and Lemma 6.11, the closedness requirement 4 in Section 6.1 is satisfied, i.e. *Prop* is closed under arbitrary products. The inclusion requirement $Prop \subseteq Type_0$ is satisfied by the fact that **PROP** is a full subcategory of ω-**Set**(0) and, the membership requirement $Prop \in Type_0$ by the fact $\Delta(\mathrm{Obj}(\mathbf{PROP})) \in \mathrm{Obj}(\omega\text{-}\mathbf{Set}(0))$, where $\Delta : \mathbf{Set} \to \omega\text{-}\mathbf{Set}$ is the embedding functor defined in the last section.

Based on these, we interpret the universe *Prop* as the following $|\,[\![\Gamma]\!]\,|$-indexed family of ω-sets, for $\gamma \in |\,[\![\Gamma]\!]\,|$,

$$[\![\Gamma \vdash Prop : Type_0]\!](\gamma) =_{\mathrm{df}} \Delta(\mathrm{Obj}(\mathbf{PROP})).$$

6.5 Remarks

We have given a sketch of a model-theoretic semantics of the language of ECC, which shows how the main constructions (types in particular) in the language may be understood in the constructive framework of ω-sets and modest sets. When a detailed interpretation of the full language including the interpretations of objects is defined (cf. [Luo91a, Str88]), we can prove the following soundness theorem of the interpretation.

Theorem 6.12. *The interpretation* $[\![\_]\!]$ *of the valid contexts and derivable judgements of* ECC *has the following properties:*

1. *If* Γ *is a valid context, then* $[\![\Gamma]\!] \in \mathrm{Obj}(\omega\text{-}\mathbf{Set})$.
2. *If* $\Gamma \vdash M : A$, *then* $[\![\Gamma \vdash M : A]\!] : [\![\Gamma]\!] \to_{FPP} [\![\Gamma, x{:}A]\!]$.
3. *If* $A \preceq A'$ *are* Γ*-types, then there is an inclusion morphism*

$$\boldsymbol{inc}_\Gamma(A, A') : [\![\Gamma, x{:}A]\!] \hookrightarrow [\![\Gamma, x{:}A']\!]$$

such that, if $\Gamma \vdash M : A$, $\Gamma \vdash N : A'$ *and* $M \simeq N$, *then* $[\![\Gamma \vdash N : A']\!] = \boldsymbol{inc}_\Gamma(A, A') \circ [\![\Gamma \vdash M : A]\!]$.

From such a model-theoretic semantics, one may gain a further understanding of the language. First, in the interpretation we have given, empty types exist. For instance, the proposition $\Pi X{:}Prop.X$ (the logical constant **false**) is in fact interpreted as the empty ω-set $(\emptyset, \emptyset)$.[27] So, there is no morphism from $[\![\langle\rangle]\!]$ to $[\![y{:}\Pi X{:}Prop.X]\!]$. By the above theorem, we have $\not\vdash M : \Pi X{:}Prop.X$ for any term M. This conforms with Theorem 5.4 of logical consistency and is an important feature of such a model-theoretic interpretation. It is one of the reasons that we view such a model-theoretic semantics as appropriate in the sense that it reflects some of the important properties of the language. There are other possible and reasonable models. For instance, one may give a truth-value model of ECC where propositions are interpreted as 0 or 1. However, some other models (e.g. domain-theoretic ones) do not capture the essential properties of the language such as logical consistency.

There are other interests in constructing semantic models of type theories. For example, semantic models are often used to justify the consistency of a logical calculus and to guide and justify new extensions or modifications. Various independence results may also be proved semantically by constructing particular models as counter-examples (cf. [Str88]). A set-theoretic semantics may also be used to give *informal* explanations for the users of the language who are usually already familiar with (naive) set theory (e.g. [LP92]).

However, it seems worth remarking that defining models for a theory of dependent types is not as easy as may have been suggested. In fact, to give a complete definition of a model (and prove its well-definedness and soundness) is often a task as tedious as proving difficult meta-theoretic properties such as normalisation. (As we have seen, proving the normalisation theorem is indeed a process of giving a particular term model.) Furthermore, many meta-theoretic properties of the language have to be used to prove the well-definedness and soundness of a model construction, which are the basis to use the model formally or theoretically, e.g. to derive the consistency property or to prove independence results.

---

[27] More precisely, $[\![\vdash \Pi X{:}Prop.X : Prop]\!]$ is defined as the function with the singleton set $\{*\}$ as its domain and $(*, (\emptyset, \emptyset))$ as its image.

7
Computational and logical theories

In this and the next chapters, we consider and discuss the use of the type theory in applications to programming, logical reasoning, and program specification and development. The study of the use of the type theory is not meant to be complete in any way, but to show the potential power of the language.

As we know, using traditional logical languages such as first-order logic, one formalises concepts and problems by setting up *extra-logical theories* such as the theory of natural numbers and the theory of sets. Type theory might be used in a similar way by viewing the logical mechanism in it as a traditional logical system and a theory in the traditional sense would then correspond to a context which declares a set of constants and assumed axioms. However, as we have mentioned in Section 2.3.5, in the intended use of the type theory, the basic mathematical and computational structures are introduced by adding new types together with the associated objects whose meanings are determined by the associated inference rules. Put in another way, basic mathematical or computational structures may be introduced into the language by considering new inductive data types. This is a rather different notion of 'theory', which may be called *computational theories*, since the notion of computation is one of the essential elements in understanding the inductive data types, which is new as compared with the traditional notion of logical theory.

The use of inductive data types (or computational theories) to introduce basic structures does not imply that the traditional role of logic in describing or characterising the properties of the considered objects is of no use anymore. On the contrary, since the type theory is a language which provides nice abstraction mechanisms as well as a powerful internal logic, we can use the language to consider a notion of *abstract theory* which is useful in formalising and reasoning about abstract concepts, and on the basis of which we can consider *abstract structured reasoning* in the sense that reasoning about related structures can be done in a structured way so that one may perform proof development *in the large* as well as in the small.

7.1 Computational theories and inductive data types

We explain the notion of computational theory by considering some simple examples of inductive data types. How inductive data types may be introduced in the type theory in general will be considered in Chapter 9.

7.1.1 The type of natural numbers

A traditional logical theory formalises a mathematical structure by introducing a set of basic symbols (say constants and function symbols) and a set of axioms. For example, if we use the type theory as a traditional logic, we may formalise the notion of natural numbers by considering a context of the following form:[28]

$$N : Type_0,\ 0 : N,\ succ : N \to N,\ ...,$$

where '...' contains the assumptions of the axioms for natural numbers, such as the following Peano's axioms:

$(P3)$ $\forall x{:}N\forall y{:}N.(succ(x) =_N succ(y)) \supset (x =_N y).$

$(P4)$ $\forall x{:}N.\ \neg(0 =_N succ(x)).$

$(P5)$ $\forall P{:}N \to Prop.\ P(0) \supset (\forall x{:}N.P(x) \supset P(succ(x))) \supset \forall z{:}N.P(z).$

In such a logical theory, the meanings of the introduced entities are determined by the logical axioms. In particular, the notion of computation does not play any essential role in such a formalisation.

In type theory, according to the idea of Martin-Löf, instead of adopting the traditional notion of logical theory, one introduces a computational theory of natural numbers as an (inductive) type N by the following rules: the formation and introduction rules

$$\frac{}{\vdash N : Type_0} \qquad \frac{}{\vdash 0 : N} \qquad \frac{\Gamma \vdash n : N}{\Gamma \vdash succ(n) : N}$$

the elimination rule

$$\frac{\begin{array}{c}\Gamma \vdash C : N \to Type_i \quad \Gamma \vdash n : N \\ \Gamma \vdash c : C(0) \quad \Gamma \vdash f : \Pi x{:}N.\ C(x) \to C(succ(x))\end{array}}{\Gamma \vdash Rec_N(c, f)(n) : C(n)}$$

[28]Or, one may introduce *constants* N etc., and add the Peano axioms as the axioms of the type theory.

and the computation (contraction) rules

$$
\begin{aligned}
Rec_N(c,f)(0) &\leadsto c,\\
Rec_N(c,f)(succ(n)) &\leadsto f(n, Rec_N(c,f)(n)).
\end{aligned}
$$

Like Π-types and Σ-types, the meaning of the type of natural numbers is determined by the above rules. The introduction rules determine how type N may be inhabited by specifying the forms of its canonical objects (0 and successors $succ(n)$), and the elimination and computation rules how type N and natural numbers may be used by means of the recursion (and induction) operator to define functional programs (and proofs, when C is a family of propositions). The elimination rule says that for any family of types C indexed by the natural numbers, if one can find constructions that produce an object of type $C(n)$ for any canonical object n of type N, then there exists a construction that produces an object of type $C(z)$ for any object z of type N. Note that, if C is a family of propositions, the elimination rule is the type-theoretic version of Peano's fifth axiom ($P5$). The computation rules determine the computational meaning of the elimination operator by specifying how computation performs when the elimination operator is applied to a natural number in canonical form.

There are two important differences between inductive data types and the traditional notion of logical theory. The first is that the notion of computation plays an essential role in giving the meaning to the type and its objects and hence how they may be used. The second is that, the possible range of the recursion operator may be non-propositional types as well as propositions. Therefore, the elimination operator is used for defining (primitive) recursive functional programs as well as logical proofs. For example, $Rec_N(c,f)$ is the function g whose definition is usually presented by the following equations in (informal) mathematics:

$$
\begin{aligned}
g(0) &=_{\mathrm{df}} c,\\
g(n+1) &=_{\mathrm{df}} f(n, g(n)).
\end{aligned}
$$

Example 7.1. Here are some simple examples of functional programs and relations defined by means of the recursion operator Rec_N.

1. The predecessor function *pred* of type $N \to N$:

$$pred(n) =_{\mathrm{df}} Rec_N(0,\ \lambda x{:}N\lambda y{:}N.x)(n).$$

2. The (infix) functions for addition, subtraction, and multiplication of type $N \to N \to N$:

$$
\begin{aligned}
m+n &=_{\mathrm{df}} Rec_N(m,\ \lambda x{:}N\lambda y{:}N.succ(y))(n).\\
m-n &=_{\mathrm{df}} Rec_N(m,\ \lambda x{:}N\lambda y{:}N.pred(y))(n).\\
m*n &=_{\mathrm{df}} Rec_N(0,\ \lambda x{:}N\lambda y{:}N.(m+y))(n).
\end{aligned}
$$

3. The (infix) binary relations 'less than or equal' and 'less than' of type $N \to N \to Prop$:

$$\begin{array}{lll} m \leq n & =_{\rm df} & \exists k{:}N.\ (m+k) =_N n. \\ m < n & =_{\rm df} & (m \leq n)\ \&\ \neg(m =_N n). \end{array}$$

Example 7.2. (Peano's fourth axiom) The Peano axioms are provable for the natural numbers introduced above. For example, to prove Peano's fourth axiom ($P4$), we may first define a predicate over N which is true for 0 and false otherwise:

$$IsZero(n) =_{\rm df} Rec_N(\mathbf{true},\ \lambda x{:}N\lambda P{:}Prop.\mathbf{false})(n).$$

Then, the following is a proof of ($P4$):

$$\lambda x{:}N\lambda h{:}(0 =_N succ(x)).\ h(IsZero, id),$$

where id is the canonical proof of **true** (see Section 5.1.2).

The above formulation of the type of natural numbers falls into a general pattern (due to Martin-Löf [ML84]) of introducing inductive data types in general. For instance, in a similar way, one can introduce finite types—inductive data types with finitely many canonical objects such as the empty type, the unit type, etc. (see Chapter 9). As an example, the type with boolean values tt and ff as its canonical objects can be introduced by the following rules: the formation and introduction rules

$$\frac{}{\vdash Bool : Type_0} \qquad \frac{}{\vdash \mathrm{tt} : Bool} \qquad \frac{}{\vdash \mathrm{ff} : Bool}$$

the elimination rule

$$\frac{\Gamma \vdash C : Bool \to Type_i \quad \Gamma \vdash b : Bool \quad \Gamma \vdash c_1 : C(\mathrm{tt}) \quad \Gamma \vdash c_2 : C(\mathrm{ff})}{\Gamma \vdash Rec_{Bool}(c_1, c_2)(b) : C(b)}$$

and the computation rules

$$\begin{array}{lll} Rec_{Bool}(c_1, c_2)(\mathrm{tt}) & \leadsto & c_1, \\ Rec_{Bool}(c_1, c_2)(\mathrm{ff}) & \leadsto & c_2. \end{array}$$

Then the elimination operator Rec_{Bool} provides means to define functions such as the 'if-then-else' function. For instance,

$$\mathrm{if}_N(b, m, n) =_{\rm df} Rec_{Bool}(m, n)(b) : Bool \to N \to N \to N.$$

As another example, the following binary function $\leq_B$ of type $N \to N \to Bool$ returns tt as its value if m is less than or equal to n and ff otherwise:

$$\leq_B\ =_{\rm df} Rec_N(\lambda x{:}N.\mathrm{tt},\ \lambda x{:}N\lambda f{:}N \to Bool.Rec_N(\mathrm{ff}, \lambda y{:}N\lambda b{:}Bool.f(y))).$$

7.1.2 The type of lists of natural numbers

Similarly, we may introduce a type of (finite) lists of natural numbers by means of the following rules:

$$\frac{}{\vdash List(N) : Type_0} \qquad \frac{}{\vdash nil_N : List(N)} \qquad \frac{\Gamma \vdash n : N \quad \Gamma \vdash l : List(N)}{\Gamma \vdash cons_N(n, l) : List(N)}$$

$$\frac{\begin{array}{c}\Gamma \vdash C : List(N) \rightarrow Type_i \quad \Gamma \vdash l : List(N) \quad \Gamma \vdash c : C(nil_N) \\ \Gamma \vdash f : \Pi n{:}N\Pi l{:}List(N).\ C(l) \rightarrow C(cons_N(n, l))\end{array}}{\Gamma \vdash Rec_{List(N)}(c, f)(l) : C(l)}$$

together with the computation rules

$$\begin{array}{rcl} Rec_{List(N)}(c, f)(nil_N) & \rightsquigarrow & c, \\ Rec_{List(N)}(c, f)(cons_N(n, l)) & \rightsquigarrow & f(n, l, Rec_{List(N)}(c, f)(l)). \end{array}$$

Example 7.3. Here are some simple examples of functional programs and relations that can be defined about lists.

1. The functions hd_N of type $List(N) \rightarrow N$ and tl_N of type $List(N) \rightarrow List(N)$:

$$\begin{array}{rcl} hd_N(l) & =_{\mathrm{df}} & Rec_{List(N)}(0,\ \lambda x{:}N\lambda l'{:}List(N)\lambda y{:}N.x)(l). \\ tl_N(l) & =_{\mathrm{df}} & Rec_{List(N)}(nil_N,\ \lambda x{:}N\lambda l'{:}List(N)\lambda y{:}N.l')(l). \end{array}$$

   When l is the empty list, $hd_N(l)$ and $tl_N(l)$ return 0 and nil_N as value, respectively.

2. The function *append* of type $List(N) \rightarrow List(N) \rightarrow List(N)$:

$$\begin{array}{rl} & append(k, l) \\ =_{\mathrm{df}} & Rec_{List(N)}(l,\ \lambda x{:}N\lambda l_1{:}List(N)\lambda l_2{:}List(N).cons(x, l_2))(k). \end{array}$$

3. The function *length* of type $List(N) \rightarrow N$:

$$length_N(l) \quad =_{\mathrm{df}} \quad Rec_{List(N)}(0,\ \lambda x{:}N\lambda l'{:}List(N).succ)(l).$$

The following is an example of a functional program for sorting a list of natural numbers.

Example 7.4. (insert sorting) By means of the recursion operator for lists, it is easy to define a functional program that implements the algorithm of insert sort, which is usually defined in the following way in functional programming:

$$\begin{array}{rcl} insert\_sort(nil) & = & nil \\ insert\_sort(n::l) & = & insert(n, insert\_sort(l)) \\ insert(n, nil) & = & n::nil \\ insert(n, m::l) & = & if\ n \leq m\ then\ n::(m::l)\ else\ m::insert(n, l). \end{array}$$

This can directly be expressed by means of $Rec_{List(N)}$ as follows. First define *insert* of type $N \to (List(N) \to List(N))$:

$$insert(n) =_{\mathrm{df}} Rec_{List(N)}(cons_N(n, nil_N), g[n]),$$

where $g[n]$ is the function of type $N \to List(N) \to List(N) \to List(N)$ defined as:

$$g[n](m, l, r) =_{\mathrm{df}} \mathrm{if}_N(n \leq_B m,\ cons_N(n, cons_N(m, l)),\ cons_N(m, r)).$$

Then define the sorting function *insert_sort* of type $List(N) \to List(N)$ as follows:

$$insert\_sort =_{\mathrm{df}} Rec_{List(N)}(nil_N,\ insert'),$$

where $insert'$ is of type $N \to List(N) \to List(N) \to List(N)$ and defined as

$$insert'(m, l, r) =_{\mathrm{df}} insert(m, r).$$

We have only given some very simple examples to explain how functional programs may be defined in type theory. More examples can be found in, for example, [NPS90, Tho91, Wan92]. From the above example, the reader must have realised that the notations involving the elimination operators are difficult to read and very cumbersome to use in practice. This calls for a further research on how one may present functional programs in the style of equational presentations as in functional programming languages but still guarantee that the programs defined are eligible (well-defined) in the type theory under consideration.

7.2 Abstract theories and abstract reasoning

The above simple examples of natural numbers and lists have explained how basic mathematical or computational structures may be introduced into type theory as inductive data types (or computational theories). However, as we have emphasized, the use of computational theories does not mean that the descriptive power of the internal logic is of less use. We explain in this section how a notion of *abstract theory* may be defined so that *abstract reasoning* can be considered. The idea[29] is that in logical reasoning, we may benefit from a notion of *abstract theory* which allows us to develop proofs and organise proof development in a structured and modular way so that one can control the complexity in large proof development. (This is a very similar idea to modular program development. See the next chapter.)

7.2.1 A notion of abstract theory

More specifically, the need to consider a notion of abstract theory, as opposed to the computational notion of theory given by inductive data types, comes essentially from several sources. The first is that, since many computational theories have some common structure and properties, one hopes to be able to reason about a class of data types rather than to reason about them one by one. Then, there is a problem of considering abstract types rather than just the specific (and concrete) data types. For example, one may hope to reason about data types with group structures in general and then to instantiate the abstract results for specific data types. Secondly, not every possibly useful concept can be formalised as an inductive data type and there is a need to talk about 'subtypes' of the existing data types. Thirdly, when using type theory (or any other logical language) in reasoning, one hopes to organise the results of proof development into an organised library of theories which has a clear structure to allow people to use.

The rich type structure in our type theory, in particular, Σ-types, type universes and the internal logic, allow us to express a notion of *abstract theory*, providing a nice mechanism for abstract and structured reasoning. We first explain the basic idea of using Σ-types to express abstract structures and mathematical theories through a simple example.

Notation In the rest of this chapter and the next chapter, we shall often omit the typing subscripts for pairs in ECC, when no confusion may occur. Furthermore, we shall use the following notational convention:

$$\sum [x_1{:}A_1,\ x_2{:}A_2,\ \ldots,\ x_n{:}A_n]$$

will denote the Σ-type

[29]The need of structuring theories in proof development was suggested to the author by Burstall and the current presentation has benefited from discussions with Coquand, Taylor and Pollack.

$$\Sigma x_1{:}A_1\Sigma x_2{:}A_2 ... \Sigma x_{n-1}{:}A_{n-1}.A_n,$$

and, for any object a of such a type, we use $x_i[a]$ as (the name of) the obvious projections over object a, e.g. $x_2[a]$ stands for $\pi_1(\pi_2(a))$ and $x_n[a]$ for $\pi_2(...\pi_2(\pi_2(a))...)$ with π_2 occurring $n-1$ times. Objects of such a type will be written as a tuple $\langle a_1, ..., a_n\rangle$.

Example 7.5. We may express an abstract theory of semigroups as consisting of two parts:

- A type of semigroup structures $\mathbf{Str}[SG] =_{\mathrm{df}} \sum[X : Type_0,\ \circ : X \to X \to X]$, and
- the (abstract) *axiom* which is a predicate $\mathbf{Ax}[SG]$ over $\mathbf{Str}[SG]$ which, when given any semigroup structure s, returns the associativity axiom for s, i.e. $\forall x, y, z{:}X.\ (x \circ (y \circ z)) =_N ((x \circ y) \circ z)$.

One may also put the two parts of the semigroup abstraction together as a Σ-type $\mathbf{Mod}(SG) =_{\mathrm{df}} \Sigma s{:}\mathbf{Str}[SG].\mathbf{Ax}[SG](s)$.

One can then prove (abstract) theorems about arbitrary semigroups. Such abstract theorems constitute a predicate $\mathbf{Thm}[SG]$ over $\mathbf{Str}[SG]$, which can in general be expressed as the following form (say, n theorems have been proved):

$$\mathbf{Thm}[SG] \equiv \lambda s{:}\mathbf{Str}[SG].\ P_1\ \&\ ...\ \&\ P_n$$

Their (abstract) proofs are then a function $\mathbf{Prfs}[SG]$ of type

$$\forall s{:}\mathbf{Str}[SG].\ \mathbf{Ax}[SG](s) \supset \mathbf{Thm}[SG](s).$$

That is, given any concrete semigroup structure (i.e. a data type and a binary operation over the type which satisfies the associativity axiom), $\mathbf{Prfs}[SG]$ will result in the proofs of the concrete versions of the theorems for the given semigroup structure.

We now generalise the above ideas to the following definition of (abstract) theory.

Definition 7.6. (abstract theories) *An* abstract theory T *is a four-tuple*

$$T = \langle \mathbf{Str}[T],\ \mathbf{Ax}[T],\ \mathbf{Thm}[T],\ \mathbf{Prfs}[T]\rangle,$$

where

- $\mathbf{Str}[T]$ *is called the* structure type *of* T*, which is a type (usually a* Σ*-type);*

- $\mathbf{Ax}[T]$ *is called the* abstract axioms *of* T*, which is a predicate over* $\mathbf{Str}[T]$*;*

- $\mathbf{Thm}[T]$ *is called the (proved)* abstract theorems *of* T*, which is a predicate over* $\mathbf{Str}[T]$*; and*

- $\mathbf{Prfs}[T]$ *is called the* abstract proofs *of the theorems of* T*, which is of type* $\forall t{:}\mathbf{Str}[T].\ \mathbf{Ax}[T](t) \supset \mathbf{Thm}[T](t)$.

The set of abstract theories is expressed by the following type:

$$\mathbf{THEORY} =_{\mathrm{df}} \sum \begin{bmatrix} \mathbf{Str} : \mathit{Type}_1, \\ \mathbf{Ax} : \mathbf{Str} \to \mathit{Prop}, \\ \mathbf{Thm} : \mathbf{Str} \to \mathit{Prop}, \\ \mathbf{Prfs} : \forall s{:}\mathbf{Str}.\ \mathbf{Ax}(s) \supset \mathbf{Thm}(s) \end{bmatrix}.$$

Remarks Several simple remarks follow.

1. Note that predicative universes and the internal notion of predicate are both important in expressing *internally* in the type theory the notion of abstract theory (and the notion of theory morphism below). For this, we have used the fourth level of the type hierarchy (types of type Type_2).

2. The theorems in an abstract theory are those *proved* ones, which in practice are always finitely many. This is in contrast with the 'obvious' choice to consider a theory as including all of the *provable* logical consequences which we would argue, is incorrectly conceived concept for theorem proving, because conceptually it does not reflect the fact that deductive reasoning advances our knowledge and in practice it is not useful.

3. It is easy to see that, in this setting, any abstract notion of universal algebras with finitely many sorts, operators, and axioms can be formalised as an abstract theory. One can also formalise categorical notions (e.g. the category of small categories) in a similar way.

We shall show below that the notion of (abstract) theory presented above nicely supports an approach to abstract reasoning and structured reasoning.

7.2.2 Abstract reasoning

The idea of abstract reasoning[30] is that, instead of re-proving a theorem for many concrete theories, we can prove an (abstract) theorem in an (abstract) theory, then simply *instantiate* the abstract proofs as concrete ones for free. The notion of abstract theories for computer-assisted reasoning is analogous to the notion of 'parameterised modules' for modular programming. It becomes more useful as the task of proof development becomes large.

How this idea of abstract reasoning by proof instantiation can be expressed by means of the notion of abstract theory is best explained by a simple example. Consider the abstract theory SG of semigroups and suppose that we have proved some (abstract) theorems $\mathbf{Thm}[SG]$ whose proofs are $\mathbf{Prfs}[SG]$. We can then, for instance, instantiate these theorems and proofs to the concrete ones for the (concrete) computational theory of natural numbers and + (or other similar computational theories) provided that we have proved that + is associative (say, with proof ass_N). The instantiated proofs are then easily constructed as

$$Prfs\_N\_SG =_{\mathrm{df}} \mathbf{Prfs}[SG](\langle N, +\rangle, ass\_N).$$

Remark The facility of abstract reasoning comes from the power of Π-abstraction. However, the type universes make it possible to formalise abstract mathematics (like the theory of semigroups) adequately and Σ-types are important for 'packaging' the formalisation in a well-structured way. Based on such a mechanism, one may build up a *theory base* consisting of well-organised (abstract) theories with proved theorems which can be used by users in many different ways. Such a theory base would be very useful for large proof development tasks.

7.2.3 Theory morphisms and proof inheritance

Besides reasoning abstractly as considered above, in larger proof development one hopes to conquer a big and complex task by dividing it into smaller and simpler ones and then putting the results together in a structured way. One aspect of this may be considered by defining a notion of *theory morphism* between abstract theories[31] so that the theorems and proofs of a smaller and weaker theory can be inherited as those of a bigger and stronger theory.

---

[30] We use the phrase 'abstract reasoning' here in the sense of Paulson [Pau87], where he points out its desirability.

[31] I am in debt to Paul Taylor for this notion of theory morphism [LPT89], with whom we started to consider abstract reasoning.

Definition 7.7. (theory morphism) *A* morphism *from an abstract theory T' to another T is a pair of functions (f, g) such that*

$$\begin{array}{lcl} f & : & \mathbf{Str}[T'] \to \mathbf{Str}[T], \\ g & : & \forall s'{:}\mathbf{Str}[T'].\ \mathbf{Ax}[T'](s') \supset \mathbf{Ax}[T](f(s')). \end{array}$$

In practice, the existence of a morphism from T' to T usually means that T' is *stronger* than T. A typical example of such a morphism is when T' is a theory (say, a theory of rings) which contains more types and/or operators and/or stronger axioms than a theory T (say, SG); there is then a 'forgetful' morphism whose first component, f, forgets the extra types and operators and whose second component gives proofs of the axioms of T under the translation of f.

Given any morphism (f, g) from T' to T, we can inherit the proofs of theorems in the weaker theory T as the proofs of the corresponding theorems in T'. The corresponding (abstract) theorems in T',

$$Thm(T, T') =_{\mathrm{df}} \lambda s'{:}\mathbf{Str}[T'].\ \mathbf{Thm}[T](f(s')),$$

are proved by the following proofs inherited from $\mathbf{Prfs}[T]$:

$$Prfs(T, T') =_{\mathrm{df}} \lambda s'{:}\mathbf{Str}[T']\lambda p'{:}\mathbf{Ax}[T'](s').\ \mathbf{Prfs}[T](f(s'), g(s', p')).$$

For example, the theorems about semigroups can be inherited as theorems about rings through a forgetful morphism. (There are indeed two forgetful morphisms which concern the operators plus and multiplication, respectively.) The idea of divide-and-conquer (and separation of concerns) is embodied in proof inheritance. Simpler and more general theorems are dealt with in simpler and weaker theories, and then inherited (or lifted) to more complex and stronger theories.

The mechanism for proof inheritance as explained above is also useful when one is developing a library of (abstract) theories since one can use it to structure the development of proofs in the library.

7.3 Discussion

We have briefly discussed two notions of theories—computational theories (inductive data types) and abstract theories. The former is inherently computational in the sense that they stand for types of concrete data objects for which the notion of computation plays an important role in their meaning explanation. The notion of abstract theory is essentially logical (as in traditional logics) but is internalised using the rich type structure in the type theory and provides powerful mechanisms for structured abstract reasoning.

It may be worth remarking that the existential types (the impredicative existential quantifier or the predicative existential types as we have defined in Section 2.3.2) are *not* useful to express mathematical theories because some of their components are 'hidden' and can not be extracted when needed. The elimination operators for the existential types are too weak and, in particular, there is no way to prove that the first component of a 'weak pair' of type $\exists x{:}A.B$ satisfies the property B. To express mathematical theories as we have shown above, strong sums (Σ-types) are needed. A comparison of strong and weak sums in the context of modular programming can be found in [Mac86].

The approach to abstract theory discussed above adopts a view of '*theories as type-predicate pairs*'. There is another approach to theory structuring [SB83, LB92] borrowing ideas from research in algebraic specification languages like Clear [BG80]. This latter approach may be called '*theories as meta-values*', as there are theory operations to 'put theories together', which are performed at the meta-level of implementation. In the Automath project, ideas like telescope of organising mathematical texts through manipulating contexts are considered [dB80, Zuc75].

Since the notion of abstract theory can be internalised in the type theory (see [Luo90a]), the proof development systems like Lego already support its use in practice (see [Pol90b] for an example of proving Tarski's fixpoint theorem using the notion of abstract theory). However, how to design a nice environment together with a friendly library of (both computational and abstract) theories to support real proof development needs much more efforts to justify.

8
Specification and development of programs

In the above chapter, we have explained the difference and use of computational and logical theories in type theory. On the basis of that conceptual framework, a nice application of the type theory is to consider specification and development of programs.

Program specification and modular program development by stepwise refinement has been an interesting research area in computer science.[32] Various formal abstraction mechanisms (e.g. algebraic specifications) have been studied to provide good methodology and tools which can be used to apply the useful principles of software development such as separation of concerns and divide-and-conquer and to guarantee the correctness of programs with respect to their specifications. Since the work by Martin-Löf, it has become known that type theories can also provide basic mechanisms for programming and program specification (cf. [ML82, NPS90]). For instance, program derivation has been studied in various type theories [NPS90, BCM89, PM89, Hay91]. However, although it is known that a type theory may be used as a programming and specification language, some important topics concerning modular design and structured specification (for example, abstract implementation and modular refinement) have not been paid enough attention in the type-theoretic setting and the potential of type theory has not been well developed in this area.

In this chapter, we consider an approach to program specification and data refinement to show that the type theory provides an adequate language for both modular design by data refinement and structured specification of (functional) programs in the type theory. This addresses a particular aspect of the use of the type theory and is a part of our work aiming at developing type theory as a rich and uniform language for programming,

[32]Among the enormous literature in this area, see, for example, [Hoa72, LZ75, GHM76, GTW78, BG80, EFH83, EM85, FGJM85, Wir86, Jon86, ST87, ST88a, WB89, EM90].

logical reasoning, structured specification, and modular program development. The material of this chapter is based on [Luo91b, Luo93].

8.1 A brief summary

The notion of program specification in the type theory is very similar to that of abstract theory discussed in the above chapter and due to Rod Burstall, who first noticed the usefulness of the notions of abstract theory and theory morphism in application to program specifications, and developed a notion of deliverable for program development [BM92, McK92].

A *specification* in the type theory consists of (a pair of) a type, whose objects are the possible structures (programs and program modules) which may realise the specification, and a predicate over the structure type, which specifies the properties that any realisation should satisfy. In particular, the structure type of a specification of an abstract data type (say of stacks) can be defined as a Σ-type, each of whose objects has as its components a type (of stacks) associated with an explicit congruence relation (between stacks) and certain operations (corresponding to the empty stack, the push operation, etc.); the predicate over the structure type would specify the required properties including that the associated binary relation (between stacks) is a congruence. The semantics is straightforward and 'model-theoretic' in the sense that a *realisation* of a specification is simply a structure (an object of the structure type) which satisfies the required properties.

In order to discuss program development by stepwise refinement, we formalise a notion of *abstract implementation* between specifications. A specification SP *refines to* (or *is implemented by*) another specification SP' through a refinement map ρ (a function from the structure type of SP' to that of SP) if the images of ρ over the realisations of SP' are realisations of SP. In such a case, the refinement map is an incomplete program which expresses the design decisions made in the refinement step. This implementation relation composes vertically (cf. [BG80]) and hence satisfies the basic requirement for stepwise development of programs.

Based on the notion of abstract implementation, we further discuss methodological issues in software development and show that the higher-order structural mechanisms in the type theory nicely support modular design and structured specification. Σ-types support *decomposition* of specifications into independent specifications (which may possibly share some common parts). We also identify two general classes of specification operations, called *constructors* and *selectors*, which are monotone with respect to the implementation relation and can be used both in structured design by modular refinement and in structuring requirements specifications.

The higher-order facilities in the type theory naturally supports *para-*

meterised specifications. A notion of implementation between parameterised specifications is defined and it is shown to compose vertically. When a parameterised specification is monotone with respect to the implementation relation between specifications, the property of horizontal composition (cf. [BG80]) holds and the design principle of divide-and-conquer can be applied as well.

The type-theoretic approach to specification and data refinement is simple and the higher-order mechanisms in the type theory provide powerful and useful supports in various aspects of modular development of programs and specifications. Note that the type theory provides a single formal system in which programs, specifications, and their implementation relationships can be uniformly formalised and discussed. Such an 'internalisation' has an immediate benefit that refinement maps (programs and design decisions) as well as proofs of implementation correctness can be developed (interactively) in a proof development system like Lego. (In fact, all of the examples and propositions in this chapter have been checked in the Lego system.) We shall relate and compare our type-theoretic approach to that of algebraic specifications, in particular by relating the notion of implementation to that of constructor implementation developed by Sannella and Tarlecki [ST88b] and discussing the differences between the two approaches.

In our discussion of specifications and program development below, the reader may always assume that we are working in the empty context, unless we have made the context explicit. We shall also omit the subscripts of the predicative universes, assuming that we are working in a large enough universe and use the principle of 'typical ambiguity' as implemented in the Lego system (see Section 2.3.5).

8.2 Specifications and data refinement

In this section, we introduce the notion of specification and show how abstract data types can be specified and how a notion of abstract implementation between specifications can be defined and used for stepwise program development by refinement.

8.2.1 Program specifications and their realisations

Since type theory provides a single language for programming and logical reasoning, program specifications can be expressed directly in its language. For example, in Martin-Löf's type theory, a specification of sorting programs for lists of natural numbers may be defined as the following Σ-type:

$$\Sigma f{:}List(N) \to List(N).\ \forall l{:}List(N).\ Sorted(l, f(l)),$$

whose objects are pairs of a program and a proof that the program is indeed a sorting program. This idea of expressing a specification as a single type (a Σ-type in the above example) follows Martin-Löf's consideration of identifying specifications with types [ML82, ML84], which does not separate the computational content (programs) with the axiomatic requirements (correctness proofs). However, such a separation of concern, as we have repeatedly argued, is both conceptually natural and pragmatically important, and this is also reflected in our conception of logical theory in the previous chapter and the notion of program specification below.

Informally, a specification in the type theory consists of (a pair of) a type, whose objects are the possible programs (and program modules) which may realise the specification, and a predicate over the type, which specifies the properties that the realisations of the specification should satisfy.

Definition 8.1. (specifications) *A* specification SP *consists of a type* $\mathbf{Str}[SP]$ *of* SP-structures, *called the* structure type of SP, *and a predicate* $\mathbf{Ax}[SP]$ *over* $\mathbf{Str}[SP]$. *The set of specifications is described by the following type:*

$$\mathbf{SPEC} =_{\rm df} \sum [\mathbf{Str} : Type,\ \mathbf{Ax} : \mathbf{Str} \to Prop]\,.$$

For any type S, *we also write* $\mathbf{Spec}(S)$ *for the class of specifications whose structure type is* S.[33]

Remark Two simple remarks about the notion of specification:

1. Having a totality of logical propositions and hence the internal notion of predicate in our type theory is important to formalise the above notion of specification so that specifications can be manipulated *inside* the type theory.

2. As mentioned above, a specification is *not* just a type, but a pair. The pragmatic significance of this is that we can separate computational contents (expressed by the structure type of a specification) from the axiomatic requirements for the programs (see also a remark in Section 8.2.3 after Definition 8.4).

[33] Formally, $\mathbf{Spec}(S)$ is defined as $S \to Prop$, that is, the type of predicates over S. In this chapter, we ignore the details of the formal transformation between $\mathbf{Spec}(S)$ and $\mathbf{SPEC}$ and use $\mathbf{Spec}(S)$ *informally* as the 'type' of specifications of the form $\langle S, P\rangle$ where P is of type $S \to Prop$.

The semantics of specifications is determined by the type theory, as given by the following notion of realisation.

Definition 8.2. (realisations) *Let SP be a specification. A* realisation *(or* concrete implementation*) of SP is an SP-structure r such that $\mathbf{Ax}[SP](r)$ is provable, that is, an object r of type $\mathbf{Str}[SP]$ such that there is an object of type $\mathbf{Ax}[SP](r)$. SP is called* realisable *(or* consistent*) if there exists a realisation.*

Note that a realisation is just a program (or program module), but *not* a pair of a program and the proof of its correctness.[34] For example, using our notion of specification and realisation, a specification *Sorting* of the sorting programs for lists of natural numbers is a pair consisting of the structure type $\mathbf{Str}[Sorting] \equiv List(N) \rightarrow List(N)$ and the predicate $\mathbf{Ax}[Sorting] \equiv \lambda f{:}List(N) \rightarrow List(N).\ \forall l{:}List(N).\ Sorted(l, f(l))$, and a realisation of *Sorting* is just a sorting function of type $List(N) \rightarrow List(N)$.

Specifications such as *Sorting* are about the programs of *concrete* data types such as the types of natural numbers and lists of natural numbers (see Section 7.1). The *adequacy* of the specifications concerning concrete data types, for instance, that *Sorting* does specify the sorting programs, is in particular based on the fact that the propositional equality used in them (for the *Sorting* example, the use of propositional equality becomes clear when a full description of the relation *Sorted* is given) reflects or faithfully describes the computational equality. In our type theory, the Leibniz equality can be used to describe the computational equality based on the property of equality reflection (Theorem 5.9). This issue of adequacy would best be explained by the following simple example. Consider the following specification ID of the identity functions over natural numbers:

$$\mathbf{Str}[ID] =_{\mathrm{df}} N \rightarrow N, \quad \mathbf{Ax}[ID](f) =_{\mathrm{df}} \forall x{:}N.(f(x) =_N x).$$

The use of the Leibniz equality ($=_N$) in the definition of $\mathbf{Ax}[ID]$ is adequate because it reflects the computational equality (and hence our intention). For any realisation id of ID and any natural number n (of type N in the empty context), we have $id(n) =_N n$ (Leibniz-equal), which implies $id(n) \simeq n$ (computationally equal), by Equality Reflection (Theorem 5.9).

[34] One may use Σ-types to put together programs and their correctness proofs, e.g. by defining a *model* of a specification SP as a pair of an SP-structure and a proof that the SP-structure satisfies $\mathbf{Ax}[SP]$. Then, the set of SP-models is given by the type $\mathbf{Mod}(SP) =_{\mathrm{df}} \Sigma s{:}\mathbf{Str}[SP].\mathbf{Ax}[SP](s)$.

8.2.2 Specifications of abstract data types

The examples of specifications considered above directly specify programs for concrete data types in the type theory. For (large) program development by stepwise refinement, we are also interested in specifications of abstract data types, i.e. specifications of program modules with loose semantics in the sense that a variety of data representations are possible to be used to implement the abstract types and the associated operations. Σ-types, together with type universes, provide a good mechanism in the type theory to describe abstract structures and can be used to express (types of) program modules. This gives us an important basis to specify abstract data types.

However, carefully considering the intention of introducing abstract data types and the methodology of data refinement for program development, one will find out that specification of abstract data types has different requirements from specification of programs for concrete data types. A particular point is that, in general, the equality over the abstract type should *not* be expressed by a propositional equality that reflects the computational equality (like the Leibniz equality in our language or the intensional/extensional equality in Martin-Löf's type theories). The reason is that such a propositional equality is in fact the finest equality relation in the type theory (see Section 5.1.3); to use it as the equality for an abstract type would not faithfully express the intention that the abstract type may further be implemented by a variety of rather different type structures (or data representations) and would prevent us from refining the specification of the abstract data type to another as expected. For example, consider an abstract type *Stack* of stacks (of natural numbers). It is natural to use array-pointer pairs to implement (or represent) a stack. However, if the equality over stacks is specified as the Leibniz equality, it would be impossible to choose such a data representation (see Example 8.6 of data refinement in Section 8.2.3). To emphasize, using a propositional equality that reflects the computational equality as the equality over an abstract type does not faithfully express our intention that the abstract type to be specified allows a variety of implementations via different data representations.

Therefore, instead of using a built-in equality such as the Leibniz equality as the equality for an abstract type, we associate the abstract type with an explicitly specified congruence relation to represent the intended equality.[35] We now give an example to explain how abstract data types

[35]The condition that the equality is a congruence seems to be the weakest reasonable requirement. For design specifications, one may start with stronger equalities (even the Leibniz equality!); but the moral here is that one should be aware of the restrictions of those equalities on the further refinement. For requirements specifications, it is not

can be specified using Σ-types and taking into account of the above consideration. We shall use the following definition in our examples:

$$\textbf{Setoid} =_{\mathrm{df}} \sum[Dom : Type,\ Eq : Dom \to Dom \to Prop].$$

A 'setoid' is a type together with a binary relation over the type; in a specification of abstract data type, that the binary relation is a congruence is specified in the axiom part of the specification.

Example 8.3. *(***Stack***)* A specification of stacks (of natural numbers) can be given as follows:

$$\mathbf{Str}[\mathbf{Stack}(N)] =_{\mathrm{df}} \sum \begin{bmatrix} Stack : \textbf{Setoid} \\ empty : Dom[Stack] \\ push : N \to Dom[Stack] \to Dom[Stack] \\ pop : Dom[Stack] \to Dom[Stack] \\ top : Dom[Stack] \to N \end{bmatrix},$$

and for any structure S of type $\mathbf{Str}[\mathbf{Stack}(N)]$,

$$\begin{array}{lrl} \mathbf{Ax}[\mathbf{Stack}(N)](S) =_{\mathrm{df}} & & \mathbf{Cong}_{\mathbf{Stack}(N)}(Eq) \\ & \& & Eq(pop(empty), empty) \\ & \& & top(empty) =_N 0 \\ & \& & \forall n{:}N \forall s{:}Dom[Stack].\ Eq(pop(push(n,s)), s) \\ & \& & \forall n{:}N \forall s{:}Dom[Stack].\ top(push(n,s)) =_N n, \end{array}$$

where $Stack$ abbreviates $Stack[S]$, Eq abbreviates $Eq[Stack[S]]$, and similar for the others; $\mathbf{Cong}_{\mathbf{Stack}(N)}(Eq)$ stands for the following proposition expressing that the binary relation between stacks is a congruence, that is, an equivalence relation which respects the operations over stacks:

$$\begin{array}{l} Equiv(Eq)\ \& \\ \forall s, s'{:}Dom[Stack].\ \ Eq(s, s') \supset \\ \quad top(s) =_N top(s')\ \&\ Eq(pop(s), pop(s'))\ \& \\ \quad \forall m, n{:}N.\ m =_N n \supset Eq(push(m, s), push(n, s')). \end{array}$$

Remark Note that in the above example, we have used the Leibniz equality for the concrete data type of natural numbers and the associated consequence Eq for the abstract type of stacks. Such a distinction reflects our

---

good to have such design decisions to be made too early.

discussion above, and can be compared to the distinction between initial semantics and loose semantics in algebraic specifications (see Section 8.5 for a further discussion).

Given a specification of an abstract data type, there are various possible realisations (concrete implementations) which are tuples of the structure type of the specification that satisfy the axiomatic requirements. For instance, one can realise the abstract type $Dom[Stack]$ by the concrete data type $List(N)$ and the stack operations such as *push* and *top* by functions such as $cons_N$ and hd_N.

8.2.3 Data refinement and implementation

Besides considering concrete implementations (realisations) of specifications, a notion of (abstract) implementation is the most important if we want to develop programs in a stepwise way by refinement between specifications. That is, we want to know what we mean by saying that a specification refines to (or is implemented by) another specification. Various notions have been proposed in the literature, starting from the early notion of abstraction function and representation function (see [Hoa72, GTW78]) to the more recent considerations (see, for example, [ST88b, EM90, WB89]). We formalise in the type theory a simple notion of refinement (implementation).

Definition 8.4. (refinement map and implementation) *Let SP and SP' be specifications. A* refinement map *from SP' to SP is a function ρ from $\mathbf{Str}[SP']$ to $\mathbf{Str}[SP]$,*

$$\rho : \mathbf{Str}[SP'] \to \mathbf{Str}[SP],$$

such that the following proposition, called satisfaction condition, *is provable:*

$$\mathbf{Sat}(\rho) =_{\mathrm{df}} \forall s' {:} \mathbf{Str}[SP'].\ \mathbf{Ax}[SP'](s') \supset \mathbf{Ax}[SP](\rho(s')).$$

If ρ is a refinement map from SP' to SP, we say that SP refines to *(or* is implemented by*) SP'* through *ρ, notation $SP \Longrightarrow_\rho SP'$.*

Notation If $\mathbf{Str}[SP] \simeq \mathbf{Str}[SP']$ and $id : \mathbf{Str}[SP'] \to \mathbf{Str}[SP]$ is the identity function $\lambda x{:}\mathbf{Str}[SP'].s$, we may write $SP \Longrightarrow SP'$ to abbreviate $SP \Longrightarrow_{id} SP'$.

Remark Several simple remarks:

1. Refinement maps *are* incomplete programs which incorporate various design decisions made during the process of refinement implementation. This is different from most of the other approaches where refinement maps are meta-level entities such as (semantic) functions in set theory.

2. Slightly different from the notion of theory morphism and that of deliverable, a refinement map is *not* a pair but just a map between the structure types which satisfies the satisfaction condition. Again, the separation of computational contents (programs) and their correctness proofs is emphasized here. Such a separation is pragmatically important in program development since refinement maps (programs) should not contain unnecessary components concerning about (proofs of) implementation correctness. In practice, this would also give a useful additional flexibility for program development by multi-step refinement: one can do several steps of refinement without worrying about the development of the correctness proofs and then verify the correctness by viewing the composition of the developed maps as one refinement map developed in a single step.

Informally, a refinement map from SP' to SP determines the following subset of realisations of the original specification SP:

$$\{\, \rho(m') \in \mathbf{Str}[SP] \mid m' \in \mathbf{Str}[SP'] \textit{ and } \mathbf{Ax}[SP'](m') \textit{ is provable} \,\},$$

i.e. the images of the refinement map over the realisations of SP'. The stepwise development of programs from a specification SP_0 would be a sequence of refinement implementation steps:

$$SP_0 \Longrightarrow_{\rho_1} SP_1 \Longrightarrow_{\rho_2} \ldots \Longrightarrow_{\rho_n} SP_n.$$

Any realisation r_n of SP_n gives a realisation r_0 of SP_0 as,

$$r_0 =_{\mathrm{df}} \rho_1(\ldots(\rho_n(r_n)))$$

and, the composition of the correctness proofs for each step will give the proof that r_0 is a realisation of SP_0. This justifies the fact that the implementation relation *composes vertically* (cf. [BG80]), as expressed by the following proposition. (Notation: For functions $f : A \to B$ and $g : B \to C$, we write $g \circ f$ as the composition of g and f which is of type $A \to C$ and defined as: $(g \circ f)(x) =_{\mathrm{df}} g(f(x))$.)

Proposition 8.5. (vertical composition) *If $SP \Longrightarrow_{\rho} SP'$ and $SP' \Longrightarrow_{\rho'} SP''$, then $SP \Longrightarrow_{\rho\circ\rho'} SP''$. As a special case, we have $SP \Longrightarrow SP'$ and $SP' \Longrightarrow SP''$ imply $SP \Longrightarrow SP''$.*

Remark As well-known, starting from a realisable specification, stepwise refinement does *not* necessarily lead to realisable specifications. It is the developer's responsibility to choose 'reasonable' and good design decisions which may lead to realisable implementing specifications and good programs that realise the requirements specifications.

Let us now see a traditional example of refinement—implementing stacks by array-pointer pairs. (This is an example for explanation, which does not necessarily a good design decision in real software development.)

Example 8.6. We consider a specification **Array**(N) for arrays (of natural numbers), define a refinement map ρ from **Array**(N) to the specification **Stack**(N) defined in Example 8.3 such that **Stack**(N) is implemented by **Array**(N) through ρ.

The specification of **Array**(N) is defined as follows: **Str**[**Array**(N)] is defined as

$$\sum \begin{bmatrix} Array : \mathbf{Setoid} \\ newarray : Dom[Array] \\ assign : N \to Dom[Array] \to N \to Dom[Array] \\ access : Dom[Array] \to N \to N \end{bmatrix}$$

and, for any structure A of type **Str**[**Array**(N)], **Ax**[**Array**(N)](A) is defined as

$$\begin{array}{ll} & \mathbf{Cong}_{\mathbf{Array}(N)}(Eq) \\ \& & \forall i{:}N.\ access(newarray, i) =_N 0 \\ \& & \forall n, i, j{:}N \forall a{:}Dom[Array]. \\ & \qquad (i =_N j \supset access(assign(n, a, i), j) =_N n) \\ & \qquad \& \ (i \neq_N j \supset access(assign(n, a, i), j) =_N access(a, j)), \end{array}$$

where $\mathbf{Cong}_{\mathbf{Array}(N)}(Eq)$ is the proposition expressing that the relation Eq between arrays is a congruence, similarly defined as $\mathbf{Cong}_{\mathbf{Stack}(N)}(Eq)$ in Example 8.3.

The refinement map ρ, given any **Array**(N)-structure A, generates the following **Stack**(N)-structure:

$$\begin{array}{lll} Dom[Stack[\rho(A)]] & =_{\mathrm{df}} & \sum[arr : Dom[Array[A]],\ ptr : N]. \\ Eq[Stack[\rho(A)]] & =_{\mathrm{df}} & \lambda s, s'{:}Dom[Stack[\rho(A)]]. \\ & & \quad ptr[s] =_N ptr[s'] \ \& \\ & & \quad \forall i{:}N.\ i < ptr[s] \supset \\ & & \qquad access(arr[s], i) =_N access(arr[s'], i). \end{array}$$

$$\begin{array}{lll} empty[\rho(A)] & =_{\rm df} & \langle newarray[A], 0\rangle. \\ push[\rho(A)] & =_{\rm df} & \lambda n{:}N\lambda s{:}Dom[Stack[\rho(A)]]. \\ & & \quad \langle assign(n, arr[s], ptr[s]), ptr[s]+1\rangle. \\ pop[\rho(A)] & =_{\rm df} & \lambda s{:}Dom[Stack[\rho(A)]].\ \langle arr[s], ptr[s]-1\rangle. \\ top[\rho(A)] & =_{\rm df} & \lambda s{:}Dom[Stack[\rho(A)]]. \\ & & \quad Rec_N(0,\ \lambda x, y{:}N.access(arr[s], ptr[s]-1))(ptr[s]). \end{array}$$

The chosen data representation uses array-pointer pairs to represent stacks. Two of such stack representations are equal if and only if the pointers (represented by natural numbers) are the same and accessing the representing arrays at any position lower than the pointers gives the same result.

ρ defined above is indeed a refinement map from **Array**(N) to **Stack**(N), that is,

$$\mathbf{Stack}(N) \Longrightarrow_\rho \mathbf{Array}(N).$$

Therefore, any realisation r of **Array**(N) will give a realisation $\rho(r)$ of **Stack**(N).

Note that the 'equality representation' (or 'representation invariants') in the traditional approaches to proofs of abstract implementation is directly reflected in the refinement map (its $Eq[Stack[\rho(A)]]$ part). The choice of the above data representation is possible because we have associated an explicit congruence rather than using a fixed equality such as the Leibniz equality for the abstract type of stacks.

An obviously important issue in a refinement development of programs is that the correctness of the (abstract) implementations must be able to be verified, when required. In other words, the satisfaction condition must be provable. The above fact of implementation correctness has been formally checked in the proof development system Lego; in fact, we have used Lego to develop the refinement map interactively on the machine.

8.3 Modular design and structured specification

Modular design and structured specification have been generally accepted as two related useful methodologies for software development. There are two issues here. First, given a requirements specification to be implemented, programmers use principles like divide-and-conquer and stepwise refinement to decompose and refine the specification until they reach desirable low-level specifications which can be concretely implemented by, say efficient enough, software modules. This is the process of modular design, which may involve many intermediate design specifications, probably proposed by some chief programmers and further implemented separately by others. Secondly, to get a good requirements specification of a large software system, people must structure the specification in a modular way so that it is understandable and may suggest some possible design decisions.

Having given a notion of implementation in the last section, we discuss in this section modular design and structured specification in our type-theoretic approach (parameterised specifications are discussed in Section 8.4). In particular, we consider various specification operations[36] which can be used either in modular design by refinement or in structuring requirements specifications. An important property of such specification operations is the monotonicity with respect to the implementation relation (see below), which will ensure independent further refinements of the argument specifications (the so-called *horizontal composition* property [BG80]).

8.3.1 Decomposition and sharing

Using the principle of divide-and-conquer in a design process, developers often decompose a specification into several independent ones (with clear interfaces) so that they can be implemented separately and their realisations can be put together to get a realisation of the original specification. Considering this, one might think that the notion of implementation given in the last section is over-simplified since at first appearance it seemed to cover only the situations where a single line of refinement is pursued. In fact, this is not the case. Using the notion of implementation and Σ-types in our type theory, one can do specification decomposition by considering the following specification operation. (This also gives us a simple example to explain why the monotonicity of specification operations offers the independency for further refinements.)

Definition 8.7. *Let SP and SP' be specifications. Then, specification $SP \otimes SP'$ is defined as follows:*

$$\mathbf{Str}[SP \otimes SP'] =_{\mathrm{df}} \mathbf{Str}[SP] \times \mathbf{Str}[SP'],$$

and for any s of type $\mathbf{Str}[SP \otimes SP']$,

$$\mathbf{Ax}[SP \otimes SP'](s) =_{\mathrm{df}} \mathbf{Ax}[SP](\pi_1(s)) \ \& \ \mathbf{Ax}[SP'](\pi_2(s)).$$

The (infix) specification operation $\otimes$ is of type $\mathbf{SPEC} \to \mathbf{SPEC} \to \mathbf{SPEC}$.

The idea to use the above specification operation to decompose a specification SP into several (say two) independent specifications (SP_1 and

[36] A *specification operation* is a function which takes specifications (and possibly some other kinds of objects) as arguments and returns a specification as the result of application. Specification operations can also be seen as parameterised specifications. See Section 8.4.

SP_2) by certain design strategy is to consider a refinement step of the following form:

$$SP \Longrightarrow_\rho SP_1 \otimes SP_2,$$

where the refinement map $\rho : \mathbf{Str}[SP_1 \otimes SP_2] \to \mathbf{Str}[SP]$ is the incomplete program expressing the design strategy at this decomposition step. The intention here is to implement the specifications SP_1 and SP_2 independently by further refinements. The soundness for such independent further refinements is guaranteed by the monotonicity of $\otimes$ with respect to the implementation relation.

Proposition 8.8. ***(monotonicity of*** $\otimes$***)*** *If* $SP_1 \Longrightarrow_{\rho_1} SP_1'$ *and* $SP_2 \Longrightarrow_{\rho_2} SP_2'$*, then*

$$SP_1 \otimes SP_2 \Longrightarrow_{\rho_1 \otimes \rho_2} SP_1' \otimes SP_2',$$

where $\rho_1 \otimes \rho_2 =_{\mathrm{df}} \lambda s' {:} \mathbf{Str}[SP_1' \otimes SP_2'].(\rho_1(\pi_1(s')), \rho_2(\pi_2(s')))$.

By the monotonicity of $\otimes$ and the vertical composition property of the implementation relation (Proposition 8.5), we have that $SP \Longrightarrow_\rho SP_1 \otimes SP_2$ and $SP_i \Longrightarrow_{\rho_i} SP_i'$ $(i = 1, 2)$ imply $SP \Longrightarrow_{\rho \circ (\rho_1 \otimes \rho_2)} SP_1' \otimes SP_2'$ and, for any realisations r_i' of SP_i' $(i = 1, 2)$, $\rho \circ (\rho_1 \otimes \rho_2)(r_1', r_2')$ is a realisation of SP.

In our discussion so far, we have only considered decomposition of a specification into several completely independent specifications. In practice, it is often the case that the sub-specifications are not completely independent but share some common structure.[37] For example, one may decompose a specification of a parser into several specifications including *AbsSyn* for an abstract syntax tree generator and *SymTab* for management of the symbol table; these later two specifications both use symbols and symbol management functions which are specified by another specification *Symbol*. Note that a parser can only work correctly when *AbsSyn* and *SymTab* use the same realisation of *Symbol*. Such a structure sharing can be dealt with using Σ-types by considering the following specification operation $\sum$, which has $\otimes$ above as a special case.

Definition 8.9. *Let* SP *be a specification and* $P : \mathbf{Str}[SP] \to \mathbf{SPEC}$. *Then,* $\sum(SP, P)$ *is the specification defined as follows:*

$$\mathbf{Str}[\textstyle\sum(SP, P)] =_{\mathrm{df}} \Sigma s{:}\mathbf{Str}[SP].\mathbf{Str}[P(s)]$$

[37]Much attention has been paid to such structure sharing in the design of both programming languages (e.g. Standard ML [Mac81, MTH90] and Pebble [BL84]) and specification languages (e.g. Clear [BG80] and Extended ML [ST87]).

and, for any s' of type $\mathbf{Str}[\sum(SP,P)]$,

$$\mathbf{Ax}[\sum(SP,P)](s') =_{\mathrm{df}} \mathbf{Ax}[SP](\pi_1(s')) \ \&\ \mathbf{Ax}[P(\pi_1(s'))](\pi_2(s')).$$

$\sum$ *is of type* $\Pi SP{:}\mathbf{SPEC}.\ (\mathbf{Str}[SP] \to \mathbf{SPEC}) \to \mathbf{SPEC}$.

Proposition 8.10. (monotonicity of $\sum$) *Let SP and SP' be specifications, $P : \mathbf{Str}[SP] \to \mathbf{SPEC}$ and $P' : \mathbf{Str}[SP'] \to \mathbf{SPEC}$. If*

1. *$SP \Longrightarrow_\rho SP'$, and*
2. *δ is a function of type $\Pi s'{:}\mathbf{Str}[SP'].\ \mathbf{Str}[P'(s')] \to \mathbf{Str}[P(\rho(s'))]$ such that*
   $\forall s'{:}\mathbf{Str}[SP'].\ P(\rho(s')) \Longrightarrow_{\delta(s')} P'(s')$ is provable,[38]

then,

$$\textstyle\sum(SP,P) \Longrightarrow_{\sum(\rho,\delta)} \sum(SP',P'),$$

where $\sum(\rho,\delta) =_{\mathrm{df}} \lambda s'{:}\mathbf{Str}[\sum(SP',P')].\ (\rho(\pi_1(s')), \delta(\pi_1(s'),\pi_2(s')))$.

Suppose P is of the form $\lambda s_0{:}\mathbf{Str}[SP_0].\ P_1(s_0) \otimes P_2(s_0)$. Then, a refinement step

$$SP \Longrightarrow_\rho \textstyle\sum(SP_0, P)$$

decomposes SP into three specifications SP_0, $P_1(s_0)$ and $P_2(s_0)$; the latter two share a common structure specified by SP_0. The above monotonicity result suggests one to decompose SP into SP_0 and (parameterised specification) P which are to be further refined independently (see Section 8.4 for refinement of parameterised specifications). Another way to look at the further refinement of $\sum(SP_0,P)$ is to consider SP_0 and the following specification SP':

$$\begin{array}{lll} \mathbf{Str}[SP'] & =_{\mathrm{df}} & \Pi s_0{:}\mathbf{Str}[SP_0].\ \mathbf{Str}[P(s_0)], \\ \mathbf{Ax}[SP'](f) & =_{\mathrm{df}} & \forall s_0{:}\mathbf{Str}[SP_0].\ \mathbf{Ax}[SP_0](s_0) \supset \mathbf{Ax}[P(s_0)](f(s_0)). \end{array}$$

In other words, we proceed to implement $P_1(s_0)$ and $P_2(s_0)$ independently, assuming that s_0 is an arbitrary realisation of SP_0. Note that SP_0 and SP' are independent of each other and they have a clear interface specified by Π. To get a realisation of $\sum(SP_0,P)$, we simply put together any realisation r_0 of SP_0 and the result of applying any realisation of SP' to

[38] P and P' are parameterised specifications and, when SP and SP' have the same structure type and ρ is the identity function, the condition for δ here is to say that the parameterised specification P refines to P' through δ. See Definition 8.16 in Section 8.4.

r_0. (The reader may have noticed that the above refinement has suggested another specification operation corresponding to the type constructor Π. We do not elaborate on this here.)

As remarked before, not all design decisions such as decompositions suggested above lead to solutions (not to say good solutions); in other words, one may go into a blind alley—some of the sub-specifications are not realisable. Here is a trivial example: Decomposing a (realisable) specification whose structure type is $\Sigma X{:}Type_0.X$ into two specifications with $Type_0$ and $\Pi X{:}Type_0.X$ as structure types, respectively, produces an unrealisable specification (the second one) since $\Pi X{:}Type_0.X$ has no object in any consistent context in the type theory (cf. Theorem 5.4). In any stage of refinement development, the programmer must be careful about such a consistency argument. If necessary, one may verify that certain intermediate design specifications are realisable. For the above situation concerning about sharing, if independent decomposition is not feasible, one has to first refine SP_0 to SP_0' (with the same structure type) so that such a decomposition for $\mathbf{\Sigma}(SP_0', P)$ is possible, or we simply find an (intended) realisation r_0 of SP_0 and then implement $P(r_0)$.

8.3.2 Constructors and selectors

Since the work by Burstall and Goguen on the specification language Clear [BG80], it has been generally accepted that specification operations play important roles both in modular design by refinement and in structuring specifications. For example, we can define the following simple specification operations which may often be used in structuring specifications:

- $\mathbf{Join}_S$: it 'puts together' the axiomatic parts of two specifications over the same structure type S: if $S \equiv \mathbf{Str}[SP] \simeq \mathbf{Str}[SP']$, then

$$\begin{aligned} \mathbf{Str}[\mathbf{Join}_S(SP, SP')] &=_{\mathrm{df}} S, \\ \mathbf{Ax}[\mathbf{Join}_S(SP, SP')](s) &=_{\mathrm{df}} \mathbf{Ax}[SP](s)\ \&\ \mathbf{Ax}[SP'](s). \end{aligned}$$

  Join is of type

$$\Pi S{:}Type.\ \mathbf{Spec}(S) \to \mathbf{Spec}(S) \to \mathbf{Spec}(S).$$

  Similarly, one may define $\mathbf{Meet}_S$ with $\mathbf{Ax}[\mathbf{Meet}_S(SP, SP')](s) =_{\mathrm{df}} \mathbf{Ax}[SP](s) \vee \mathbf{Ax}[SP'](s)$, and other possibly useful operators by means of logical operators.

- **Extend**: it extends a specification by some extra structure components and/or some axioms. Given a specification SP, an extension Ext_Str of $\mathbf{Str}[SP]$, which is a function of type $\mathbf{Str}[SP] \to Type$, and some axioms (a predicate) Ext_Ax over the extended structure type (i.e. $\Sigma s{:}\mathbf{Str}[SP].\ Ext\_Str(s)$), define the specification $E \equiv \mathbf{Extend}(SP, Ext\_Str, Ext\_Ax)$ by

$$\begin{array}{rcl}\mathbf{Str}[E] & =_{\mathrm{df}} & \Sigma s{:}\mathbf{Str}[SP].\ Ext\_Str(s),\\ \mathbf{Ax}[E](s') & =_{\mathrm{df}} & \mathbf{Ax}[SP](\pi_1(s'))\ \&\ Ext\_Ax(s').\end{array}$$

Extend is of type

$$\Pi SP{:}\mathbf{SPEC}\ \Pi f{:}\mathbf{Str}[SP] \to Type$$
$$\Pi g{:}(\Sigma s{:}\mathbf{Str}[SP].f(s)) \to Prop.\ \mathbf{SPEC}.$$

There are various specification operations which can be defined. Instead of studying them one by one (e.g. considering whether they are monotone), we define two general classes of specification operations called *constructors*[39] and *selectors*, which are determined by functions between structure types.

Definition 8.11. (constructors and selectors) *Let S and S' be types and $\rho : S' \to S$. The specification operations* $\mathbf{Con}_\rho$ *and* $\mathbf{Sel}_\rho$ *are defined as follows:*

1. $\mathbf{Con}_\rho$*, the constructor determined by ρ, is a specification operation of type* $\mathbf{Spec}(S') \to \mathbf{Spec}(S)$ *defined as: for any SP' with* $\mathbf{Str}[SP'] \simeq S'$,

$$\begin{array}{rcl}\mathbf{Str}[\mathbf{Con}_\rho(SP')] & =_{\mathrm{df}} & S,\\ \mathbf{Ax}[\mathbf{Con}_\rho(SP')](s) & =_{\mathrm{df}} & \exists s'{:}S'.\ \mathbf{Ax}[SP'](s')\ \&\ \rho(s') =_S s.\end{array}$$

2. $\mathbf{Sel}_\rho$*, the selector determined by ρ, is a specification operation of type* $\mathbf{Spec}(S) \to \mathbf{Spec}(S')$ *defined as: for any specification SP with* $\mathbf{Str}[SP] \simeq S$,

$$\begin{array}{rcl}\mathbf{Str}[\mathbf{Sel}_\rho(SP)] & =_{\mathrm{df}} & S',\\ \mathbf{Ax}[\mathbf{Sel}_\rho(SP)](s') & =_{\mathrm{df}} & \mathbf{Ax}[SP](\rho(s')).\end{array}$$

Intuitively, the constructor $\mathbf{Con}_\rho$ applied to specification SP' constructs as its realisations the images of ρ over the SP'-realisations, while the selector $\mathbf{Sel}_\rho$ applied to SP selects the inverse images of the SP-realisations by ρ. Interesting specification operations can be defined by using selectors and constructors. For example, **Join** and **Extend** discussed above can be defined in the following way:

[39]The name 'constructor' comes from the similarity of this class of specification operations with Sannella and Tarlecki's notion of constructor. See Section 8.3.3.

- The operation $\mathbf{Join}_S$ can be defined as

$$\mathbf{Join}_S(SP, SP') =_{\text{df}} \mathbf{Sel}_d(SP \otimes SP'),$$

where $d =_{\text{df}} \lambda s{:}S.\langle s, s\rangle : S \to S \times S$ is the diagonal function over S.

- The operation **Extend** can be defined as

$$\mathbf{Extend}(SP, Ext\_Str, Ext\_Ax) =_{\text{df}} \mathbf{Join}_S(\mathbf{Sel}_{\pi_1}(SP), (S, Ext\_Ax)),$$

where $S \equiv \Sigma s{:}\mathbf{Str}[SP].\ Ext\_Str(s)$ and $\pi_1 : S \to \mathbf{Str}[SP]$ is the first projection function.

The constructors can be used to play a role of 'renaming' and information hiding similar to the operation **derive** in specification language ASL [SW83, Wir86]. **derive** in ASL is based on a signature morphism from the signature of the resulting specification to that of the argument specification. Such an signature morphism σ, when it is a signature inclusion, corresponds to a (forgetful) map ρ from the structure type of the argument specification to that of the resulting specification; and in such a case, $\mathbf{Con}_\rho(SP)$ corresponds to **derive** SP *from* σ. Similarly, the operation **translate** (see [ST88a]) can be simulated as selectors.

It is also easy to verify the following basic properties of constructors and selectors.

Proposition 8.12. *Let* $\rho : S' \to S$.

- *Realisability:*

  1. *if* $SP' : \mathbf{Spec}(S')$ *is realisable, so is* $\mathbf{Con}_\rho(SP')$;
  2. *if* $\mathbf{Sel}_\rho(SP)$ *is realisable, so is* SP.

- *Monotonicity:*

  1. *for* $SP_1', SP_2' : \mathbf{Spec}(S')$, $SP_1' \Longrightarrow SP_2'$ *implies* $\mathbf{Con}_\rho(SP_1') \Longrightarrow \mathbf{Con}_\rho(SP_2')$;
  2. *for* $SP_1, SP_2 : \mathbf{Spec}(S)$, $SP_1 \Longrightarrow SP_2$ *implies* $\mathbf{Sel}_\rho(SP_1) \Longrightarrow \mathbf{Sel}_\rho(SP_2)$.

8.3.3 Constructor/selector implementation

The constructor operations are very similar in spirit to the notion of constructors (functions between algebra classes) introduced in [ST88b], although they are semantically different. Sannella and Tarlecki have proposed the idea to suggest the following refinement methodology: starting from an initial specification SP to be implemented, one uses constructors to specify some specification which implements SP and goes on to implement the argument specifications of the constructors used in this step. Such a method applies to our setting as well. In fact, we can define a similar notion of constructor/selector implementation, which turns out to be equivalent to the notion of implementation we have defined. This enables us to relate our approach to that in algebraic specifications and gives a better understanding of the notion of implementation.

Definition 8.13. (constructor/selector implementation) *Let SP and SP' be specifications and ρ be of type $\mathbf{Str}[SP'] \to \mathbf{Str}[SP]$.*

1. *SP is implemented by SP' through constructor ρ (notation $SP \stackrel{c}{\Longrightarrow}_\rho SP'$) if $SP \Longrightarrow \mathbf{Con}_\rho(SP')$.*
2. *SP is implemented by SP' through selector ρ (notation $SP \stackrel{s}{\Longrightarrow}_\rho SP'$) if $\mathbf{Sel}_\rho(SP) \Longrightarrow SP'$.*

Proposition 8.14. *Let SP and SP' be specifications and $\rho : \mathbf{Str}[SP'] \to \mathbf{Str}[SP]$. Then, the following are equivalent:*

$$SP \Longrightarrow_\rho SP', \quad SP \stackrel{c}{\Longrightarrow}_\rho SP', \quad SP \stackrel{s}{\Longrightarrow}_\rho SP'.$$

Proof The first and the last statements are computationally equal and they are logically equivalent to the second. □

8.4 Parameterised specification

Parameterisation is a powerful abstraction tool both for modular design and for structured specification. It may enhance the reusability of program modules and their specifications. A type theory with good structural facilities can provide powerful higher-order parameterisation mechanisms for parameterised specifications as well as parameterised program modules.

In fact, we have seen an example of the use of parameterised specifications in Section 8.3.1, where we considered implementation of a specification of the form $\sum(SP_0, P)$. We pointed out there that there are at least two design decisions such a form of specifications may suggest: one is to decompose it into two independent specifications SP_0 and SP', where SP' is a specification of parameterised program modules (using the type constructor Π); another is to directly use the monotonicity property of the specification operation Σ to consider further refinements of the specification SP_0 and the *parameterised specification* P. Taking this latter view, we must consider parameterised specifications and their implementations.

Of course, the need and usefulness of parameterised specifications in modular design and structuring specifications can not only be explained by a simple example. We would not elaborate it here. Among the large amount of literature on this are [BG80, SW83, EM85] and in particular [SST92] where a recent account on this issue in algebraic specification can be found.

8.4.1 Parameterised specifications

Parameterised specifications are functions in the type theory which applied to its arguments return specifications as results. In other words, parameterised specifications have types of the following forms:

$$\Pi x_1{:}A_1 ... \Pi x_n{:}A_n.\ \mathbf{SPEC} \quad \mathit{or} \quad \Pi x_1{:}A_1 ... \Pi x_n{:}A_n.\ \mathbf{Spec}(S),$$

where $n \geq 1$. Note that the forms of arguments to which a parameterised specification can apply are not restricted here; they can be any kinds of objects including structures (program modules), specifications and any kinds of parameterised objects.

For example, we may parameterise the specification of stacks (see Example 8.3) in two different ways. First, given any (non-empty) concrete data type A with a congruence relation, the parameterised specification returns a specification of stacks for that concrete data type. This can be done in the obvious way in our type theoretic setting, for example, the stack parameterised over concrete data types would look like

$$\mathbf{Stack} \equiv \lambda X{:}\mathit{Type}\lambda x{:}X\lambda R{:}X \to X \to \mathit{Prop}.\ \mathbf{Stack}(X, x, R),$$

where $\mathbf{Stack}(X, x, R)$ is the same as $\mathbf{Stack}(N)$ except that N, 0 and $=_N$ are replaced by X, x and R, respectively. (Depending on different intentions of how **Stack** is to be used, one may require that R be a congruence by adding another argument to **Stack** or remove the argument R by using the Leibniz's equality over X.) Such a parameterisation is over concrete program modules and the parameterised specification P involved in specification of the form $\Sigma(SP_0, P)$ is of such a kind.

Considering structured specifications and modular design, we may parameterise a specification over specifications. This is what it normally means by parameterised specification in the algebraic approach to specifications (cf. Clear [BG80] and other specification languages). For example, given any specification of an abstract data type (e.g. of sets, stacks or arrays), we may want to extend them by a specification of stacks to get a specification of stacks of sets, stacks or arrays, etc.. Instead of doing them one by one, we want to parameterise the specification of stacks over such specifications. The example below explains how this can be done.

There is something to say before we give the example. A parameterised specification **STACK** extending specifications by stacks can not take an arbitrary specification as its argument; the structure type of an eligible argument specification must have a distinguished type with some object. In the algebraic approach to specifications, this is usually done by considering a special specification (usually called **Elem**) as the parameter specification, which has only one sort and one constant of the sort (see [BG80] for example). Satisfaction (or matching) of an argument specification to a parameter specification is through a signature morphism from the parameter specification to the argument. In other words, we need to talk about the 'components' of the structure type of specifications. A way to do this in the type theory is to use functions to indicate the components of a structure type. For example, for any type S, a function of type

$$\mathbf{Elem}(S) =_{\mathrm{df}} S \to \sum[X{:}\mathbf{Setoid},\ x{:}Dom[X]]$$

can be used as a *component indicator* which, given any structure of type S, identifies a type (with a binary relation) and an object of the type. For instance, the following function (cf. Example 8.6)

$$ind\_array =_{\mathrm{df}} \lambda A{:}\mathbf{Str}[\mathbf{Array}(N)].\ (Array[A], newarray[A])$$

is of type $\mathbf{Elem}(\mathbf{Str}[\mathbf{Array}(N)])$ and may be used in application of parameterised specification **STACK** below to generate a specification of stacks of arrays of natural numbers.

Example 8.15. ***(*****STACK*****)*** We define a parameterised specification **STACK** which, when applied to a specification whose structure type has a distinguished non-empty setoid, returns as result a specification which extends the argument specification by a stack specification over the indicated setoid. We shall use the specification operation **Extend** to define **STACK**. First, we define two preliminary functions for extensions of structure type and axioms, respectively.

- *Ext_Str_Stack* is a function of type $\Pi S{:}Type.\ \mathbf{Elem}(S) \to S \to Type$.

Given a type S, a function *Elem* of type $\mathbf{Elem}(S)$, and an object s of type S, $Ext\_Str\_Stack(S, Elem, s)$ is defined to be the same as the structure type of $\mathbf{Stack}(N)$ in Example 8.3 except that we replace N by $Dom[X[Elem(s)]]$.

- *Ext_Ax_Stack* is the function of type

$$\Pi S{:}Type\ \Pi Elem{:}\mathbf{Elem}(S).$$
$$(\Sigma s{:}S.Ext\_Str\_Stack(S, Elem, s)) \to Prop.$$

Given a type S, *Elem* of type $\mathbf{Elem}(S)$, and s' of type $\Sigma s{:}S.Ext\_Str\_Stack(S, Elem, s))$, $Ext\_Ax\_Stack(S, Elem, s')$ is the proposition defined the same as the axiom part of $\mathbf{Stack}(N)$ in Example 8.3 except that we replace N, 0 and $=_N$ by $Dom[X[Elem(\pi_1(s'))]]$, $x[Elem(\pi_1(s'))]$, and $Eq[X[Elem(\pi_1(s'))]]$, respectively.

Now, we define parameterised specification **STACK** as follows:

$$\mathbf{STACK} =_{\mathrm{df}}$$
$$\lambda S{:}Type \lambda Elem{:}\mathbf{Elem}(S) \lambda SP{:}\mathbf{Spec}(S).$$
$$\mathbf{Extend}(SP, Ext\_Str\_Stack(S, Elem), Ext\_Ax\_Stack(S, Elem)),$$

which is of type

$$\Pi S{:}Type\ \Pi Elem{:}\mathbf{Elem}(S).$$
$$\mathbf{Spec}(S) \to \mathbf{Spec}(\Sigma s{:}S.Ext\_Str\_Stack(S, Elem, s)).$$

Applying **STACK** to, for example, the specification $\mathbf{Array}(N)$ (see Example 8.6) with the component indicator *ind_array* defined above will result in the specification of stacks of arrays of natural numbers

$$\mathbf{STACK}(\mathbf{Str}[\mathbf{Array}(N)], ind\_array, \mathbf{Array}(N)).$$

8.4.2 Implementation of parameterised specifications

In a design process, it is often natural to decompose a specification into several specifications some of which are parameterised specifications. For example, when a specification is of the form $P(SP)$ or $\sum(SP, P)$, a decomposition into SP and parameterised specification P may be desirable. Such a need calls for a notion of implementation between parameterised specifications.

Definition 8.16. (implementation of parameterised specifications) *Let P and P' be parameterised specifications over the same parameter type Par. A refinement map from P' to P is a function*

$$\delta : \Pi s{:}Par.\ \mathbf{Str}[P'(s)] \to \mathbf{Str}[P(s)]$$

such that the following satisfaction condition is provable:

$$\mathbf{Sat}(\delta) =_{\mathrm{df}} \forall s{:}Par.\ P(s) \Longrightarrow_{\delta(s)} P'(s)$$

If δ is a refinement map from P' to P, we say that P refines to (or is implemented by) P' through δ, notation $P \Longrightarrow_{\delta} P'$.

Remark A parameterised specification P is implemented by P' if P' implements P pointwisely through a *uniform* refinement map. The essential idea of pointwise implementation comes from [SW83]. Note that the polymorphism and type dependency in type theory gives a nice way to express a (uniform) family of refinement maps as a single polymorphic function. One may have noticed the similarity of this definition with the notion of natural transformation between functors in category theory. Although the above definition is already rather general, one may further consider implementation between two parameterised specifications with possibly different parameter types. We do not expand this discussion here.

The above notion of implementation composes vertically.

Proposition 8.17. (vertical composition) *Let P, P', and P'' be parameterised specifications with the same parameter type Par. If $P \Longrightarrow_{\delta} P'$ and $P' \Longrightarrow_{\delta'} P''$, then $P \Longrightarrow_{\delta \bullet \delta'} P''$, where $\delta \bullet \delta' =_{\mathrm{df}} \lambda s{:}Par.\ \delta(s) \circ \delta'(s)$.*

Example 8.18. Following Example 8.15, we can similarly define a parameterised specification (cf. Example 8.6)

$$\begin{aligned}&\mathbf{ARRAY} =_{\mathrm{df}}\\ &\quad \lambda S{:}Type\lambda Elem{:}\mathbf{Elem}(S)\lambda SP{:}\mathbf{Spec}(S).\\ &\quad \mathbf{Extend}(SP, Ext\_Str\_Array(S, Elem), Ext\_Ax\_Array(S, Elem)).\end{aligned}$$

$\mathbf{ARRAY}(S, Elem, SP)$ extends the argument specification SP by a specification of arrays. For any type S and any component indicator $Elem$ of type $\mathbf{Elem}(S)$, we can find a refinement map δ (cf. Example 8.6) such that $\mathbf{STACK}(S, Elem) \Longrightarrow_{\delta} \mathbf{ARRAY}(S, Elem)$.

There are two kinds of parameter types which often occur: the structure type of some specification, which we have seen in a specification of the form $\sum(SP, P)$, or a type of specifications (e.g. **Spec**(S) or **SPEC**). In the latter case, it is important to consider the property of *horizontal composition* of the implementation relation [BG80], since it guarantees that we can implement a specification of the form $P(SP)$ by implementing SP and the parameterised specification P separately. The above notion of implementation also enjoys the property of horizontal composition, when a parameterised specification is monotone with respect to the implementation relation between specifications.

Definition 8.19. (monotonicity) *Let Par be* **SPEC** *or* **Spec**(S). *A parameterised specification P of type Par* $\rightarrow$ **SPEC** *is* monotone *if and only if there is a function f of type*

$$\Pi A, B{:}Par.\ (\mathbf{Str}[B] \rightarrow \mathbf{Str}[A]) \rightarrow (\mathbf{Str}[P(B)] \rightarrow \mathbf{Str}[P(A)])$$

such that $\forall A, B{:}Par \forall \rho{:}\mathbf{Str}[B] \rightarrow \mathbf{Str}[A].\ (A \Longrightarrow_{\rho} B) \supset (P(A) \Longrightarrow_{f(\rho)} P(B))$ *is provable. If so, we say P is monotone via f.*

Proposition 8.20. (horizontal composition) *Let Par be* **SPEC** *or* **Spec**(S), $SP, SP' : Par$ *and* $P, P' : Par \rightarrow$ **SPEC**. *Then,* $P(SP) \Longrightarrow_{\rho} P'(SP')$ *for some* ρ, *if the following conditions hold:*

$$SP \Longrightarrow_{\rho_0} SP', \quad P \Longrightarrow_{\delta} P', \quad \textit{and} \quad P \textit{ or } P' \textit{ is monotone.}$$

Proof Define

$$\rho =_{\mathrm{df}} \begin{cases} f(SP, SP', \rho_0) \circ \delta(SP') & \text{if } P \text{ is monotone via } f, \\ \delta(SP) \circ g(SP, SP', \rho_0) & \text{if } P' \text{ is monotone via } g. \end{cases}$$

Then, we have $P(SP) \Longrightarrow_{\rho} P'(SP')$. □

The property of horizontal composition shows that we can implement a specification of the form $P_0(SP_0)$ by independent refinements $P_0 \Longrightarrow_{\delta_1} \dots \Longrightarrow_{\delta_m} P_m$ and $SP_0 \Longrightarrow_{\rho_1} \dots \Longrightarrow_{\rho_n} SP_n$, when the parameterised specifications involved are monotone.

Finally, we remark that the above definition of monotonicity and proposition for horizontal composition can easily be generalised to the case where parameterised specifications have more than one specification as arguments (Par is of the form $Par_1 \times \dots \times Par_n$ where Par_i is either **SPEC** or **Spec**(S_i)).

8.5 Discussion

We have considered a type-theoretic approach to specification and development of programs in the type theory, whose higher-order logical and structural mechanisms provide useful tools for abstraction and modularisation. A notable advantage of this approach is that it provides a uniform language for modular programming, structured specification, logical reasoning, and modular development of programs. We have been able to formalise internally the notions such as abstract implementation in the type theory, and this enables us to use a computer implementation of the type theory (Lego) to develop the refinement maps (programs) and the correctness proofs of implementations.

From the above, it is clear that our work has been highly influenced by the existing works on specifications including algebraic specification, especially by the methodological developments so far. Comparative studies of the type-theoretic approach with other approaches need further research. Some works along this line have been in progress. For example, Reus and Streicher [RS93] have shown that the laws of module algebra in algebraic specifications can be translated into the type-theoretic approach and proved to be sound. In the following, we give a brief discussion on several aspects of the type-theoretic approach to highlight some of the differences as well as similarities with other approaches such as algebraic specification.

The most important aspect to be emphasized is that we have used type theory as a *uniform* language—it is a functional programming language, a specification language and a language for logical reasoning. What has been studied above is specification and modular development of functional programs *in* the type theory. Therefore, we are *not* looking for a general semantic understanding of specifications for the sake of itself, but rather considering a single language which incorporates both programs and their specifications. This is different from the traditional style of specifications using, e.g. Hoare logic which is a logical language built on top of a programming language such as Pascal. It is also different from the algebraic approach to specifications where a general semantical study of specifications is considered, but the operational (or computational) notion of program and program modules seems to be ignored and programs are semantically modelled by the notion of algebra (based on set theory). As algebras are *not* computational programs, there is a need in the algebraic approach to fill up the gap between specifications and the programs in ordinary programming languages (cf. the development of languages such as Extended ML [ST87]) and between the algebraic semantics of specifications and the operational semantics of programs (e.g. the semantics given by term-rewriting). Our study of using type theory for program specification and development offers a single language (the type theory) which has a simple operational semantics on the basis of which programs and specifications in the language are understood.

Compared with set theory, type theory is a more manageable formalism, as shown by its proof-theoretic properties and the success in computer implementation of various proof development systems based on type theory. However, although they are different, types have fundamental similarities with sets (e.g. type equality is extensional as explained in Section 2.3.3), which allow us to formalise many pragmatic applications nicely in the type theory. Our internal formalisation of the various notions for modular refinement such as abstract implementation is such an example. Therefore, as to formalisation of specifications and their refinement, the conceptual simplicity in model-theoretic approaches to specifications (cf. for example, [ST88b]) and the computational simplicity that allows a direct computer implementation of the language of type theory. This is why we have mentioned in Section 8.1 that the semantics of specifications and their refinement is 'model-theoretic', in the sense that types (Σ-types) are used to represent sets of program modules and functions (functional programs in the type theory) are used to represent refinement maps which are programs in the type theory, and this allows us to *internalise* those notions which are usually defined at the meta level (e.g. in set theory).

For the readers who are familiar with algebraic specifications, the following remarks on some technical points may be helpful. In type theory, we have a distinction between concrete data types and the abstract data types, as discussed in Section 8.2. This is comparable to the distinction in between the initial semantics and the loose semantics in algebraic specifications, where specifications are the only kind of entities to be considered. The types such as N of natural numbers are data types in the type theory, which in algebraic specifications are specified with initial semantics, while the specifications of abstract data types have a variety of possible realisations, which in algebraic specifications are considered as having loose semantics. Based on such a view, a Σ-type is regarded as representing a class of program modules (which in algebraic specification are semantically considered as a class of algebras) and structure mappings between Σ-types correspond to functions between classes of algebras. Note that, in our setting, the notions of signature and signature morphisms are not necessary, as we are working in type theory, which is comparable to working in a 'syntactically manageable set theory'. However, there is an essential difference here; that is, the refinement maps are themselves (computational) programs rather than non-computational functions in set theory.

Finally, we remark that the use of type theory suggested above, in particular, the representational use of type-predicate pairs, provides a general conceptual framework which may be used in other applications of type theory (cf. [WL93]).

9
Towards a unifying theory of dependent types

As we made clear in the Introduction, one of our major goals in studying type theory is to develop a powerful computational and logical language for modular program development, structured specification and logical reasoning. The study of the Extended Calculus of Constructions, especially the ideas of how to organise the conceptual universe of types reflected in it, have indicated a particular but coherent approach. The language of ECC, developed as a first step towards a unifying theory of dependent types, has given us a good basis for studying many important issues and interesting applications. In this chapter, we consider a further development of the type theory, as described in [Luo92]. The conceptual universe of the type theory has been briefly described in Section 1.4 and many of the associated ideas have been reflected in the development of ECC. The further development below introduces a large class of inductive data types (computational theories) into the language of the type theory, based on the idea of using inductive schemata to introduce inductive types as considered by Coquand and Mohring [CPM90] and Dybjer [Dyb91].

The language of the resulting theory of dependent types UTT is presented by means of a meta-language—(a typed version of) Martin-Löf's logical framework. The main reason for us to use a meta-language (logical framework) to present our language of type theory, rather than presenting it directly as we did for ECC, is that it allows us to give a clearer and more satisfactory presentation of the type theory. There is a clear distinction between the language of the type theory and the meta-level mechanisms that are used to define the type theory, with the understanding that the former is the language that is to be used (e.g. in programming and reasoning) and the latter is a language that provides schematical mechanisms for language designers to specify languages (type theory in our case) and meta-level definitional mechanisms. In particular, this presentation allows one to understand the structure of the conceptual universe of types in our type theory more clearly, and enables us to elaborate our views on some of the related technical and philosophical issues such as the notion of pure logical truth, hierarchical understanding of the language of type theory, intensionality of computational equality, and the relationship between the logical universe and predicative universes, which in the previous chapters have only been briefly discussed.

9.1 A logical framework with inductive schemata

There are various ways that a *logical framework* may be used. The Edinburgh Logical Framework [HHP87] has been studied for formalisation of logical systems based on the idea of judgements-as-types. Martin-Löf's logical framework (for its presentation, see Part III of [NPS90]) has been proposed by Martin-Löf to present his intensional type theory. In the following, we consider a typed version of Martin-Löf's logical framework, explain how to use it as a meta-language to specify type theories, and define a notion of inductive schemata in logical framework which is to be used to introduce inductive data types in our type theory.

9.1.1 Martin-Löf's logical framework

We consider LF, a typed version of Martin-Löf's logical framework.[40] LF is a simple type system with terms of the following forms:

$$\mathbf{Type},\quad El(A),\quad (x{:}K)K',\quad [x{:}K]k',\quad f(k),$$

where the free occurrences of variable x in K' and k' are bound by the binding operators $(x{:}K)$ and $[x{:}K]$, respectively.

Since LF is to be used as a meta-language to specify type theories, types in LF will be called *kinds*, in order to be distinguished from the types in the specified type theories. There are five forms of judgements in LF:

- Γ **valid**, which asserts that Γ is a valid context;
- $\Gamma \vdash K$ **kind**, which asserts that K is a kind;
- $\Gamma \vdash k : K$, which asserts that k is an object of kind K;
- $\Gamma \vdash k = k' : K$, which asserts that k and k' are equal objects of kind K; and
- $\Gamma \vdash K = K'$, which asserts that K and K' are equal kinds.

[40] For those familiar with the presentation of Martin-Löf's logical framework in [NPS90], it may be helpful to note that the difference is that besides some inessential notational changes, we have the typed functional operations of the form $[x{:}K]k$ instead of the untyped $(x)k$.

Contexts and assumptions

$$\frac{}{\langle\rangle\ \textbf{valid}} \qquad \frac{\Gamma \vdash K\ \textbf{kind} \quad x \notin FV(\Gamma)}{\Gamma, x{:}K\ \textbf{valid}} \qquad \frac{\Gamma, x{:}K, \Gamma'\ \textbf{valid}}{\Gamma, x{:}K, \Gamma' \vdash x : K}$$

General equality rules

$$\frac{\Gamma \vdash K\ \textbf{kind}}{\Gamma \vdash K = K} \qquad \frac{\Gamma \vdash K = K'}{\Gamma \vdash K' = K} \qquad \frac{\Gamma \vdash K = K' \quad \Gamma \vdash K' = K''}{\Gamma \vdash K = K''}$$

$$\frac{\Gamma \vdash k : K}{\Gamma \vdash k = k : K} \qquad \frac{\Gamma \vdash k = k' : K}{\Gamma \vdash k' = k : K} \qquad \frac{\Gamma \vdash k = k' : K \quad \Gamma \vdash k' = k'' : K}{\Gamma \vdash k = k'' : K}$$

Equality typing rules

$$\frac{\Gamma \vdash k : K \quad \Gamma \vdash K = K'}{\Gamma \vdash k : K'} \qquad \frac{\Gamma \vdash k = k' : K \quad \Gamma \vdash K = K'}{\Gamma \vdash k = k' : K'}$$

Substitution rules

$$\frac{\Gamma, x{:}K, \Gamma'\ \textbf{valid} \quad \Gamma \vdash k : K}{\Gamma, [k/x]\Gamma'\ \textbf{valid}}$$

$$\frac{\Gamma, x{:}K, \Gamma' \vdash K'\ \textbf{kind} \quad \Gamma \vdash k : K}{\Gamma, [k/x]\Gamma' \vdash [k/x]K'\ \textbf{kind}} \qquad \frac{\Gamma, x{:}K, \Gamma' \vdash K'\ \textbf{kind} \quad \Gamma \vdash k = k' : K}{\Gamma, [k/x]\Gamma' \vdash [k/x]K' = [k'/x]K'}$$

$$\frac{\Gamma, x{:}K, \Gamma' \vdash k' : K' \quad \Gamma \vdash k : K}{\Gamma, [k/x]\Gamma' \vdash [k/x]k' : [k/x]K'} \qquad \frac{\Gamma, x{:}K, \Gamma' \vdash k' : K' \quad \Gamma \vdash k_1 = k_2 : K}{\Gamma, [k_1/x]\Gamma' \vdash [k_1/x]k' = [k_2/x]k' : [k_1/x]K'}$$

$$\frac{\Gamma, x{:}K, \Gamma' \vdash K' = K'' \quad \Gamma \vdash k : K}{\Gamma, [k/x]\Gamma' \vdash [k/x]K' = [k/x]K''} \qquad \frac{\Gamma, x{:}K, \Gamma' \vdash k' = k'' : K' \quad \Gamma \vdash k : K}{\Gamma, [k/x]\Gamma' \vdash [k/x]k' = [k/x]k'' : [k/x]K'}$$

Fig. 9.1. The general inference rules of LF.

Dependent product kinds

$$\frac{\Gamma \vdash K\ \mathbf{kind} \quad \Gamma, x{:}K \vdash K'\ \mathbf{kind}}{\Gamma \vdash (x{:}K)K'\ \mathbf{kind}} \qquad \frac{\Gamma \vdash K_1 = K_2 \quad \Gamma, x{:}K_1 \vdash K_1' = K_2'}{\Gamma \vdash (x{:}K_1)K_1' = (x{:}K_2)K_2'}$$

$$\frac{\Gamma, x{:}K \vdash k : K'}{\Gamma \vdash [x{:}K]k : (x{:}K)K'} \qquad \frac{\Gamma \vdash K_1 = K_2 \quad \Gamma, x{:}K_1 \vdash k_1 = k_2 : K}{\Gamma \vdash [x{:}K_1]k_1 = [x{:}K_2]k_2 : (x{:}K_1)K}$$

$$\frac{\Gamma \vdash f : (x{:}K)K' \quad \Gamma \vdash k : K}{\Gamma \vdash f(k) : [k/x]K'} \qquad \frac{\Gamma \vdash f = f' : (x{:}K)K' \quad \Gamma \vdash k_1 = k_2 : K}{\Gamma \vdash f(k_1) = f'(k_2) : [k_1/x]K'}$$

$$\frac{\Gamma, x{:}K \vdash k' : K' \quad \Gamma \vdash k : K}{\Gamma \vdash ([x{:}K]k')(k) = [k/x]k' : [k/x]K'} \qquad \frac{\Gamma \vdash f : (x{:}K)K' \quad x \notin FV(f)}{\Gamma \vdash [x{:}K]f(x) = f : (x{:}K)K'}$$

***The kind* Type**

$$\frac{\Gamma\ \mathbf{valid}}{\Gamma \vdash \mathbf{Type}\ \mathbf{kind}} \qquad \frac{\Gamma \vdash A : \mathbf{Type}}{\Gamma \vdash El(A)\ \mathbf{kind}}$$

Fig. 9.2. Dependent product kinds and **Type** in LF.

The rules for inferring judgements in LF are given in Fig. 9.1 and 9.2. Figure 9.1 contains the general inference rules in LF—the rules for context validity and variable assumption, the general equality rules (the judgemental equality is an equivalence relation), the equality typing rules (equal kinds have the same objects and object equality), and the substitution rules for objects and equal objects.

Figure 9.2 contains the rules about the kind-forming operators. The following are the brief explanations of the kinds and their objects in LF, whose use in specifying type theories is to be further explained later, and the notion of definitional equality.

Dependent product kinds

For any kind K and any family of kinds $K'[x]$ indexed by objects of kind K, $(x{:}K)K'[x]$ is the dependent product kind whose objects are the *functional operations* which for any object k of kind K, yield objects of kind $K'[k]$. The canonical objects of a dependent product kind is of the abstraction form $[x{:}K]k'$, and the application of a functional operation f to an object k is expressed by $f(k)$.

Notation We shall often write $(K_1)K_2$ for the dependent product kind

$(x{:}K_1)K_2$ when x does not occur free in K_2. For application of functional operations, we shall often write $f(k_1, ..., k_n)$ for $f(k_1)...(k_n)$.

Remark Kinds and functional operations provide us the meta-level schematical mechanism for specification of type theories and should not be confused with Π-types and functions in the type theory to be specified. We shall come back to this point later.

Types and kinds of their objects

In the logical framework, there is a special kind **Type**, each of whose objects A generates a kind $El(A)$. When specifying a type theory in LF, **Type** corresponds to the conceptual universe of types of the type theory to be specified, and for any type A, i.e. any object of kind **Type**, kind $El(A)$ corresponds to the collection of objects of type A.

The following terminology will be useful later.

Definition 9.1. (types, kinds, and small kinds) *A is called a* Γ-type *if* $\Gamma \vdash A : \mathbf{Type}$. *$K$ is called a* Γ-kind *if* $\Gamma \vdash K$ **kind**. *A Γ-kind is called* small *if it is either of the form $El(A)$ or of the form $(x{:}K_1)K_2$ for some small Γ-kind K_1 and small $(\Gamma, x{:}K_1)$-kind K_2.*

Notation When no confusion may occur, we shall often omit the kind-forming operator El to write, for example, $(x{:}A)B$, $\Gamma \vdash a : A$, $\Gamma \vdash a = b : A$ and $\Gamma \vdash A = B$ for $(x{:}El(A))El(B)$, $\Gamma \vdash a : El(A)$, $\Gamma \vdash a = b : El(A)$ and $\Gamma \vdash El(A) = El(B)$, respectively.

Definitional equality

We shall say that two objects of the same kind are *definitionally equal* if they are $\beta\eta$-convertible, that is, they are identical subject to the meta-level $\beta\eta$-equality (cf. the last two equality rules for dependent product kinds in Fig. 9.2). More precisely, for any type theory T specified in the logical framework, two objects k and k' of kind K are *definitionally equal* (in T), notation $\Gamma \vdash^T k =_{\beta\eta} k' : K$, if and only if $\Gamma \vdash k : K$ and $\Gamma \vdash k' : K$ are derivable (in T) and k and k' are convertible w.r.t. the following contraction rules:

$$\begin{array}{rcl} ([x{:}K]k')(k) & \leadsto & [k/x]k', \\ [x{:}K]f(x) & \leadsto & f \quad (x \notin FV(f)). \end{array}$$

This notion of definitional equality should not be confused with the notion of computational equality for the type theories to be specified by means of

LF. The point here is that $\beta\eta$-equality is a suitable equality for definitional abbreviations, while the computational equality is *not* just a definitional equality for meta-level abbreviation but an essential feature of the object language (the specified type theory). If two objects in a specified type theory are definitionally equal, they are certainly computationally equal (or better, identical, since definitional equality is regarded as a meta-level notion).

It should be made clear that η-equality is definitional, but in our view *not* computational.[41] In other words, η-rule should not hold for the computational equality between functions of Π-types in the type theory, but it should hold for the functional *operations* in the definitional mechanism provided by the meta-language. One of the reasons that η-rule is preferable in a definitional mechanism based on λ-calculus may be explained by the following simple example. Recall that such a mechanism, as in (informal) mathematics and in a proof development system (e.g. Lego), usually allows us to write

$$g(x_1, ..., x_n) = k, \quad or \quad g[x_1{:}K_1]...[x_n{:}K_n] = k,$$

to mean that g is defined as $[x_1{:}K_1]...[x_n{:}K_n]k$. Now, consider the following examples of definitions:

$$F[f{:}(K)K][x{:}K] = f(x). \qquad F'[f{:}(K)K] = f.$$

Intuitively (and naturally), we would have a very strong intention to hold that the above two definitions define the same functional operation, that is, F and F' are definitionally equal. However, as it is clear, this is only true when η-rule is regarded as definitionally valid.

There are other reasons in favour of the inclusion of the η-rule in LF, as we shall explain in Section 9.3.3.

9.1.2 Specifying type theories in LF

Now, let us briefly explain how to use LF to specify type theories. In general, a specification of a type theory in LF will consist of a collection of declarations of new constants and a collection of computation rules (usually about the new constants). Formally, declaring a new constant k of kind K by writing

$$k : K,$$

is to extend the type theory (specified by means of LF) to which the constant is introduced by the following inference rule:

[41] This is the view taken by Martin-Löf as reflected in his formulation of his intensional type theory.

$$\frac{\Gamma \ \textbf{valid}}{\Gamma \vdash k : K}$$

and asserting a computation rule by writing

$$k = k' : K \quad for \quad k_i : K_i \ (i = 1, ..., n),$$

is to extend the type theory by the following equality inference rule,

$$\frac{\Gamma \vdash k_i : K_i \ (i = 1, ..., n) \quad \Gamma \vdash k : K \quad \Gamma \vdash k' : K}{\Gamma \vdash k = k' : K}$$

As explained above, the special kind **Type** in LF corresponds to the conceptual universe of types in the type theory to be specified. For example, one may introduce a new (constant) type, the type N of natural numbers, by declaring the following new constants:

$$\begin{array}{rcl} N & : & \textbf{Type} \\ 0 & : & N \\ succ & : & (N)N \\ Rec_N & : & (C{:}(N)\textbf{Type})(c{:}C(0))(f{:}(x{:}N)(C(x))C(succ(x))) \\ & & (n{:}N)C(n) \end{array}$$

and asserting the following computation rules about them:

$$\begin{array}{rcl} Rec_N(C, c, f, 0) & = & c \ : \ C(0) \\ Rec_N(C, c, f, succ(n)) & = & f(n, Rec_N(C, c, f, n)) \ : \ C(succ(n)) \end{array}$$

for C, c, f, and n of the appropriate kinds so that the terms concerned are well-typed. (Since the information for the required kinds of such terms is usually clear from the declarations of relevant constants, we will omit such explanations later in asserting computation rules.) It is not difficult to see that the type of natural numbers have derivable rules that correspond to those we have considered in Section 7.1.1 except that here the meta-level kind **Type** and dependent product kinds play the (more proper) role that was done by $Type_i$ and Π-types there.[42]

[42]Comparing the presentation of type theories in LF with those directly formulated such as ECC, we would remark that the kind **Type** is also different from *Type* as implemented in the Lego system and used in Chapter 8. The former is a meta-level entity while the latter should be regarded as a notational abbreviation for some suitable universe $Type_i$ and is hence a type in the type theory.

Since we take LF seriously as a *meta-language* that provides schematical and definitional mechanisms, we will be careful in distinguishing the entities in the specified type theory from the meta-level entities such as the kind of types, dependent product kinds, and functional operations. The fact that the meta-language is itself a type system might sometimes cause a confusion and hence a misunderstanding of the use of the specified type theory. However, if we are careful, the distinction can be made easily. In particular, using a type theory, the entities that we are mainly concerned with are types (objects of kind **Type**) and their objects (objects of kinds of the form $El(A)$), while the other kinds and functional operations are only used as meta-level schematical and definitional mechanisms.[43] Therefore, it is worth pointing out what the judgements *in the specified type theory* are.

Let T be any type theory specified in LF as suggested above. Then, a T-*context* is a context of the form $x_1{:}El(A_1), ..., x_n{:}El(A_n)$, and T has the following five forms of judgements (where Γ is any T-context):

- Γ **valid**, which asserts that Γ is a valid T-context;
- $\Gamma \vdash A : \mathbf{Type}$, which asserts that A is a type;
- $\Gamma \vdash a : El(A)$, which asserts that a is an object of type A;
- $\Gamma \vdash a = b : El(A)$, which asserts that a and b are computationally equal objects of type A in the sense that they compute to the same value; and
- $\Gamma \vdash A = B : \mathbf{Type}$, which asserts that A and B are equal types in the sense that they have the same objects.

A judgement in a type theory specified in LF is *derivable* if it is derivable in the system of LF extended by the constants and computation rules specifying the type theory.[44]

The judgements of the above forms are those judgements with which the user of the specified type theory is concerned. Note that the meta-level expressions such as $(x{:}K)K'$ and $[x{:}K]k'$ are *not* regarded as expressions in the type theory specified in LF, but rather as meta-level expressions

[43] This situation is similar to the usual practice of using schemata (informally) to discuss logical languages (e.g. logical rules). The difference here is that the meta-language is also formal.

[44] One may define a T-derivation as a derivation of a judgement in T in the system of LF extended by the constants and computation rules specifying T. However, one may also safely regard the parts of such a derivation concerning the dependent product kinds and functional operations as meta-level reasoning and hence omit them from the notion of derivation in the specified type theory.

used for definitional abbreviations when they occur in an expression of the type theory. For example, C, f, and *succ* in $Rec_N(C, c, f, succ(n))$, are not objects in the specified type theory, but meta-level functional operations. A user of a specified type theory may use the definitional mechanism to help himself in the use of the type theory, but his ultimate concern is only the language of the specified type theory.

The above discussion is meant to help people to understand our use of LF as a meta-language. To summarise, once a type theory is specified, the user uses the type theory rather than the LF language, except that he may use LF as a definitional mechanism which may be implemented in a proof development system. In particular, in such a use of logical framework as meta-language, one does *not* use the meta-logic embedded in LF to reason about objects in the type theory, but should use the internal logic in the specified type theory for reasoning.

The notion of computational equality for a type theory T between objects is different from that of the definitional equality. In any context Γ (not necessarily a T-context), two objects a and b of type A are *computationally equal (in* Γ*)* if $\Gamma \vdash a = b : A$ is derivable.

9.1.3 Inductive schemata

The type theory UTT to be specified in the next section contains inductive data types which are introduced by means of a notion of inductive schemata, which is very similar to Coquand and Mohring's notion of constructor in [CPM90], with the difference that we consider the inductive schemata at the meta-level (in the logical framework), while they consider it based on the Π-types in the calculus of constructions with universes.

Definition 9.2. (inductive schemata) *Let* Γ *be a valid context and* X *be a variable such that* $X \notin FV(\Gamma)$.

- Φ *is a* strictly positive operator in Γ w.r.t. X, *notation* $\mathrm{POS}_{\Gamma;X}(\Phi)$, *if* Φ *is of the form* $(x_1{:}K_1)...(x_n{:}K_n)X$, *where* $n \geq 0$ *and* K_i *is a small* $(\Gamma, x_1{:}K_1, ..., x_{i-1}{:}K_{i-1})$*-kind for* $i = 1, ..., n$.[45]
- Θ *is an* inductive schema in Γ w.r.t. X, *notation* $\mathrm{ISCH}_{\Gamma;X}(\Theta)$, *if*
  1. $\Theta \equiv X$, *or*
  2. $\Theta \equiv (x{:}K)\Theta_0$, *where* K *is a small* Γ*-kind and* $\mathrm{ISCH}_{\Gamma,x:K;X}(\Theta_0)$, *or*
  3. $\Theta \equiv (\Phi)\Theta_0$, *where* $\mathrm{POS}_{\Gamma;X}(\Phi)$ *and* $\mathrm{ISCH}_{\Gamma;X}(\Theta_0)$.

[45] Note that K_i being a $(\Gamma, x_1{:}K_1, ..., x_{i-1}{:}K_{i-1})$-kind guarantees that X does not occur free in K_i.

Any inductive schema w.r.t. X is of the form $(x_1{:}M_1)...(x_m{:}M_m)X$, where M_i is either a small kind such that $X \notin FV(M_i)$ or a strictly positive operator w.r.t. X. A strictly positive operator is an inductive schema where M_i's are all small kinds such that $X \notin FV(M_i)$. Using inductive schemata to introduce inductive types into type theory, the smallness condition of the kinds occurring in inductive schemata is important. For example, neither $(\mathbf{Type})X$ nor $(\mathbf{Type})((A)\mathbf{Type})X$ is an inductive schema since **Type** is not a small kind.

The variable X in a strictly positive operator or an inductive schema plays the role of a placeholder. We shall use the following notational conventions.

Notations For any strictly positive operator Φ and inductive schema Θ w.r.t. X, $\Phi[A]$ and $\Theta[A]$ stand for $[A/X]\Phi$ and $[A/X]\Theta$, respectively. (To generalise this convention, if X does not occur free in a kind K, $K[A]$ is just K.) Note that, for any Γ-type A, $\Phi[A]$ and $\Theta[A]$ are small Γ-kinds, if $\textsc{Pos}_{\Gamma;X}(\Phi)$ and $\textsc{Isch}_{\Gamma,X}(\Theta)$. We shall write $\bar{\Theta}$ for a sequence of inductive schemata $\Theta_1, ..., \Theta_n$ $(n \geq 0)$, and $\textsc{Isch}_{\Gamma;X}(\bar{\Theta})$ to express that $\bar{\Theta}$ is a sequence of inductive schemata in Γ w.r.t. X.

Definition 9.3. (constant expressions) *Let $\bar{\Theta}$ be any finite sequence of inductive schemata in Γ w.r.t. X. Then, a* constant expression w.r.t. $\bar{\Theta}$ *is an expression of the form $\kappa[\bar{\Theta}]$, where the free occurrences of X become bound (by the binding operator $[\_]$). κ is called the* constant letter *of the constant expression $\kappa[\bar{\Theta}]$.*

Definition 9.4. (*LF *with inductive schemata) *The* logical framework with inductive schemata, LF$_\theta$, *is the extension of* LF *by constant expressions with the following equality rule:*

$$\frac{\textsc{Isch}_{\Gamma;X}(\bar{\Theta},\bar{\Theta}') \quad \Gamma \vdash \kappa[\bar{\Theta}] : K \quad \Gamma \vdash \kappa[\bar{\Theta}'] : K \qquad \Gamma, X{:}\mathbf{Type} \vdash \Theta_i = \Theta_i' \quad (i = 1, ..., n)}{\Gamma \vdash \kappa[\bar{\Theta}] = \kappa[\bar{\Theta}'] : K}$$

where $\bar{\Theta}$ and $\bar{\Theta}'$ are of the same length n, and $\kappa[\bar{\Theta}]$ and $\kappa[\bar{\Theta}']$ are constant expressions with the same constant letter.

With the above extension, one is allowed to declare new constant expressions as well as new constants.[46] Let $\bar{\Theta}$ be a sequence of inductive

[46] For simplicity, we assume that the set of constants and the set of constant letters for constant expressions are disjoint. In particular, a constant is *not* identified with a constant expression w.r.t. the empty sequence of inductive schemata.

schemata $\bar{\Theta}$ in Γ. Then, declaring a new constant expression w.r.t. $\bar{\Theta}$ to be of Γ-kind K by writing

$$\kappa[\bar{\Theta}] : K,$$

means that the judgement $\Gamma \vdash \kappa[\bar{\Theta}] : K$ is added as an axiom (an inference rule with no premises).

Remark Note that two constant expressions are computationally equal only if they have the same constant letter. In particular, two constant expressions $\kappa[\bar{\Theta}]$ and $\kappa'[\bar{\Theta}]$ with κ and κ' different are not computationally equal even when they are declared to have the same kind. This allows one, for example, to introduce different inductive data types with the same structure (say, two types of natural numbers which may be used to represent different entities in one's particular application).

9.2 The formulation of UTT

The type theory UTT consists of an internal logic, a large class of inductive data types, and predicative universes. We shall specify UTT in LF_θ, starting with the definition of the internal logical mechanism.

9.2.1 SOL: the internal logical mechanism

The internal logic consists of a universe *Prop* of logical propositions and their proof types. They are introduced by declaring the following constants:

$$\begin{aligned}
Prop &: \mathbf{Type} && (9.1)\\
\mathbf{Prf} &: (Prop)\mathbf{Type} && (9.2)\\
\forall &: (A{:}\mathbf{Type})((A)Prop)Prop && (9.3)\\
\Lambda &: (A{:}\mathbf{Type})(P{:}(A)Prop)((x{:}A)\mathbf{Prf}(P(x)))\mathbf{Prf}(\forall(A,P)) && (9.4)\\
\mathbf{E}_\forall &: (A{:}\mathbf{Type})(P{:}(A)Prop)(R{:}(\mathbf{Prf}(\forall(A,P)))Prop)\\
&\quad ((g{:}(x{:}A)\mathbf{Prf}(P(x)))\mathbf{Prf}(R(\Lambda(A,P,g))))\\
&\quad (z{:}\mathbf{Prf}(\forall(A,P)))\mathbf{Prf}(R(z)) && (9.5)
\end{aligned}$$

and asserting the following computation rule:

$$\mathbf{E}_\forall(A,P,R,f,\Lambda(A,P,g)) = f(g) \ : \ \mathbf{Prf}(R(\Lambda(A,P,g))). \qquad (9.6)$$

We shall call the (logical) type theory as formulated above in LF as SOL.

The logical universe *Prop* is impredicative since universal quantification $\forall(A,P)$ can be formed for *any* type A and (meta-level) predicate P over A. In particular, A can be *Prop* itself or more complex. However, it is worth remarking that one cannot use $\forall$ to quantify over meta-level kinds such as **Type**, (A)**Type**, or $(A)Prop$.

Notation For universal quantification, when no confusion may occur, we shall often use the usual notations, writing $\forall x{:}A.P(x)$ for $\forall(A,P)$ and $\Lambda x{:}A.f(x)$ for $\Lambda(A,P,f)$. Note that a usual elimination (application) operator **App** of kind $(A{:}\mathbf{Type})(P{:}(A)Prop)(\mathbf{Prf}(\forall(A,P)))(a{:}A)\mathbf{Prf}(P(a))$ can be defined as

$$\begin{array}{ll} & \mathbf{App}(A,P,F,a) \\ =_{\mathrm{df}} & \mathbf{E}_{\forall}(A,P,[G{:}\mathbf{Prf}(\forall(A,P))]P(a),[g{:}(x{:}A)\mathbf{Prf}(P(x))]g(a),F), \end{array}$$

which satisfies the equality (the β-rule for Λ and **App**):

$$\mathbf{App}(A,P,\Lambda(A,P,g),a) = g(a) : \mathbf{Prf}(P(a)).$$

We shall often omit the typing information to simply write $\mathbf{App}(F,a)$ instead of $\mathbf{App}(A,P,F,a)$.

The type theories we shall consider below all contain SOL (that is, the above constants and the computation rule) as its logical language. We can introduce the following terminology for such a type theory.

Definition 9.5. *A term P is called a* Γ-proposition *if* $\Gamma \vdash P : Prop$. *A* Γ*-type A is* propositional *if* $\Gamma \vdash A = \mathbf{Prf}(P) : \mathbf{Type}$ *for some* Γ*-proposition P, and* non-propositional, *otherwise. A* Γ*-proposition P is* provable *if* $\Gamma \vdash p : \mathbf{Prf}(P)$ *for some p, and such a p is called a* proof *of P. We shall call a functional operation of kind* $(El(A_1))...(El(A_n))Prop$ *a* (meta-level) predicate over types $A_1,...,A_n$.

Similar to what we have shown for ECC, many of the usual logical operators can be defined by means of the impredicative universal quantification. The logical implication between propositions P_1 and P_2 can be defined as

$$\begin{array}{rcl} P_1 \supset P_2 & =_{\mathrm{df}} & \forall x{:}\mathbf{Prf}(P_1).P_2 \\ & = & \forall(\mathbf{Prf}(P_1),[x{:}\mathbf{Prf}(P_1)]P_2). \end{array}$$

The other logical operators (**true**, **false**, &, $\vee$, $\neg$, and $\exists$) can be defined as in Definition 5.3, with the understanding that $\forall$ and $\supset$ are introduced and defined as above. However, the type theory SOL by itself is only a second-order logic (hence the name). In particular, there are no *types* of internal predicates or internal relations in SOL over which universal quantification may be possible. (The meta-level predicates form *kinds* of the form $(A)Prop$ to which the universal quantifier $\forall$ cannot be applied.) As a consequence, the Leibniz equality can *not* be defined in SOL. When one introduces function space between types, the internal logic will become higher-order since logical quantification over types of internal predicates (of the form $A \to Prop$) becomes possible, and the Leibniz equality is then definable (see below).

Remark In LF, one may introduce dependent product types by declaring the following constants:

$$\begin{array}{rcl} \Pi & : & (A{:}\mathbf{Type})((A)\mathbf{Type})\mathbf{Type} \\ \lambda & : & (A{:}\mathbf{Type})(B{:}(A)\mathbf{Type})((x{:}A)B(x))\Pi(A,B) \\ \mathbf{E}_\Pi & : & (A{:}\mathbf{Type})(B{:}(A)\mathbf{Type})(C{:}(\Pi(A,B))\mathbf{Type}) \\ & & ((g{:}(x{:}A)B(x))C(\lambda(A,B,g)))\ (z{:}\Pi(A,B))C(z) \end{array}$$

and asserting the following computation rule:

$$\mathbf{E}_\Pi(A,B,C,f,\lambda(A,B,g)) = f(g) : C(\lambda(A,B,g)).$$

Then, SOL together with the Π-types is *essentially* a formulation of the calculus of constructions [CH88] in LF. However, such a formulation in LF is slightly different from the direct one in that the logical η-rule for the Π-types w.r.t. the Leibniz equality is provable in the above LF-formulation but not in the direct one. See Section 9.3.3.

9.2.2 Inductive data types

We now introduce inductive data types in UTT based on the notion of inductive schemata defined in Section 9.1.3. We first consider the general formulation and then give examples and explanations.

A schematic formulation of inductive types in UTT

The idea is that any finite sequence of inductive schemata specifies a collection of introduction rules (each schema in the sequence determines one of them) and hence generates an inductive data type whose meaning is given by the introduction rules (and the associated elimination and computation rules). The essential idea is not new and has been considered by, for example, Gentzen [Gen35], Prawitz [Pra73, Pra74], etc. for traditional logical systems, and by Martin-Löf [ML84], Backhouse [Bac88], Dybjer [Dyb91], and Coquand and Mohring [CPM90] for type theories.

First, we introduce two notational definitions to be used below to formulate the elimination and computation rules for inductive data types.

Definition 9.6.

1. *Let* $\Theta \equiv (x_1{:}M_1)...(x_m{:}M_m)X$ *be an inductive schema and* $\langle \Phi_{i_1}, ..., \Phi_{i_k} \rangle$ *the subsequence of* $\langle M_1, ..., M_m \rangle$*, which consists of the strictly positive operators. Then, for* $A : \mathbf{Type}$*,* $C{:}(A)\mathbf{Type}$ *and* $z : \Theta[A]$*, define kind* $\Theta^\circ[A, C, z]$ *as follows:*

$$\begin{array}{lll} \Theta^\circ[A, C, z] & =_{\rm df} & (x_1{:}M_1[A])...(x_m{:}M_m[A]) \\ & & (\Phi^\circ_{i_1}[A, C, x_{i_1}])...(\Phi^\circ_{i_k}[A, C, x_{i_k}])\ C(z(x_1, ..., x_m)). \end{array}$$

   In the special case when Θ *is a strictly positive operator* Φ *(i.e.* $X \notin FV(M_1, ..., M_m)$*),* $\Phi^\circ[A, C, z] \equiv (x_1{:}M_1)...(x_m{:}M_m)C(z(x_1, ..., x_m))$*.*

2. *Let* $\Phi \equiv (x_1{:}K_1)...(x_m{:}K_m)X$ *be a strictly positive operator w.r.t.* X*. Define* $\Phi^\natural[A, C, f, z]$ *of kind* $\Phi^\circ[A, C, z]$ *for* $A : \mathbf{Type}$*,* $C : (A)\mathbf{Type}$*,* $f : (x{:}A)C(x)$ *and* $z : \Phi[A]$*, as follows:*

$$\Phi^\natural[A, C, f, z] =_{\rm df} [x_1{:}K_1]...[x_m{:}K_m]f(z(x_1, ..., x_m)).$$

   When $m = 0$*, we simply have* $\Phi^\natural[A, C, f, z] \equiv f(z)$*.*

With the above notations, we can now introduce the inductive data types in UTT as follows. Let Γ be a valid context and $\bar{\Theta} \equiv \langle \Theta_1, ..., \Theta_n \rangle$ ($n \in \omega$) a sequence of inductive schemata in Γ. Then, $\bar{\Theta}$ generates a Γ-type which is introduced by declaring the following constant expressions w.r.t. $\bar{\Theta}$:

$$\begin{array}{rcll} \mathcal{M}[\bar{\Theta}] & : & \mathbf{Type} & (9.7) \\ \iota_i[\bar{\Theta}] & : & \Theta_i[\mathcal{M}[\bar{\Theta}]] \quad (i = 1, ..., n) & (9.8) \\ \mathbf{E}[\bar{\Theta}] & : & (C{:}(\mathcal{M}[\bar{\Theta}])\mathbf{Type}) & \\ & & (f_1{:}\Theta_1^\circ[\mathcal{M}[\bar{\Theta}], C, \iota_1[\bar{\Theta}]])\ ...\ (f_n{:}\Theta_n^\circ[\mathcal{M}[\bar{\Theta}], C, \iota_n[\bar{\Theta}]]) & \\ & & (z{:}\mathcal{M}[\bar{\Theta}])C(z) & (9.9) \end{array}$$

and asserting the following n computation rules for $i = 1, ..., n$:

$$\begin{array}{rll} & \mathbf{E}[\bar{\Theta}](C, \bar{f}, \iota_i[\bar{\Theta}](\bar{x})) & \\ = & f_i(\bar{x},\ \Phi^\natural_{i_1}[\mathcal{M}[\bar{\Theta}], C, \mathbf{E}[\bar{\Theta}](C, \bar{f}), x_{i_1}], ..., \Phi^\natural_{i_k}[\mathcal{M}[\bar{\Theta}], C, \mathbf{E}[\bar{\Theta}](C, \bar{f}), x_{i_k}]) & \\ : & C(\iota_i[\bar{\Theta}](\bar{x})) & (9.10) \end{array}$$

where it is assumed that Θ_i be of the form $(x_1{:}M_1)...(x_{m_i}{:}M_{m_i})X$, $\langle \Phi_{i_1}, ..., \Phi_{i_k} \rangle$ be the subsequence of $\langle M_1, ..., M_{m_i} \rangle$ that consists of the strictly positive operators, and $\bar{f}$ stand for $f_1, ..., f_n$ and $\bar{x}$ for $x_1, ..., x_{m_i}$.

The above formulation of inductive data types conforms with the pattern developed by Martin-Löf to introduce inductive types in type theory. In general, for any inductive type $A \equiv \mathcal{M}[\bar{\Theta}]$, each of its introduction rules corresponds to an inductive schema $\Theta_i \equiv (x_1{:}M_1)...(x_{m_i}{:}M_{m_i})X$ in $\bar{\Theta}$ and introduces an introduction operator $\iota_i[\bar{\Theta}]$ whose kind is

$$(x_1{:}M_1[A])...(x_{m_i}{:}M_{m_i}[A])A.$$

That is, given any objects k_j of kind $M_j[A]$ (with $k_1,...,k_{j-1}$ substituted for $x_1,...,x_{j-1}$ in $M_j[A]$, respectively), $\iota_i[\bar{\Theta}](k_1, ..., k_{m_i})$ is an object of type A. The objects of such a form are *canonical objects* of type A. For example, if $\bar{\Theta}_N \equiv \langle X, (X)X\rangle$, then $N =_{\text{df}} \mathcal{M}[\bar{\Theta}_N]$ is the type of natural numbers and its introduction rules allow us to define

$$0 =_{\text{df}} \iota_1[\bar{\Theta}_N] : N \quad \textit{and} \quad \textit{succ} =_{\text{df}} \iota_2[\bar{\Theta}_N] : (N)N.$$

The elimination operator $\mathbf{E}[\bar{\Theta}]$ introduces an induction (or recursion) principle which informally says that, for any family of types C indexed by objects of type A, any f_i showing that $C(\iota_i[\bar{\Theta}](k_1, ..., k_{m_i}))$ is inhabited (i.e. $C(u)$ is inhabited for every canonical object u of type A), and any object a of type A, $C(a)$ is inhabited—$\mathbf{E}[\bar{\Theta}](C, f_1, ..., f_n, a)$ is of type $C(a)$. The computation rules above give the computational meaning to the elimination operator by specifying what it computes to when applied to a canonical object of type A. For the example of natural numbers, we can define

$$Rec_N =_{\text{df}} \mathbf{E}[\bar{\Theta}_N],$$

whose kind is the same as given in the example in Section 9.1.2, and so are the computational rules for natural numbers.

Note that the recursion principle ranges over *all types*, as expressed by C being an arbitrary family of types. This conforms with the use of **Type** as the formal counterpart of the conceptual universe of types. In other words, it is the types in our conceptual universe that we are concerned with, not more and not less. On the one hand, we do not allow any elimination over a larger collection of entities (say, all kinds); kinds are out of our conceptual domain to be captured by the specified type theory and therefore it does not make sense to impose elimination rules ranging over them. On the other hand, the inductive types are inductive w.r.t. the conceptual universe of types, rather than a subuniverse of it.[47]

[47]Considered in this way, the use of universes $Type_i$ in Chapter 7 to introduce inductive data types does *not* reflect our intention properly, although we know in ECC every type has a name in a predicative universe and technically it works there.

Remark As formulated above, every sequence of inductive schemata corresponds to one inductive data type up to computational equality. As remarked before, with the notion of constant expressions, it is possible to introduce more than one copy of an inductive data type which will not be identified by the computational equality. For instance, for a sequence of inductive schemata $\bar{\Theta}$, we may introduce another inductive data type with the same structure as $\mathcal{M}[\bar{\Theta}]$ by choosing different constant expressions such as $\mathcal{M}'[\bar{\Theta}]$, $\iota_i'[\bar{\Theta}]$ and $\mathbf{E}'[\bar{\Theta}]$. But for our purpose here, the above formulation is enough.

Examples

The following are some examples of inductive data types.

1. The empty type: $\emptyset =_{\mathrm{df}} \mathcal{M}[]$. ($\emptyset$ is generated by the empty sequence of inductive schemata.)
2. The unit type: $\mathbf{1} =_{\mathrm{df}} \mathcal{M}[X]$.
3. The type of Booleans: $Bool =_{\mathrm{df}} \mathcal{M}[X, X]$.
4. The type of natural numbers: $N =_{\mathrm{df}} \mathcal{M}[X, (X)X]$.
5. Lists: $List =_{\mathrm{df}} [A{:}\mathbf{Type}]\ \mathcal{M}[X, (A)(X)X]$.
6. Function space: $\rightarrow\ =_{\mathrm{df}} [A{:}\mathbf{Type}][B{:}\mathbf{Type}]\ \mathcal{M}[((A)B)X]$.
7. Dependent product: $\Pi =_{\mathrm{df}} [A{:}\mathbf{Type}][B{:}(A)\mathbf{Type}]\ \mathcal{M}[((x{:}A)B(x))X]$.
8. Product: $\times =_{\mathrm{df}} [A{:}\mathbf{Type}][B{:}\mathbf{Type}]\ \mathcal{M}[(A)(B)X]$.
9. Strong sum: $\Sigma =_{\mathrm{df}} [A{:}\mathbf{Type}][B{:}(A)\mathbf{Type}]\ \mathcal{M}[(x{:}A)(B(x))X]$.
10. Disjoint sum: $+ =_{\mathrm{df}} [A{:}\mathbf{Type}][B{:}\mathbf{Type}]\ \mathcal{M}[(A)X, (B)X]$.
11. Binary trees: $BT =_{\mathrm{df}} [A{:}\mathbf{Type}]\mathcal{M}[X, (A)(X)(X)X]$.
12. ω-branching trees: $InfT =_{\mathrm{df}} [A{:}\mathbf{Type}]\mathcal{M}[X, (A)((N)X)X]$.
13. Well-ordering types:[48]
    $W =_{\mathrm{df}} [A{:}\mathbf{Type}][B{:}(A)\mathbf{Type}]\ \mathcal{M}[(x{:}A)((B(x))X)X]$.

[48] The well-ordering type construction is conceptually a very general one. With η-equality rules, well-ordering types can be used to represent a large class of inductive data types [GL93]. However, in an intensional type theory, such representations are not possible.

One may define many more examples. It is easy to check that the definitions above do give the desirable rules.

A remark is that we have used the functional operations in the meta-language to define the meta-level type constructors (from 5 to 13 above). These functional operations (e.g. *List*, Π) are not entities in UTT, but rather the meta-level type constructors standing for *families of inductive data types*. For instance, for any type A and any family of types B indexed by objects of A (now represented by a type-valued functional operation B), $\Pi(A, B)$ and $\Sigma(A, B)$ are the dependent product type and the strong sum type of A and B, respectively. We can define the introduction and elimination operators for Π-types and Σ-types as follows, where $A : \mathbf{Type}$, $B : (A)\mathbf{Type}$, $\bar{\Theta}_{\Pi(A,B)} \equiv ((x{:}A)B(x))X$, and $\bar{\Theta}_{\Sigma(A,B)} \equiv (x{:}A)(B(x))X$:

$$\lambda(A, B) =_{\mathrm{df}} \iota_1[\bar{\Theta}_{\Pi(A,B)}], \quad \mathbf{E}_{\Pi}(A, B) =_{\mathrm{df}} \mathbf{E}[\bar{\Theta}_{\Pi(A,B)}].$$

$$\mathbf{pair}(A, B) =_{\mathrm{df}} \iota_1[\bar{\Theta}_{\Sigma(A,B)}], \quad \mathbf{E}_{\Sigma}(A, B) =_{\mathrm{df}} \mathbf{E}[\bar{\Theta}_{\Sigma(A,B)}].$$

For the other inductive data types, this is similar.

For Π-types and Σ-types, the application operator and the projection operators can be defined as follows:

$$\begin{array}{lll}
\mathbf{app} & =_{\mathrm{df}} & [A{:}\mathbf{Type}][B{:}(A)\mathbf{Type}][F{:}\Pi(A,B)][a{:}A] \\
 & & \mathbf{E}_{\Pi}(A, B, [G{:}\Pi(A,B)]B(a), [g{:}(x{:}A)B(x)]g(a), F). \\
\pi_1 & =_{\mathrm{df}} & [A{:}\mathbf{Type}][B{:}(A)\mathbf{Type}][z{:}\Sigma(A,B)] \\
 & & \mathbf{E}_{\Sigma}(A, B, [z{:}\Sigma(A,B)]A, [x{:}A][y{:}B(x)]x, z). \\
\pi_2 & =_{\mathrm{df}} & [A{:}\mathbf{Type}][B{:}(A)\mathbf{Type}][z{:}\Sigma(A,B)] \\
 & & \mathbf{E}_{\Sigma}(A, B, [z{:}\Sigma(A,B)]B(\pi_1(A,B,z)), [x{:}A][y{:}B(x)]y, z).
\end{array}$$

In the above examples, we have listed the function spaces and Π-types (also, products and Σ-types) separately for illustration. In fact, as usual (e.g. in ECC), the function spaces are special cases of Π-types (and the products are special cases of Σ-types). It is easy to verify that the function space $A \to B$ and the product $A \times B$[49] introduced above are definitionally equal to $\Pi(A, [x{:}A]B)$ and $\Sigma(A, [x{:}A]B)$, respectively. (To check this, the equality rule given in Definition 9.4 is used.)

We would like to remark that every *type* A in the type theory has a 'copy' of itself, that is, the type $\mathcal{M}[(A)X]$. With the rules for the inductive data types, one can show that A and $\mathcal{M}[(A)X]$ are isomorphic in the sense that one can define the following functional operations

$$f \quad =_{\mathrm{df}} \quad \iota_1[(A)X] \ : \ (A)\mathcal{M}[(A)X],$$

[49]We shall use infix notation when appropriate.

$$g \quad =_{\mathrm{df}} \quad \mathbf{E}[(A)X]([z{:}\mathcal{M}[(A)X]]A, [x{:}A]x) \ : \ (\mathcal{M}[(A)X])A,$$

and for any a of type A and any u of type $\mathcal{M}[(A)X]$, $f(g(u)) = u : \mathcal{M}[(A)X]$ and $g(f(a)) = a : A$. However, if A is *not* a type but a small kind (e.g. $A \equiv (A_1)A_2$ with A_1 and A_2 being types), the above construction breaks down because $[z{:}\mathcal{M}[(A)X]]A$ is not a well-typed functional operation (and one cannot have elimination over kinds!) and g is not well-defined.

The above also explains that Π-types $\Pi(A, B)$ are *not* internal copies of the kinds $(x{:}A)B$. In fact, the objects of the meta-level dependent product kinds are *weakly extensional* in the sense that the η-rule holds for the meta-level functional operations (definitional equality), while the functions of Π-types are intensional and the η-rule does not hold for λ and **app** (computational equality) in general.

Having the function spaces in UTT, we have introduced the types of internal predicates (or relations) such as $A \to Prop$. Therefore, we are now able to define the Leibniz equality over any type A as follows: for a and b of type A, $a =_A b$ is defined as the following proposition:

$$\forall P{:}A \to Prop.\ \mathbf{app}(P, x) \supset \mathbf{app}(P, y),$$

where we use $\mathbf{app}(P, z)$ to abbreviate $\mathbf{app}(A, [x{:}A]Prop, P, z)$. The Leibniz equality is an intensional equality but it is weakly extensional in the sense that, for the inductive data types, the logical η-rules w.r.t. the Leibniz equality are provable (see Section 9.3.3).

9.2.3 Predicative universes

In UTT, besides the impredicative universe *Prop*, we also introduce the predicative universes $Type_i$ ($i \in \omega$). In the following declarations of constants and constant expressions, and assertions of computational rules, $i \in \omega$ is an arbitrary natural number.

The predicative universes are types whose objects are names of types—for any object a in $Type_i$, $\mathbf{T}_i(a)$ is the type named by a:

$$Type_i : \mathbf{Type}, \qquad \mathbf{T}_i : (Type_i)\mathbf{Type}. \tag{9.11}$$

Each predicative universe $Type_i$ has a name $type_i$ in $Type_{i+1}$:

$$type_i : Type_{i+1}, \qquad \mathbf{T}_{i+1}(type_i) = Type_i : \mathbf{Type}. \tag{9.12}$$

The impredicative universe of propositions has a name *prop* in $Type_0$:

$$prop : Type_0, \qquad \mathbf{T}_0(prop) = Prop : \mathbf{Type}. \tag{9.13}$$

Every type with a name in $Type_i$ has a name in $Type_{i+1}$:

$$\mathbf{t}_{i+1} : (Type_i)Type_{i+1}, \qquad \mathbf{T}_{i+1}(\mathbf{t}_{i+1}(a)) = \mathbf{T}_i(a) : \mathbf{Type}. \tag{9.14}$$

The proof type of any proposition in $Prop$ has a name in $Type_0$:

$$\mathbf{t}_0 : (Prop)Type_0, \qquad \mathbf{T}_0(\mathbf{t}_0(P)) = \mathbf{Prf}(P) : \mathbf{Type}. \tag{9.15}$$

Finally, the inductive types generated by the inductive schemata have names in the appropriate predicative universes, whose introduction conforms with the predicativity of $Type_i$. We need the following auxiliary definition of $\textsc{Types}_\Gamma(\bar{\Theta})$, the set of types occurring in the sequence of inductive schemata $\bar{\Theta}$ together with the contexts in which they are well-typed.

Definition 9.7. *Let K, Φ and Θ be a small Γ-kind, a strictly positive operator and an inductive schema in Γ w.r.t. X, respectively. The sets $\textsc{Types}_\Gamma(K)$, $\textsc{Types}_\Gamma(\Phi)$ and $\textsc{Types}_\Gamma(\Theta)$ are defined as follows:*

$$\textsc{Types}_\Gamma(K) =_{\mathrm{df}} \begin{cases} \{(\Gamma, A)\} & \text{if } K \equiv El(A) \\ \textsc{Types}_\Gamma(K_1) \cup \textsc{Types}_{\Gamma,x:K_1}(K_2) & \text{if } K \equiv (x{:}K_1)K_2 \end{cases}$$

$$\textsc{Types}_\Gamma(\Phi) =_{\mathrm{df}} \begin{cases} \emptyset & \text{if } \Phi \equiv X \\ \textsc{Types}_\Gamma(K_1) \cup \textsc{Types}_{\Gamma,x:K_1}(\Phi_0) & \text{if } \Phi \equiv (x{:}K_1)\Phi_0 \end{cases}$$

$$\textsc{Types}_\Gamma(\Theta) =_{\mathrm{df}} \begin{cases} \emptyset & \text{if } \Theta \equiv X \\ \textsc{Types}_\Gamma(K_1) \cup \textsc{Types}_{\Gamma,x:K_1}(\Theta_0) & \text{if } \Theta \equiv (x{:}K_1)\Theta_0 \\ \textsc{Types}_\Gamma(\Phi_1) \cup \textsc{Types}_\Gamma(\Theta_0) & \text{if } \Theta \equiv (\Phi_1)\Theta_0 \end{cases}$$

For $\bar{\Theta} \equiv \Theta_1, ..., \Theta_n$, $\textsc{Types}_\Gamma(\bar{\Theta}) =_{\mathrm{df}} \bigcup_{1\le i\le n} \textsc{Types}_\Gamma(\Theta_i)$.

Now, let $\bar{\Theta}$ be any finite sequence of inductive schemata in Γ. If, for any $(\Gamma', A) \in \textsc{Types}_\Gamma(\bar{\Theta})$, A has a name a in $Type_i$ in Γ', that is, for some a, we have

$$\Gamma' \vdash a : Type_i \quad \textit{and} \quad \Gamma' \vdash \mathbf{T}_i(a) = A : \mathbf{Type},$$

then the following constant expression $\mu_i[\bar{\Theta}]$ is declared (in context Γ), which is a name of the inductive type $\mathcal{M}[\bar{\Theta}]$ in $Type_i$:[50]

$$\mu_i[\bar{\Theta}] : Type_i, \qquad \mathbf{T}_i(\mu_i[\bar{\Theta}]) = \mathcal{M}[\bar{\Theta}] : \mathbf{Type}. \tag{9.16}$$

[50]We may also enforce the name uniqueness for inductive data types by asserting $\mathbf{t}_{i+1}(\mu_i[\bar{\Theta}]) = \mu_{i+1}[\bar{\Theta}] : Type_{i+1}$. However, this is not essential.

To be more precise, the introduction of names of inductive data types into the predicative universes amounts to the following two inference rules, where $\textsc{IsCh}_{\Gamma;X}(\bar{\Theta})$:

$$\frac{\Gamma' \vdash a : Type_i \quad \Gamma' \vdash \mathbf{T}_i(a) = A : \mathbf{Type} \quad ((\Gamma', A) \in \textsc{Types}_\Gamma(\bar{\Theta}))}{\Gamma \vdash \mu_i[\bar{\Theta}] : Type_i}$$

$$\frac{\Gamma' \vdash a : Type_i \quad \Gamma' \vdash \mathbf{T}_i(a) = A : \mathbf{Type} \quad ((\Gamma', A) \in \textsc{Types}_\Gamma(\bar{\Theta}))}{\Gamma \vdash \mathbf{T}_i(\mu_i[\bar{\Theta}]) = \mathcal{M}[\bar{\Theta}] : \mathbf{Type}}$$

In other words, an inductive data type has a name in the predicative universe $Type_i$ if and only if the types that occur in its generating sequence of inductive schemata have names in $Type_i$. For example, the type of natural numbers has a name in any predicative universe $Type_i$. For the Π-types, $\Pi(A, B)$ has a name in $Type_i$ if and only if A has a name in $Type_i$ and $B(x)$ has a name in $Type_i$, assuming $x{:}A$. (These conform with what we have had for ECC). Note that the above rules have finitely many premises since the set $\textsc{Types}_\Gamma(\bar{\Theta})$ is always finite and the omitted premise $\textsc{IsCh}_{\Gamma;X}(\bar{\Theta})$ is also finitary.

Remark Using a logical framework with inductive schemata, we have introduced inductive data types *independently* of the existence of the predicative universes. In other words, an inductive data type whose formation does not involve $Type_j$ for $j \geq i$ exists independently of these universes and its name in $Type_i$ is introduced when the universe is introduced. Note that the predicative universes in our theory are *not* inductively defined; there is no elimination rule to impose induction principle over a universe. In fact, being aware of the potential infinity of conceptions in type formation, it does not seem to be reasonable to consider the predicative universes as closed for finitely many type constructors. For the impredicative universe of propositions, there seems to be a choice which we shall discuss later.

By means of predicative universes, one can define *inductive families of types*. For example, supposing that type A has a name in $Type_i$, we can define an inductive family of types $Listn_A : (N)\mathbf{Type}$ such that for any natural number $n : N$, $Listn_A(n)$ is the type of lists of objects in A of length n. $Listn_A$ can be defined by first defining a functional operation $listn_A$ of kind $(N)Type_i$ by induction over N as follows:

$$\begin{aligned} listn_A(0) &= \mu_i[X], \\ listn_A(n+1) &= \mu_i[(A)(\mathbf{T}_0(listn_A(n)))X], \end{aligned}$$

and then $Listn_A =_{\mathrm{df}} [x{:}N]\mathbf{T}_i(listn_A(x)) : (N)\mathbf{Type}$. For any natural number $n : N$, $Listn_A(n) = A \times ... \times A$ (n times) and $Listn_A(0)$ is the unit type. With these definitions, one can then define the following 'introduction operators' (where $\star =_{\mathrm{df}} \iota_1[X]$ is the canonical object of the unit type)

$$\begin{array}{lll} nil_A & =_{\mathrm{df}} & \star \; : \; Listn_A(0), \\ cons_A & =_{\mathrm{df}} & [n{:}N]\ \mathbf{pair}(A, [x{:}A]Listn_A(n)) \\ & : & (n{:}N)(a{:}A)(l{:}Listn_A(n))Listn_A(succ(n)), \end{array}$$

and an elimination operator Rec_{Listn_A} of kind

$$\begin{array}{l} (C{:}(n{:}N)(Listn_A(n))\mathbf{Type}) \\ (C(0, nil_A))\ ((n{:}N)(x{:}A)(l{:}Listn_A(n))(C(n,l))C(succ(n), cons_A(x,l))) \\ (n{:}N)(l{:}Listn_A(n))C(n,l), \end{array}$$

which satisfies the following computational equalities:

$$\begin{array}{l} Rec_{Listn_A}(C, c, f, 0, nil_A) \; = \; c \; : \; C(0, nil_A), \\ Rec_{Listn_A}(C, c, f, succ(n), cons_A(n, a, l)) \\ \quad = \; f(n, a, l, Rec_{Listn_A}(C, c, f, n, l)) \; : \; C(succ(n), cons_A(n, a, l)). \end{array}$$

We omit the definition of Rec_{Listn_A} here.

Remark We would like to distinguish between *families of inductive types* such as Π and *List* and *inductive families of types*[51] such as $Listn_A$. Obviously, each type in a family of inductive types is an *inductive type* (e.g. $List(A) = \mathcal{M}[X, (A)(X)X]$ is itself an inductive type). However, a type in an inductive family of types may not necessarily be an inductive type. For example, $Listn_{Prop}(1) = Prop$ is not an inductive type. The key difference is that an inductive family of types has an induction principle for the whole family of types which may be rather subtly related to each other, while for a family of inductive types this may not be the case. So far, we have not directly introduced inductive schemata to include inductive families of types in UTT as formulated above. However, the current notion of inductive schemata in LF_θ can be extended to do so (see Section 9.3.5 below).

9.2.4 A summary

The theory of dependent types UTT has been formally presented above in the logical framework with inductive schemata. It consists of

[51] Inductive families of types are also often called *inductive relations* when one does not distinguish data types from logical propositions.

1. SOL, the impredicative universe of logical propositions, introduced by (9.1) to (9.6);
2. the inductive data types covered by a general form of inductive schemata, introduced by (9.7) to (9.10); and
3. the predicative universes, introduced by (9.11) to (9.16).

As it is clear, ECC is essentially the language consisting of SOL with Π-types, Σ-types, and the predicative universes. Therefore, UTT can be seen as a further extension of ECC by a large class of inductive data types, and we claim that UTT also has the nice meta-theoretic properties that we have considered for ECC. In particular, we conjecture that UTT has strong normalisation property (subject to the obvious notion of computation). The strong normalisation theorem may be proved by extending the method of quasi-normalisation we have used to prove strong normalisation of ECC.[52] The realisability model sketched in Chapter 6 can be extended to UTT [Ore92]. The inductive data types (and inductive families of data types, see Section 9.3.5) have been implemented in the Lego proof development system by Claire Jones on the basis of Pollack's implementation of rewrite rules [LP92].

9.3 Discussion

The issues to be discussed below concern with some of the important questions in the study of type theory and the associated design decisions that we have made above in the development of our type theory. In discussing them, we hope to elaborate our ideas and points of view, some of which have been briefly mentioned before. The discussion will be based on the above formulation of UTT and some technical aspects are also considered.

9.3.1 The internal logic and pure logical truths

One of the ideas that we have argued for is that in type theory there should be a clear conceptual distinction between the notion of logical proposition and that of data type. (See Section 1.3.4 and Section 2.3.1.) In our view, some types in the conceptual universe of types are *logical* in the sense that they are used to represent collections of proofs of logical propositions that describe properties of the objects of types representing entities in the application domains to be reasoned about. Since data types and their objects represent entities in various possible applications (including programming,

[52]The meta-theory of UTT is studied by Healfdene Goguen at Edinburgh in his forthcoming PhD thesis.

specification, theorem proving, and more; not just mathematical entities!), it is not natural to identify logical propositions with them in the language and it is much more natural to have a clear distinction. Such a distinction is reflected in ECC and the above formulation of UTT in that the logical universe of propositions gives a distinguishable sublanguage (the internal logic) for logical reasoning.

Pure logical truths

As we have briefly mentioned in Section 2.3.1, with a distinction between logical propositions and data types in the conceptual universe of types, it is possible to consider a notion of 'pure logical truth' which would be helpful for one to understand the independence (and universality) of the internal logic. The use of logical framework as a meta-language to formulate the type theory allows us to discuss this issue formally.

Intuitively, a provable proposition is (or represents) a truth; it is a *pure logical truth* if it is true (provable) essentially by the very meanings of the logical operators occurring in it, regardless of the properties of the other (e.g. computational) entities involved. In other words, one may say that a provable proposition is a pure logical truth if it is true by its logical structure and its truth is invariant under the possible changes of non-logical entities that occur in it.[53] In type theory, such a consideration may lead to a notion of pure logical truth for its internal logic. However, it is far from clear how a notion of pure logical truth can and should be formalised so that it really reflects the above intuitive idea, and if a formal treatment is possible, there may be different ways to proceed. The following is a tentative attempt.

The idea is to take the internal logical mechanism of a type theory to be a 'logical province' of the type theory and consider pure logical truths as generated by the logical inference rules for the basic logical operators from the substitutional instances of certain truth schemata in the internal logic. In the following, we first consider SOL, as described in Section 9.2.1, as the logical province to consider the notion of pure logical truth.

Notation For any type theory T specified in logical framework, we write $\Gamma \vdash^T J$ for '$\Gamma \vdash J$ is derivable in T'.

[53] The reader may recall some of the arguments and analysis by Quine [Qui86, Qui62] concerning logical truths. For us, the issue of interest is not what a logical truth *is* in general, but rather which provable propositions (in a type theory) are pure logical truths, assuming that a proposition (formula) represents a truth if it is provable (has a proof).

Definition 9.8. (truth schemata) *Let K be a kind in* SOL *of the form*

$$K \equiv (z_1{:}K_1)...(z_n{:}K_n)\mathbf{Prf}(F[\bar{z}]),$$

where $n \geq 0$ and K_i of one of the following forms:

$$K_i \equiv \begin{cases} \mathbf{Type}, \\ (y_1{:}El(A_1))...(y_{m_i}{:}El(A_{m_i}))El(Prop) \quad (m_i \geq 0). \end{cases}$$

Then, K is a truth schema *(notation* $\text{TSCH}(K)$*) if*

$$\vdash^{\text{SOL}} k : K \quad \textit{for some } k.$$

Such a k is called a schematic proof *of the truth schema K.*

Definition 9.9. (pure logical truths) *Let T be any type theory specified in logical framework which contains* SOL *as its sublanguage, and $\Gamma \equiv x_1{:}El(A_1), ..., x_m{:}El(A_m)$ be any valid T-context.*

Then, a Γ-proposition P in T is a pure logical truth in Γ *or* Γ-plt (in *T) if one of the following holds:*

1. *For some truth schema $K \equiv (z_1{:}K_1)...(z_n{:}K_n)\mathbf{Prf}(F[z_1, ..., z_n])$,*

   $$P \equiv F[k_1, ..., k_n],$$

   for some $k_1, ..., k_n$ such that $\Gamma \vdash^T k_i : [k_1, ..., k_{i-1}/z_1, ..., z_{i-1}]K_i$ ($i = 1, ..., n$).

2. *P is definitionally equal to another Γ-plt, that is, $\Gamma \vdash^T P =_{\beta\eta} P' : Prop$ for some Γ-plt P'.*

3. *$P \equiv \forall x{:}A.P'$ for some $(\Gamma, x{:}El(A))$-plt P'.*

4. *$P \equiv P'[a]$ for some Γ-plts P_0 and $\forall x{:}\mathbf{Prf}(P_0).P'[x]$ and some a such that $\Gamma \vdash^T a : \mathbf{Prf}(P_0)$.*

If a Γ-plt is obtained by means of the first two clauses only, it is then called a basic Γ-plt *(w.r.t. truth schema K).*

The notion of pure logical truth given by the above definition can be characterised by the following rules, where for any T-context Γ, $\Gamma \models P$ means that P is a Γ-plt (in the type theory under consideration).

$$(\textsc{sch}) \quad \frac{\textsc{Tsch}((z_1{:}K_1)...(z_n{:}K_n)\mathbf{Prf}(F[z_1,...,z_n])) \quad \Gamma \vdash k_i : [k_1,...,k_{i-1}/z_1,...,z_{i-1}]K_i \ (i=1,...,n)}{\Gamma \models F[k_1,...,k_n]}$$

$$(\textsc{defn}) \quad \frac{\Gamma \models P \quad \Gamma \vdash P =_{\beta\eta} P' : Prop}{\Gamma \models P'}$$

$$(\textsc{gen}) \quad \frac{\Gamma, x{:}El(A) \models P}{\Gamma \models \forall x{:}A.P}$$

$$(\textsc{inst-p}) \quad \frac{\Gamma \models \forall x{:}\mathbf{Prf}(P_0).P[x] \quad \Gamma \models P_0 \quad \Gamma \vdash a : \mathbf{Prf}(P_0)}{\Gamma \models P[a]}$$

Given the above definition of pure logical truths, it is clear that every pure logical truth is necessarily provable in the type theory T under consideration. To be precise, for any basic Γ-plt $P_0 \equiv F[k_1,...,k_n]$ w.r.t. truth schema K with schematic proof k, we have that $k(k_1,...,k_n)$ is a Γ-proof of P_0. If p is a proof of $(\Gamma, x{:}A)$-plt P, then Γ-plt $\forall x{:}A.P$ has a proof $\Lambda x{:}A.p$. For any Γ-plt $\forall x{:}\mathbf{Prf}(P_0).P[x]$ with proof p, and any $\Gamma \vdash a : \mathbf{Prf}(P_0)$, $\mathbf{App}(p,a)$ is a proof of $P[a]$.

Example 9.10. The following basic examples of pure logical truths are considered in any type theory T that contains SOL.

1. Any provable proposition P in SOL is a basic pure logical truth w.r.t. truth schema $\mathbf{Prf}(P)$.

2. If $\forall X_1{:}Prop...\forall X_n{:}Prop.F[X_1,...,X_n]$ is provable in SOL, then for any propositions P_i in T, $F[P_1,...,P_n]$ is a basic plt w.r.t. $(X_1{:}Prop)...(X_n{:}Prop)\mathbf{Prf}(F[X_1,,,.X_n])$. As special cases of this, the instances of the propositional logical laws such as $P \supset P$ are pure logical truths.

3. Let $K \equiv (X{:}\mathbf{Type})(f{:}(X)Prop)\mathbf{Prf}(\forall x{:}X.\ \forall(X,f) \supset f(x))$. Then, for any type A and any meta-level predicate $f : (A)Prop$,

$$\forall x{:}A.\ \forall(A,f) \supset f(x)$$

is a basic plt w.r.t. K.

4. If T contains function spaces of the form $A \to Prop$, the Leibniz equality (over type A) is definable. Then, for any type A, we have

$$x{:}A \models x =_A x, \qquad x, y, z{:}A \models (x =_A y) \supset (y =_A z) \supset (x =_A z).$$

The reflexivity law is a plt because $(Z{:}Prop)\mathbf{Prf}(Z \supset Z)$ is a truth schema from which we can apply rule (SCH) to substitute Z in $Z \supset Z$ by $\mathbf{app}(P, x)$ in context $x{:}A, P{:}A \to Prop$ and then quantify over P by applying rule (GEN). To see that the transitivity law is a plt, consider the following truth schema:

$$\begin{array}{l} (X{:}\mathbf{Type})(f_x, f_y, f_z{:}(X)Prop) \\ \mathbf{Prf}((\forall P{:}X.f_x(P) \supset f_y(P)) \\ \qquad \supset (\forall P{:}X.f_y(P) \supset f_z(P)) \\ \qquad \supset (\forall P{:}X.f_x(P) \supset f_z(P))), \end{array}$$

and instantiate X by $A \to Prop$ and f_k by $[P{:}A \to Prop]\mathbf{app}(P, a)$ $(a \in \{x, y, z\})$, respectively.

Note that the 'elimination rule' (INST-P) for instantiating a pure logical truth in the form of universal quantification is restricted to the case that the domain of the quantification is the proof type of a plt. One cannot instantiate a pure logical truth of the form $\forall x{:}\mathbf{Prf}(P).Q$ to obtain another pure logical truth when P is not a pure logical truth. To illustrate, the following rule is a special case of (INST-P) for logical implication:

$$\frac{\Gamma \models P \quad \Gamma \models P \supset Q}{\Gamma \models Q}$$

However, *neither* of the following rules are in general valid for deriving pure logical truths, where we use $\Gamma \vdash P$ for 'P is provable in Γ in the type theory under consideration':

$$\frac{\Gamma \vdash P \quad \Gamma \models P \supset Q}{\Gamma \models Q} \qquad\qquad \frac{\Gamma \models P \quad \Gamma \vdash P \supset Q}{\Gamma \models Q}$$

For otherwise, if either of the above two rules were valid, then every provable proposition P would be a pure logical truth since $\Gamma \models P \supset P$ and $\Gamma \vdash \mathbf{true} \supset P$.

For the implication operator, we remark that the following rules are also valid (admissible) for deriving plts:

$$\frac{\Gamma \models P \quad \Gamma \vdash R : Prop}{\Gamma \models R \supset P} \qquad \frac{\Gamma \models P \supset Q \quad \Gamma \models Q \supset R}{\Gamma \models P \supset R} \qquad \frac{\Gamma \models P \supset Q \supset R}{\Gamma \models Q \supset P \supset R}$$

The definitions of the usual logical operators in SOL are coherent with respect to the notion of pure logical truth. For example, the following rules are valid for deriving pure logical truths.

$$\frac{\Gamma \models P \quad \Gamma \models Q}{\Gamma \models P \,\&\, Q} \qquad \frac{\Gamma \models P \,\&\, Q}{\Gamma \models P} \qquad \frac{\Gamma \models P \,\&\, Q}{\Gamma \models Q}$$

$$\frac{\Gamma \models P \quad \Gamma \vdash Q : Prop}{\Gamma \models P \vee Q} \qquad \frac{\Gamma \models P \quad \Gamma \vdash Q : Prop}{\Gamma \models Q \vee P}$$

$$\frac{\Gamma \models P \vee Q \quad \Gamma \models P \supset R \quad \Gamma \models Q \supset R}{\Gamma \models R}$$

As explained above, intuitively, a provable proposition is a pure logical truth if it is true essentially by its logical structure and the very meanings of the logical operators occurring in it. In the above definition of pure logical truths, we have considered SOL as the logical province and taken the universal quantification as the (only) basic logical operator. Therefore, a proposition is a pure logical truth if it is true essentially because of the meaning of universal quantification.

Not all provable propositions are pure logical truths in the above sense. Some propositions are only true because of the very meanings of the *non*-logical entities occurring in them. The point here is that, when a non-logical entity (e.g. an inductive data type and its objects and elimination operator) is introduced, its meaning is given by the particular rules that determine how it should be used. In particular, for an inductive data type, the elimination rule gives an induction principle to be used to prove logical propositions and the computation rule determines the meaning of the elimination operator and the relationship between the objects of the inductive data type and the others. Many logical propositions are not logical truths unless one understands the meanings of the non-logical entities in it according to their computational meaning.

In our type theory, typical examples of 'impure' logical truths are:

1. propositions which are only provable by means of the elimination rules of non-logical data types; the logical η-rules to be considered in Section 9.3.3 are such examples, which include $\forall u{:}\emptyset.\mathbf{false}$, $\forall u{:}\mathbf{1}.(u =_{\mathbf{1}} \star)$, etc.;

2. propositions which are only provable by means of the computation rules of non-logical data types; such examples include $1+1 =_N 2$, $(0 \neq_N 1)$, $\pi_1(\mathbf{pair}(a,b)) =_A a$ and the logical filling-up rules to be considered in Section 9.3.3;

3. propositions that concern with the inhabitability of certain types; for example, $\exists x{:}N.\mathbf{true}$.

A good illustrative example is the symmetry law for the Leibniz equality. We have seen above that the reflexivity and transitivity laws for the Leibniz equality are pure logical truths in any type theory that contains SOL and the types of the form $A \to Prop$. If one considers SOL as the logical province, the symmetry law $(x =_A y) \supset (y =_A x)$ seems to cause a problem and fail to be a plt according to the very definition of the Leibniz equality. Recall that the definition of the Leibniz equality does not directly take into the account that the discernibility over properties is symmetric and its symmetry is proved by means of the fact that it is possible to *define* a particular internal predicate over A, that is, $P_0 =_{\mathrm{df}} \lambda a{:}A.(a =_A x)$, and to prove the following proposition:

$$Q_0 \equiv (x =_A y) \supset (x =_A x) \supset (y =_A x).$$

If Q_0 were a plt, then so would be the symmetry law since $(x =_A x)$ is a plt. Following this idea, we can define a meta-predicate f_0 as $f_0(P) =_{\mathrm{df}} \mathbf{app}(P,x) \supset \mathbf{app}(P,y)$, and have

$$x, y{:}A \models \forall(A \to Prop, f_0) \supset f_0(P_0),$$

that is,

$$x, y{:}A \models (x =_A y) \supset \mathbf{app}(P_0, x) \supset \mathbf{app}(P_0, y).$$

However, the above plt is *not* Q_0, although it is *computationally* equal to Q_0. Therefore, such an argument does not show that Q_0 (or the symmetry law) is a plt. Put in another way, because one takes SOL as the logical province and the types such as $A \to Prop$ as non-logical, Q_0 is not a plt because it is only true by the very meaning of the type $A \to Prop$ together with that of universal quantification.

It is *not* our intention to use the above example of symmetry law to show that the symmetry law for a propositional equality is not a plt. On the contrary, we believe that such basic equality laws should be plts. (See below for a further discussion on logical equality.) The point illustrated by this example is that, in general, the computational meaning of non-logical entities is essential for the provability of many logical propositions which are not pure logical truths. The examples of impure logical truths in the second class mentioned above are quite similar to the symmetry law. For instance, the truth of $1 + 1 =_N 2$ or $0 \neq_N 1$ depends on the computational meaning of the elimination operator for natural numbers.

Another subtle point is whether the following rule should be be regarded as a basic rule for deriving pure logical truths:

$$(\textsc{inst-t}) \qquad \frac{\Gamma \models \forall x{:}A.P[x] \quad \Gamma \vdash a : A \quad A \text{ non-propositional}}{\Gamma \models P[a]}$$

That is, if $\forall x{:}A.P[x]$ is a plt and A is a non-propositional type with object a, should we be able to conclude that $P[a]$ is a plt? First, (INST-T) seems to be a reasonable rule. However, a more careful thought reveals that the above rule is not quite consistent with our conception that a pure logical truth is true by its logical structure. Put in another way, the above rule allows one to conclude that certain logical propositions are plts although their logical structures do not guarantee their inhabitance. For example, if the above rule were valid for deriving plts, the proposition $\exists x{:}A.\mathbf{true}$ would be a plt as soon as A is an inhabited non-propositional type in the type theory. However, not all non-propositional types are inhabited. For example, $\exists x{:}\emptyset.\mathbf{true}$ is not a truth (in the empty context).

Logical equality

In our logical province SOL, we have not included any propositional equality as a basic logical operator. To include a propositional equality as a basic logical operator is natural and pragmatically important. In our setting, there are two ways to consider this, either to use the definable Leibniz equality, or to introduce a new equality relation. First, since we are working with an impredicative type theory and pragmatically function spaces are used in most of the applications, the possibility of defining a propositional equality according to the Leibniz principle is rather attractive. A question raised by the above discussion on pure logical truth, in particular the problem with the symmetry law, is whether one should view an equality defined according to the Leibniz principle as a basic logical operator, which should then be included into the logical province, or as a derived one whose meaning is determined by that of the defining operator (universal quantifier).

Taking the view that the Leibniz equality defined as before should be included into the logical province, one can include the 'logical' types of internal predicates (and relations) into the logical province. Then, one considers higher-order logic HOL as the logical province and can discuss pure logical truths is similar as above except that SOL is replaced by HOL in the definition of truth schemata. Such a consideration is natural since there is no reason to consider types such as $A \to Prop$ as non-logical (see Section 9.3.2 below for a related discussion).

However, the other view seems to be equally reasonable. That is, there is no reason why we should not consider SOL as the logical province and the universal quantifier as the only basic logical operator, and takes the definable logical equality as a derived notion whose understanding is based on that of the universal quantifier. What about the problem of symmetry law? The answer (or argument) is that the problem comes from a different source, that is, the *asymmetric* definition of the Leibniz equality, which does *not* capture the discernibility principle directly. If one defined the Leibniz equality $x =_A y$ as

$$\forall P{:}A \to Prop.(\mathbf{app}(P,x) \supset \mathbf{app}(P,y)) \;\&\; (\mathbf{app}(P,y) \supset \mathbf{app}(P,x)),$$

its basic laws would all become pure logical truths when SOL is considered as the logical province. From this analysis, the choice between SOL and HOL as logical province is still open.

Introducing a new equality relation Eq of kind $(A{:}\mathbf{Type})(x{:}A)(y{:}A)Prop$ into the logical type theory SOL (and UTT) is another possibility that one may consider. This can be done in a similar way as the introduction of the weak intensional equality in Martin-Löf's type theory, for example, by declaring the following new constants:

$$\begin{array}{rcl} Eq & : & (A{:}\mathbf{Type})(x{:}A)(y{:}A)Prop \\ eq & : & (A{:}\mathbf{Type})(x{:}A)\mathbf{Prf}(Eq(A,x,x)) \\ \mathbf{E}_{Eq} & : & (A{:}\mathbf{Type})(C{:}(x{:}A)(y{:}A)(\mathbf{Prf}(Eq(A,x,y)))\mathbf{Type}) \\ & & ((x{:}A)C(A,x,x,eq(A,x))) \\ & & (x{:}A)(y{:}A)(z{:}\mathbf{Prf}(Eq(A,x,y)))C(x,y,z) \end{array}$$

and asserting the following computation rule:

$$\mathbf{E}_{Eq}(A,C,f,a,a,eq(A,a)) = f(a) : C(A,a,a,eq(A,a)).$$

Then, the logical province can be considered to be SOL with equality, and will contain two basic logical operators, the universal quantification and the propositional equality. An advantage of this approach is that the logical equality does not depend on the presence of the types of internal predicates or their meaning explanation. We should remark that, the elimination operator as formulated above allows elimination over all families of types that may be dependent on proofs of the logical equality. One may consider weaker versions so that it either only eliminates over families of propositions or is non-dependent of the proofs. An interesting fact to note is that, with the above equality introduced, the Leibniz equality becomes strong in the sense that the following logical proposition is provable:

$$((a =_A b) \supset Eq(A, a, b)) \;\&\; (Eq(A, a, b) \supset (a =_A b)).$$

This is a phenomenon very similar to what happens to the existential types when small Σ-types are introduced (see Section 2.3.2).

The above tentative study of pure logical truths is preliminary and by no means conclusive. A more thorough study of the notion of pure logical truth is needed. We believe that such a study should lead to a better understanding of the language of type theory, and in particular, its internal logic. It can also be regarded as a first step towards a compositional understanding of logical truths in type theory.

9.3.2 Further separation of propositions and data types

The relationship between logical propositions and data types is worth being further discussed. Let us assume that in the predicative universes reside the application oriented or real-world entities of concern (e.g. the computational entities such as programs and data types). As pointed out in Section 2.3.1, in ECC (and UTT as presented above), we have incorporated two specific relationships between the logical world and the computational world, which are as follows.

1. The proof type of a logical proposition is regarded as a data type in the computational world. This is reflected in ECC by the universe inclusion $Prop \subseteq Type_0$, and in UTT the introduction of the names $\mathbf{t}_0(P)$ of $\mathbf{Prf}(P)$ in $Type_0$ ((9.15) in Section 9.2.3).

2. The logical universe of propositions ($Prop$) is regarded as a data type and so are the types of internal predicates and relations such as $A \rightarrow Prop$. This is reflected in ECC by asserting that $Prop$ is of type $Type_0$, and in UTT by the introduction of the name $prop$ of $Prop$ in $Type_0$ ((9.13) in Section 9.2.3).

The first above reflects our desire of viewing proofs as computational entities and the second the desire of considering entities such as program specifications as computational entities to be manipulated in the computational world.

We would like to point out that neither of these two is necessary and it seems to be equally reasonable to exclude either or both of them as it is to include them as we have done. If the (direct) presentation of the type theory ECC makes it difficult to see how they (especially the second) may be excluded, the presentation of the type theory in the logical framework has made it clear how this can be done: one simply exclude either or both of (9.15) and (9.13) in Section 9.2.3. It is also clear from this presentation that the above two aspects are technically independent.

The question to answer is what effects it has to exclude either or both of them. Excluding proof types from the computational universes implies that, for example, proofs are not regarded as programs, and when one proves generic properties such as $\forall a{:}Type_i\forall x{:}\mathbf{T}_i(a).P(a,x)$ about computational objects, the proof types and their objects are not within the domain of consideration. This does not make any dramatic difference if one does not seriously use proof objects to construct programs. In other words, if one takes the view that the internal logic is simply for *description* of properties of the objects under concern and the proof objects are not really considered as in the application domain, then excluding proof types from the application universes may in fact be a good choice. (Note that this does not mean that the proofs cannot be studied in the type theory. Types such as $\mathbf{Prf}(P) \to A$ are still types in the type theory, but they are not, e.g. types of programs any more if we view $Type_0$ as an application-oriented universe.) However, if one considers proofs as programs or objects to be studied in their own right together with the computational objects, then one would include proof types in the application domain (predicative universes).

Whether to exclude the name of the logical universe of propositions from the predicative universes is a matter worth more careful consideration, since it changes the type theory and its use more dramatically. Conceptually, it seems reasonable since one can simply ask why the *logical* types such as *Prop* and $A \to Prop$ should be regarded as computational. Without a good answer given, one would say that they should be excluded from the computational universes. However, in many applications, logical propositions, predicates, and relations are *within* the concern and need to be manipulated together with the computational objects. The notion of program specification discussed in Chapter 8 is a good example where a specification is a pair consisting of a type of program modules and an (internal) predicate over the type. In order to manipulate specifications as computational objects (as in the consideration of data refinement and parameterised specifications), one would consider computational types and predicates in the same world. If we had excluded the name of *Prop* from objects of the predicative universes, we would not have been able to consider specifications as objects to be computationally manipulated.[54] Again,

[54]Another problem would be that 'setoids' could not be regarded as parts of program modules. Separating the binary relation from the program part seems to be natural, but it causes a slight problem in parameterised specifications when specifications are supplied as arguments (the only problem we know so far for this separation). I would

this does not mean that they cannot be manipulated. **SPEC** is still a type, although not regarded as containing computational objects.

Considering these problems in such a way, it seems that there is no definite structure that could be imposed so that it is suitable to every application. The solution is that one should be allowed to formulate different application universes and organise their structures and relationships according to the natural conceptions. The separation of logical universe from the computational (application) universes is a basic example and such problems will be met with in many other places. We should repeat and emphasize that we regard the conceptual universe of types of the type theory as open: there can be more types to be added and more sophisticated type structures and relationships between types to be considered. Adding particular (predicative) universes for particular applications is one of the possibilities.

We have mentioned that the type universes in our type theory are not inductively closed in the sense that there are no induction principles imposed upon them (cf. [NPS90]). The inductive closedness is a formal notion concerning the (formal) universes such as $Type_i$ and $Prop$, and should not be confused with the philosophical openness of the conceptual universe of types. We have said that $Type_i$, as a universe containing potentially infinitely many ways of type construction, should not be closed. Considered in this way, the logical universe $Prop$ seems to be different, since there are only finitely many ways (only one way by means of the universal quantification, in our type theory) to construct logical propositions. Therefore, it is *possible* to formulate an induction principle for it, that is, to declare an elimination operator as follows:

$$\begin{aligned}\mathbf{E}_{Prop} \quad : \quad & (C{:}(Prop)\mathbf{Type})((A{:}\mathbf{Type})(g{:}(A)Prop)C(\forall(A,g))) \\ & (P{:}Prop)C(P),\end{aligned}$$

and to assert the following computation rule:

$$\mathbf{E}_{Prop}(C, f, \forall(A,g)) = f(A,g) : C(\forall(A,g)).$$

The above induction (recursion) principle says that the propositions of the form $\forall(A,P)$ are the canonical objects of type $Prop$, and if a family of types indexed by propositions is uniformly inhabited for every proposition of the form $\forall(A,P)$, then it is uniformly inhabited for every proposition. However, we do not yet know how such an induction principle can be used significantly.

---

like to thank A. Tarlecki who brought my attention to this specific issue.

Regarding the propositions of type *Prop* in UTT, we remark that there is a slightly stronger elimination operator for the proof types which might be introduced as:

$$\begin{array}{rl}\mathbf{E}'_\forall & : \ (A{:}\mathbf{Type})(P{:}(A)Prop)(C{:}(\mathbf{Prf}(\forall(A,P)))\mathbf{Type}) \\ & \quad ((g{:}(x{:}A)\mathbf{Prf}(P(x)))C(\Lambda(A,P,g)))\ (z{:}\mathbf{Prf}(\forall(A,P)))C(z).\end{array}$$

$\mathbf{E}'_\forall$ is different from $\mathbf{E}_\forall$ in that, by means of $\mathbf{E}'_\forall$ one can define functions from a proof type to any type, instead of just to proof types. With $\mathbf{E}'_\forall$ as the elimination operator, $\mathbf{Prf}(\forall(A,P))$ is isomorphic to the inductive data type $\Pi(A,[x{:}A]\mathbf{Prf}(P(x)))$, although they are not computationally equal. Without identifying proof types with the Π-types, we have left room for more flexible model interpretations such as proof-irrelevant model interpretations.

9.3.3 Intensionality and η-equality rules

In Section 2.3.3, we have discussed the issue of intensionality and extensionality and argued for the intensionality of computational equality. The notion of computational equality in our type theory UTT is intensional and in our view captures the notion of computation satisfactorily. The computational equality is not even weakly extensional in the sense that η-rules do not hold for it between the objects of the inductive types in the type theory. For example, the following equality judgements concerning Π-types and Σ-types are not derivable in general:

$$\Gamma \vdash \lambda(A,B,\mathbf{app}(A,B,z,x)) = z : \Pi(A,B) \quad (x \notin FV(z)),$$

$$\Gamma \vdash \mathbf{pair}(A,B,\pi_1(A,B,z),\pi_2(A,B,z)) = z : \Sigma(A,B),$$

where z may be a variable rather than a canonical object of type $\Pi(A,B)$ or $\Sigma(A,B)$. Such weak-extensional η-rules should not be regarded as computational simply because they do not make any proper sense for a notion of computation. Using such a rule in either direction, from the left to the right or from the right to the left, does not contribute to computation or the meaning explanation. As already remarked above, this is in contrast with the definitional equality for the meta-level functional operations for which η-rule does hold.

A more reasonable way to read the η-rules is to read them as saying that every Γ-object of an inductive data type is equal to a canonical object of the type. This is the case for the inductive data types from the meaning-theoretic point of view because for any canonical object of an inductive type the η-equality does hold (for instance, when z is of the form $\lambda(A,B,f)$ or $\mathbf{pair}(A,B,a,b)$ in the above examples), because the computation rules can be applied in such cases. Being understood in such a way, the facts expressed by η-rules are consequences of certain induction principle about the inductive types and therefore it is expected that the η-rules do hold for logical equality. In other words, in our setting, it would be expected that for the inductive data types, it should be *provable* that every object of an inductive data type is propositionally equal to an object in canonical form.

This is the case for the inductive data types in UTT. For every inductive data type, the η-rule holds for the Leibniz equality, as the proposition below shows.[55] Before giving the general formulation of the logical η-rules for arbitrary inductive data types and proving its provability in UTT, we first consider some examples. In the following, we shall use $\Pi x{:}A.B(x)$, $\lambda x{:}A.f(x)$ and $\mathbf{app}(F,a)$ to abbreviate $\Pi(A,B)$, $\lambda(A,B,f)$ and $\mathbf{app}(A,B,F,a)$, respectively.

Example 9.11. We shall write η_A for the logical η-rules for the inductive data type A, stating that every object of an inductive data type is Leibniz-equal to a canonical object of the type.

1. $\eta_{\Pi(A,B)} = \forall u{:}\Pi(A,B)\ \exists F{:}\Pi(A,B).\ (u =_{\Pi(A,B)} \lambda x{:}A.\mathbf{app}(F,x))$.
2. $\eta_{\Sigma(A,B)} = \forall u{:}\Sigma(A,B)\ \exists x{:}A\exists y{:}B(x).\ (u =_{\Sigma(A,B)} \mathbf{pair}(x,y))$.
3. $\eta_{\emptyset} = \forall u{:}\emptyset.\mathbf{false}$.
4. $\eta_{\mathbf{1}} = \forall u{:}\mathbf{1}.(u =_{\mathbf{1}} \star)$.
5. $\eta_N = \forall u{:}N.\ (u =_N 0) \vee \exists n{:}N.(u =_N succ(n))$.
6. $\eta_{A+B} = \forall u{:}A+B.\ (\exists a{:}A.u =_A i(a)) \vee (\exists b{:}B.u =_B j(b))$, where $i : (A)A+B$ and $j : (B)A+B$ are the introduction operators of $A+B$.

To prove the logical η-rules, one uses the induction principle given by the elimination operator of the corresponding inductive data types. In some of the cases such as Π-types, the η-rule for definitional equality is essentially used.

To state the logical η-rules for arbitrary inductive data types, we need a notational definition. Let

$$K \equiv (x_1{:}K_1)(x_2{:}K_2[x_1])...(x_n{:}K_n[x_1,...,x_{n-1}])El(A[x_1,...,x_n])$$

[55] Recall that at the end of Section 2.3.3, we pointed out a problem of the direct presentation of type theory as that of ECC, in which the logical η-rules are not provable for the Π-types and Σ-types because their elimination rules (the application rule (*app*) and the rules for the projection operators) are weaker.

be any small kind. The following definitions of type K^*, k^* for k of kind K, and a° for a of type K^*, and the fact that $k^{*\circ} = k : K$ are defined and proved simultaneously by induction on the structure of K.

1. Define type K^* as follows:

$$K^* =_{\mathrm{df}} \Pi y_1{:}K_1^* \Pi y_2{:}K_2[y_1^\circ]^* ... \Pi y_n{:}K_n[y_1^\circ, ..., y_{n-1}^\circ]^*.\ A[y_1^\circ, ..., y_n^\circ].$$

2. For any object k of kind K, define object k^* of type K^* as follows:

$$k^* =_{\mathrm{df}} \lambda y_1{:}K_1^* \lambda y_2{:}K_2[y_1^\circ]^* ... \lambda y_n{:}K_n[y_1^\circ, ..., y_{n-1}^\circ]^*.\ k(y_1^\circ, ..., y_n^\circ).$$

3. For any object a of type K^*, define object a° of kind K as follows:

$$\begin{array}{rcl} a^\circ & =_{\mathrm{df}} & [x_1{:}K_1][x_2{:}K_2[x_1]]...[x_n{:}K_n[x_1, ..., x_{n-1}]]. \\ & & \mathbf{app}(...(\mathbf{app}(\mathbf{app}(a, x_1^*), x_2^*)..., x_n^*). \end{array}$$

4. For any object k of kind K, $k^{*\circ} = k : K$. The proof is by induction on the structure of K. If $n = 0$, then $k^{*\circ} \equiv k$ by definition. If $n > 0$, then

$$\begin{array}{rcl} k^{*\circ} & = & [x_1{:}K_1][x_2{:}K_2[x_1]]...[x_n{:}K_n[x_1, ..., x_{n-1}]].\ k(x_1^{*\circ}, ..., x_n^{*\circ}) \\ & = & [x_1{:}K_1][x_2{:}K_2[x_1]]...[x_n{:}K_n[x_1, ..., x_{n-1}]].\ k(x_1, ..., x_n) \\ & = & k \end{array}$$

   where the second step is by induction hypothesis and the last step by the η-rule for functional operations in the logical framework.

As a simple example to illustrate, for $K \equiv (A)B$ where A abd B are types, we have

$$K^* =_{\mathrm{df}} A \to B, \quad k^* =_{\mathrm{df}} \lambda y{:}A.k(y^\circ), \quad a^\circ =_{\mathrm{df}} [x{:}A]\mathbf{app}(a, x^*),$$

and

$$k^{*\circ} \equiv [x{:}A]\mathbf{app}(\lambda y{:}A.k(y^\circ),\ x^*) = [x{:}A]k(x^{*\circ}) = [x{:}A]k(x) = k.$$

Remark Note that the η-rule for definitional equality is essential for the well-definedness of the above types and objects. The object constructions between small kinds and types do not give an isomorphism up to computational equality. In general, we do not have $a^{\circ *} = a : K^*$, since the η-rule does not hold for Π-types.

Definition 9.12. ***(logical η-rules)*** *Let $\bar{\Theta} \equiv \Theta_1, ..., \Theta_n$ be any finite sequence of inductive schemata and $A \equiv \mathcal{M}[\bar{\Theta}]$ the inductive data type generated by $\bar{\Theta}$.*

1. *Let u be an object of the inductive type A. For $i = 1, ..., n$, if $\Theta_i \equiv (x_1{:}M_1)...(x_{m_i}{:}M_{m_i})X$, $\eta_i(u)$ is defined to be the following proposition:*

$$\eta_i(u) =_{\mathrm{df}} \exists x_1{:}M_1[A]^* ... \exists x_{m_i}{:}M_{m_i}[A]^*. \ (u =_A \iota_i(x_1^\circ, ..., a_{m_i}^\circ)).$$

2. *The* logical η-rule *for the inductive data type A, η_A, is defined as the following proposition:*

$$\eta_A =_{\mathrm{df}} \forall u{:}A. \bigvee_{i=1,...,n} \eta_i(u),$$

where the disjunction $\bigvee_{i=1,...,n} \eta_i(u)$ is **false** *if $n = 0$.*

Proposition 9.13. ***(logical validity of η-rules)*** *For any sequence of inductive schemata $\bar{\Theta}$, $\eta_{\mathcal{M}[\bar{\Theta}]}$ is provable.*

Besides the logical η-rules, there is another class of logical equalities concerning the inductive data types, which state that every functional operation with an inductive data type as its domain can be expressed by means of certain canonical use of the elimination operator for the inductive data type. We call such a logical equality rule a *filling-up rule*, which is provable as the following proposition shows.

Proposition 9.14. ***(logical validity of filling-up rules)*** *Let $\bar{\Theta}$ be a sequence of inductive schemata, $C : (\mathcal{M}[\bar{\Theta}])\mathbf{Type}$ and $f : (z{:}\mathcal{M}[\bar{\Theta}])C(z)$. Then, the following proposition is provable:*

$$\forall u{:}\mathcal{M}[\bar{\Theta}]. \ (f(u) =_{C(u)} \mathbf{E}[\bar{\Theta}](C, f \circ \bar{\iota}, u)),$$

where $f \circ \bar{\iota}$ stands for $f \circ \iota_1, ..., f \circ \iota_n$ and $(f \circ \iota_i)(a_1, ..., a_n, y_1, ..., y_k) =_{\mathrm{df}} f(\iota_i(a_1, ..., a_n))$.

The logical η-rules express that every object of an inductive data type is equal to a canonical object and the filling-up rules express that the elimination operator covers all of the use of the inductive data type. From this point of view, the above propositions may be regarded as an internal (or logical) justification of the intrinsic harmony between the introduction and elimination rules.

9.3.4 Understanding of the type theory

Understanding a language is necessary for its correct use. Here, we discuss very briefly two aspects of understanding the language of type theory: its operational meaning understanding and its hierarchical understanding. The former concerns the understanding of judgements, types, and their objects, and the latter is about the relationship between types and the structure of (the conceptual universe of types reflected by) the language.

We have briefly sketched in the Introduction the basic elements of an operational meaning theory (in particular, a verificationistic one) as applied to type theory and emphasized in Section 1.2.3 an understanding of a judgement, a type, or an object is not complete unless one has mastered the two complementary aspects of its use. For inductive data types, the two aspects of their use are captured by their introduction rules and elimination/computation rules, respectively. The introduction rules determine the forms of the canonical objects of an inductive data type and the elimination rule governs the way that the type and its objects may be used to define functional operations which when applied to the objects of the type yield objects of other types. In a verificationistic view, it is the introduction rules that determine the meaning of an inductive data type, that is, how its objects can be formed. Then, it is the responsibility of the language designer to make sure that the elimination rule is in harmony with the introduction rules, that is, the other aspect of use of the inductive data type and its objects conforms with the meaning given by the introduction rules. A technical way to show such a harmony is to prove the normalisation theorem, which in the usual circumstances implies that every object of a type computes to a canonical object and therefore that there is no abuse of the types and objects in the language from the verificationistic point of view.

It should be remarked that, taking the view that the introduction rules are meaning-giving, the harmony of elimination/computation rules w.r.t. the introduction rules shown by the normalisation theorem is only a necessary but *not* a sufficient condition to justify the *adequacy* (or completeness) of the other aspect of use represented by the elimination/computation rules. It is obvious that the elimination/computation rules could be too weak to capture some of the eligible and reasonable use granted by the meaning given by the introduction rules.[56]

Another way to consider an operational meaning theory is to regard the other aspect of use that is determined by the elimination rule(s) as more basic and meaning-giving, called as pragmatist view by Dummett [Dum91].

[56] A good example of such inadequacy is the problem about the elimination rule for the intensional equality in Martin-Löf's type theory, as discussed by Streicher [Str93] and Coquand [Coq92].

Different from simple logical systems as Dummett has considered, it seems difficult to give a formal or precise account of such a view for type theories (theories of dependent types, in particular), because the elimination rules could not even be formulated without considering the canonical forms of the objects and therefore the verificationistic approach has been dominating here. However, this is not a sufficient reason for taking the introduction rules to be meaning-giving or more basic. In fact, it should be taken that it is *both* of the aspects of use that determine the meaning of a type (object, judgement). In other words, for any given language in use, one can only understand the use of its constructions by grasping the two complementary aspects of use. Grasping only one of them may run the risk that the understanding is not complete.[57]

Seeking for (or allowing a possibility to obtain) an good operational meaning understanding has often been the main reason that we are unwilling to introduce some of the less disciplined constructions (from meaning-theoretic point of view) into our language of type theory. For example, we have not considered the law of excluded middle as an axiom in the internal logic of our type theory. This is not because we are against classical logic for its own sake (as some intuitionists are), but because it makes the operational meaning explanation and the understanding of the language more difficult. One might declare a constant of the proof type of $EM \equiv \forall P{:}Prop.\neg P \vee P$ to impose the law of excluded middle. However, this would mean that EM has a special non-canonical proof, which makes the verificationistic meaning explanation difficult, if not impossible.

The operational understanding of type theory is mainly concerned with the use of individual types, objects, and judgements. When explaining the meanings of the constructions in a type theory (or any language), a principle of compositionality is often used. For example, the explanation of a Π-type $\Pi(A, B)$ is usually based on the meaning explanation of type A and that of the family of types B. It is desirable to understand a language of type theory hierarchically. In other words, one first tries to understand the simple and basic types and their objects, and then to understand more complex types and their objects. When the types involved are formed in a predicative way, the complexity of them can usually be intuitively determined by their forms. (cf. the formal complexity measure of types defined in Section 4.2.) For example, in the conceptual universe of our type theory, any type A and any family of types B are considered to be

[57]This is not saying that it is impossible to obtain a complete understanding by taking one of the two aspects as the central concept. However, it seems that unless the other complementary aspect of use permitted by the language is complete or adequate w.r.t. the meaning-giving aspect of use, or the relationship between the two aspects is stable (a word used by Dummett), such an understanding would always be subject to possible weakness or incompleteness.

less complex than $\Pi(A, B)$, any predicative universe is considered to be more complex than any type that has a name in that universe, and the internal logic is supposed to be understood in a relatively independent way w.r.t. the rest of the language (cf. the above consideration of the notion of pure logical truth). A hierarchical understanding of the language is then to understand the language in the order given by the intuitive complexity of types. This is one of the reasons that we have emphasized that the introduction of an inductive data type should be independent of that of the predicative universes in which it has a name, for otherwise, the introduction of the inductive type would be dependent on that of the universe which has a higher complexity. In other words, the understanding of a predicative universe should be based on the understanding of the types in the universe and the understanding of the latter should be independent on that of the former.

Note that in a hierarchical understanding, we require only that the formation of the less complex constructions do not depend on that of the complex ones. A stronger requirement of compositionality is the so-called *compositional understanding* of a language (cf. [Dum91]), which means that the hierarchical understanding is in certain prefect state in the sense that the understanding of the less complex constructions are *independent* of that of any of the more complex ones. Such an independent and complete understanding, if possible, would be of great value in the use of the language such as type theory in applications. Technically, this amounts to a requirement of conservativity requirement over the structure of the conceptual universe of types saying that, considering a language as being built up hierarchically, the extension of a language by a new construction (say, adding a new data type, or a new universe into a type theory) is conservative over the original language. It seems that it is very difficult to meet this strong compositionality requirement for type theories. However, I certainly do not wish to say that this requirement is only wishful thinking and it seems that there is no reason why it should not be the case for artificial (mathematical and programming) languages.

9.3.5 Inductive families of types

In the above discussion, we have considered the conceptual universe of types as essentially consisting of individual types. The types in the conceptual universe, as we have conceived of it, may be related to each other, but such relationships are understood on the basis of understanding individual types involved. For example, the understanding of a Π-type $\Pi(A, B)$ is based on the (independent) understanding of the type A and the family of types B. And, so far, to understand a family of types is simply to understand *each* type in the family as an individual type. In other words, the types in a family are simply put together by means of parameterisation represented as a type-valued meta-level functional operation.

Analysed like this, one may say that the structure of the conceptual universe of types we have considered so far is relatively simple, although we have introduced rather powerful ideas in type construction such as the introduction of universes of (names of) types. It is not difficult to see that the relationships between types in a conceptual universe may be further enriched. For example, we can think that some types are very closely related and form a collection of types, the understanding of each of which requires the understanding of the whole collection of types and the relationships between them.

Inductive families of types are typical examples of such collections of types, which we have briefly discussed at the end of Section 9.2.3. For example, the inductive family of types $Listn_A$ defined there is a collection of types which one cannot claim to have understood because one has understood the individual types and type constructors involved. (Even one could say so, most of the people would argue that the understanding would be unnatural and an unnatural understanding is not a good one.) Instead, the inductive family of types $Listn_A$ may better be understood as a whole collection of types whose inductive structure is given by the introduction operators nil_A and $cons_A$ and the elimination and computation rules (expressed for the whole collection of types). From this point of view, it would be natural to introduce inductive families of types directly into the language of type theory to reflect such a richer structure of the conceptual universe of types. When inductive families of types are introduced, the conceptual universe of types in the type theory is still formally represented by the kind **Type** in the logical framework, but it is enriched in such a way that some types are introduced as a whole collection of types and they are supposed to be understood as a whole collection uniformly. For example, an inductive family of types indexed by natural numbers $Vec(A) : (N)\mathbf{Type}$ can be introduced for any type A by declaring the following new constants:

$$\begin{array}{rcl}
Vec(A) & : & (N)\mathbf{Type} \\
nil(A) & : & Vec(A)(0) \\
cons(A) & : & (n{:}N)(a{:}A)(l{:}Vec(A)(n))Vec(A)(succ(n)) \\
Rec_{Vec}(A) & : & (C{:}(n{:}N)(Vec(A)(n))\mathbf{Type}) \\
& & (C(0, nil(A))) \\
& & ((n{:}N)(x{:}A)(l{:}Vec(A)(n))(C(n,l))C(succ(n), cons(A)(x,l))) \\
& & (n{:}N)(l{:}Vec(A)(n))C(n,l),
\end{array}$$

and asserting the following computation rules:

$$Rec_{Vec}(A)(C, c, f, 0, nil(A)) \;=\; c \;:\; C(0, nil(A)),$$

$$Rec_{Vec}(A)(C, c, f, succ(n), cons(A)(n, a, l))$$
$$= f(n, a, l, Rec_{Vec}(A)(C, c, f, n, l)) \ : \ C(succ(n), cons(A)(n, a, l)).$$

It is not difficult to see that $Vec(A)$ is very similar to $Listn_A$ with the difference that $Vec(A)$ is directly introduced while $Listn$ is defined by means of the existing type constructors (using products to represent lists of a fixed length and universes to facilitate the transfinite induction in defining the inductive family).[58]

In general, we can extend the notion of inductive schemata to allow direct introduction of inductive families of types (cf. [CPM90, Dyb91]), so that the schemata do not just generate inductive types (of kind **Type**), but also directly generate inductive families of types $\mathcal{M}\{K\}[\bar{\Theta}] : K$ with K of the form $(z_1{:}P_1)...(z_n{:}P_n)\mathbf{Type}$, in such a way that the collection of types $\mathcal{M}\{K\}[\bar{\Theta}](p_1, ..., p_n)$ form an inductive family of types whose meanings are given by a uniform set of rules generated by the schemata, which also determine the relationships between the types in the family. The following is an informal but precise sketch of how the notion of inductive schemata should be extended for our type theory to introduce inductive families of types.

The extension is to allow the placeholder X in an inductive schema to stand for a family of types rather than just a type as before, and then to extend the other constructions of introducing inductive data types accordingly. More precisely, let

$$K \equiv (z_1{:}P_1)...(z_m{:}P_m)\mathbf{Type},$$

where $m \geq 0$. Then, for introducing inductive families of types of kind K, the strictly positive operators are of the form

$$(x_1{:}K_1)...(x_n{:}K_n) \ X(p_1, ..., p_m),$$

where $n \geq 0$, K_i's are small kinds such that $X \notin FV(K_i)$ and p_j is of kind $[p_1, ..., p_{j-1}/z_1, ..., z_{j-1}]P_j$; the inductive schemata are of the form

$$(x_1{:}M_1)...(x_n{:}M_n) \ X(p_1, ..., p_m),$$

where $n \geq 0$, p_i is of kind $[p_1, ..., p_{i-1}/z_1, ..., z_{i-1}]P_i$, and M_i is either a small kind such that $X \notin FV(M_i)$ or a strictly positive operator of the above form. With this extended notion of inductive schemata, the equality

58 Another difference is that $Listn_A$ can only be defined when A has a name in some universe, while there is no such a restriction for $Vec(A)$.

rule for constant expressions of the form $\kappa\{K\}[\bar{\Theta}]$ becomes, for sequences of inductive schemata of the above form $\bar{\Theta}$ and $\bar{\Theta}'$ of the same length n,

$$\frac{\begin{array}{c}\Gamma \vdash \kappa\{K\}[\bar{\Theta}] : K'' \quad \Gamma \vdash \kappa\{K'\}[\bar{\Theta}'] : K'' \\ \Gamma \vdash K = K' \quad \Gamma, X{:}K \vdash \Theta_i = \Theta_i' \quad (i = 1, ..., n)\end{array}}{\Gamma \vdash \kappa\{K\}[\bar{\Theta}] = \kappa\{K'\}[\bar{\Theta}'] : K''}$$

Then, any finite sequence of inductive schemata $\bar{\Theta} \equiv \langle \Theta_1, ..., \Theta_n \rangle$ of the above form generates an inductive family of types $\mathcal{M}\{K\}[\bar{\Theta}]$ of kind K, which is introduced by declaring the following constant expressions $\mathcal{M}\{K\}[\bar{\Theta}]$, $\iota_i\{K\}[\bar{\Theta}]$ and $\mathbf{E}\{K\}[\bar{\Theta}]$ which, for readability, are written below as $\mathcal{M}$, ι_i and $\mathbf{E}$, respectively:

$$\begin{array}{lcl}\mathcal{M} & : & (z_1{:}P_1)...(z_m{:}P_m)\mathbf{Type} \\ \iota_i & : & \Theta_i[\mathcal{M}] \quad (i = 1, ..., n) \\ \mathbf{E} & : & (C{:}(z_1{:}P_1)...(z_m{:}P_m)(\mathcal{M}(z_1, ..., z_m))\mathbf{Type}) \\ & & (f_1{:}\Theta_1^\circ[\mathcal{M}, C, \iota_1]) \ ... \ (f_n{:}\Theta_n^\circ[\mathcal{M}, C, \iota_n]) \\ & & (z_1{:}P_1)...(z_m{:}P_m)(z{:}\mathcal{M}(z_1, ..., z_n)) \ C(z_1, ..., z_m, z)\end{array}$$

and asserting the following n computation rules for $i = 1, ..., n$:

$$\begin{array}{cl} & \mathbf{E}(C, f_1, ..., f_n, z_1, ..., z_m, \iota_i(x_1, ..., x_{m_i})) \\ = & f_i(x_1, ..., x_{m_i}, \\ & \quad \Phi_{i_1}^\natural[\mathcal{M}, C, \mathbf{E}(C, f_1, ..., f_n), x_{i_1}], ..., \\ & \quad \Phi_{i_k}^\natural[\mathcal{M}, C, \mathbf{E}(C, f_1, ..., f_n), x_{i_k}]) \\ : & C(z_1, ..., z_m, \iota_i(x_1, ..., x_{m_i}))\end{array}$$

where it is assumed that Θ_i be of the form

$$(x_1{:}M_1)...(x_{m_i}{:}M_{m_i}) \ X(p_1, ..., p_m),$$

$\langle \Phi_{i_1}, ..., \Phi_{i_k} \rangle$ be the subsequence of $\langle M_1, ..., M_{m_i} \rangle$ that consists of the strictly positive operators, and the notational definitions of Θ_i° and $\Phi_{i_j}^\natural$ be accordingly extended so that

$$\begin{array}{lcl}\Theta_i^\circ[\mathcal{M}, C, \iota_i] & =_{\mathrm{df}} & (x_1{:}M_1[\mathcal{M}])...(x_{m_i}{:}M_{m_i}[\mathcal{M}]) \\ & & (\Phi_{i_1}^\circ[\mathcal{M}, C, x_{i_1}])...(\Phi_{i_k}^\circ[\mathcal{M}, C, x_{i_k}]) \\ & & C(p_1, ..., p_m, \iota_i(x_1, ..., x_{m_i})),\end{array}$$

and for $\Phi_{i_j} \equiv (y_1{:}N_1)...(y_l{:}N_l) \ X(q_1, ..., q_m)$,

$$\Phi_{i_j}^\natural[\mathcal{M}, C, \mathbf{E}(C, f_1, ..., f_n), x_{i_j}]$$

$$=_{\rm df} \quad [y_1{:}N_1]...[y_l{:}N_l]\mathbf{E}(C, f_1, ..., f_n, q_1, ..., q_m, x_{i_j}(y_1, ..., y_l)).$$

With the above extension, the above example $Vec(A)$ can be defined as

$$Vec =_{\rm df} [A{:}\mathbf{Type}]\mathcal{M}\{(N)\mathbf{Type}\}[X(0),\ (x{:}N)(A)(X(x))X(succ(x))].$$

The generated rules are exactly what we have given above.

When predicative universes are introduced, the names of the types in an inductive family are introduced into the appropriate universes in a similar way as before. In other words, if $K \equiv (z_1{:}P_1)...(z_m{:}P_m)\mathbf{Type}$ and for any $(\Gamma', A) \in \textsc{Types}_\Gamma(\bar{\Theta})$,[59] A has a name a in $Type_i$ in Γ', then

$$\begin{array}{l} \mu_i\{K\}[\bar{\Theta}] \ :\ (z_1{:}P_1)...(z_m{:}P_m)Type_i, \\ \mathbf{T}_i(\mu_i\{K\}[\bar{\Theta}](p_1,,,.p_m)) = \mathcal{M}\{K\}[\bar{\Theta}](p_1,,,.p_m) : \mathbf{Type}. \end{array}$$

9.3.6 Subtyping and other implementation issues

In UTT, every object has a unique type up to the computational equality. Universe inclusions in ECC are replaced by the explicit lifting operators $\mathbf{t}_i$. If one wants to introduce subtyping, the inductive schemata provide a general guideline to introducing subtyping relations between inductive types. For example, the subtyping relation between Π and Σ-types in ECC is a special case of a general notion of subtyping between inductive data types (see [Luo92]). However, we remark that subtyping is usually a rather subtle feature and sometimes may cause problems. For instance, if we introduced universe subtyping into UTT as suggested above, the property of subject reduction would fail to hold because of the stronger version of elimination rules, although it only fails for rather trivial cases. In general, subtyping is an interesting implementation issue and further study is needed to consider how it may be dealt with satisfactorily.

Defining UTT by means of a logical framework also raises an interesting issue in implementation of proof development systems like Lego. Although the notion of computational equality (between objects of types) is intensional, it is desirable to have a weakly extensional meta-level definitional mechanism in the sense that η-rule holds for the meta-level functional operations. This suggests that the meta-level definitional mechanism be incorporated into an implementation of the type theory. The implementation is *not* a direct implementation of the logical framework, but an implementation of the type theory together with an implemented meta-level definitional mechanism.

---

[59] $\textsc{Types}_\Gamma(\bar{\Theta})$ is defined as in Definition 9.7 except that the clauses $\Phi \equiv X$ and $\Theta \equiv X$ are replaced by $\Phi \equiv X(p_1, ..., p_m)$ and $\Theta \equiv X(p_1, ..., p_m)$, respectively.

9.4 Final remarks

We have considered type theory as a uniform language for programming, specification, and reasoning. The conceptual type structure of the type theory studied in this monograph reflects its intended use. In computer science, the study of type theory so far has only established a basis for its further and possibly large-scale applications, although it is a very promising starting point. There are a lot of topics and problems to be further studied before a type-theoretic language can become useful in real applications. For instance, as a programming language, the programs written in type theory are not as user-friendly as one would expect and the efficiency of computation is also an issue to be further studied. How such problems can be resolved and whether there are essential limitations in large-scale applications are yet to be seen.

Bibliography

[ACN90] L. Augustsson, Th. Coquand, and B. Nordström. A short description of another logical framework. In G. Huet and G. Plotkin, editors, *Preliminary Proc. of Logical Frameworks*, 1990.

[AGM92] S. Abramsky, D. Gabbay, and T. Maibaum. *Handbook of Logic in Computer Science*, volume 2. Clarendon Press, 1992.

[Bac88] R. Backhouse. On the meaning and construction of the rules in Martin-Löf's theory of types. In A. Avron *et al.*, editor, *Workshop on General Logic.* LFCS Report Series, ECS-LFCS-88-52, Dept. of Computer Science, University of Edinburgh, 1988.

[Bar92] H.P. Barendregt. Lambda calculi with types. In [AGM92], 1992.

[BB85] C. Böhm and A. Berarducci. Automatic synthesis of typed λ-programs on term algebras. *Theoretical Computer Science*, 39, 1985.

[BCM89] R. Backhouse, P. Chisholm, and G. Malcolm. Do-it-youself type theory. *Formal Aspects of Computing*, 1(1), 1989.

[Ber90] S. Berardi. *Type Dependence and Constructive Mathematics.* PhD thesis, Universita di Torino, Italy, 1990.

[BG80] R. Burstall and J. Goguen. The semantics of Clear, a specification language. *Lecture Notes in Computer Science*, 86, 1980.

[Bis67] E. Bishop. *Foundations of Constructive Analysis.* McGraw-Hill, 1967.

[BL84] R. Burstall and B. Lampson. Pebble, a kernel language for modules and abstract data types. *Lecture Notes in Computer Science*, 173, 1984.

[BM92] R. Burstall and J. McKinna. Deliverables: a categorical approach to program development in type theory. LFCS report ECS-LFCS-92-242, Dept of Computer Science, University of Edinburgh, 1992.

[C+86] R.L. Constable *et al.*. *Implementing Mathematics with the NuPRL Proof Development System.* Pretice-Hall, 1986.

[CF58] H.B. Curry and R. Feys. *Combinatory Logic*, volume 1. North Holland Publishing Company, 1958.

[CG90] Th. Coquand and J.H. Gallier. A proof of strong normalization for the theory of constructions using a Kripke-like interpretation. In *Preliminary Proc. of the Workshop on Logical Frameworks*, Antibes, 1990.

[CGW87] Th. Coquand, C. Gunter, and G. Winskel. Domain theoretic models of polymorphism. Tech. Report 116, Computer Laboratory, University of Cambridge, 1987.

[CH85] Th. Coquand and G. Huet. Constructions: a higher order proof system for mechanizing mathematics. *Lecture Notes in Computer Science*, 203, 1985.

[CH88] Th. Coquand and G. Huet. The calculus of constructions. *Information and Computation*, 76(2/3), 1988.

[Chu40] A. Church. A formulation of the simple theory of types. *J. Symbolic Logic*, 5(1), 1940.

[Coq85] Th. Coquand. *Une Theorie des Constructions.* PhD thesis, University of Paris VII, 1985.

[Coq86a] Th. Coquand. An analysis of Girard's paradox. In *Proc. 1st Ann. Symp. on Logic in Computer Science.* IEEE, 1986.

[Coq86b] Th. Coquand. A calculus of constructions. manuscript, 1986.

[Coq92] Th. Coquand. Pattern matching with dependent types. Talk given at the BRA workshop on Proofs and Types, Bastad, 1992.

[CPM90] Th. Coquand and Ch. Paulin-Mohring. Inductively defined types. *Lecture Notes in Computer Science*, 417, 1990.

[D+91] G. Dowek *et al.*. *The Coq Proof Assistent: User's Guide (version 5.6).* INRIA-Rocquencourt and CNRS-ENS Lyon, 1991.

[dB80] N.G. de Bruijn. A survey of the project AUTOMATH. In J. Hindley and J. Seldin, editors, *To H. B. Curry: Essays on Combinatory Logic, Lambda Calculus and Formalism.* Academic Press, 1980.

[Dev79] K. Devlin. *Fundamentals of Contemporary Set Theory.* Springer-Verlag, 1979.

[Dum75] M. Dummett. The philosophical basis of intuitionistic logic. In H. Rose and J. Shepherdson, editors, *Proc. of the Logic Colloquium, 1973*. North Holland, 1975. Reprinted in P. Benacerraf and H. Putnam (eds.), Philosophy of Mathematics: selected readings, Cambridge University Press.

[Dum91] M. Dummett. *The Logical Basis of Metaphysics*. Duckworth, 1991.

[Dyb91] P. Dybjer. Inductive sets and families in Martin-Löf's type theory and their set-theoretic semantics. In G. Huet and G. Plotkin, editors, *Logical Frameworks*. Cambridge University Press, 1991.

[EFH83] H. Ehrig, W. Fey, and H. Hansen. ACT ONE: an algebraic specification language with two levels of semantics. Technical Report 83-03, Technical University of Berlin, Fachbereich Informatik, 1983.

[Ehr88] T. Ehrhard. A categorical semantics of constructions. *Proc. 3rd Ann. Symp. on Logic in Computer Science, Edinburgh*. IEEE, 1988.

[EM85] H. Ehrig and B. Mahr. *Fundamentals of Algebraic Specification 1: Equations and Initial Semantics*. Springer, 1985.

[EM90] H. Ehrig and B. Mahr. *Fundamentals of Algebraic Specification 2: Module specifications and Constraints*. Springer, 1990.

[FGJM85] K. Futatsugi, J. Goguen, J.-P. Jouannaud, and J. Meseguer. Principles of OBJ2. *Proc. Principles of Programming Languages*. ACM, 1985.

[Gal90] J.H. Gallier. On Girard's 'Candidats de Reductibilité'. In P. Odifreddi, editor, *Logic and Computer Science*. Academic Press, 1990.

[Gen35] G. Gentzen. Untersuchungen über das logische schliessen. *Mathematische Zeitschrift*, 39, 1935.

[GHM76] J.V. Guttag, E. Horowitz, and D.R. Musser. Abstract data types and software validation. *Comm. ACM*, 21(12), 1976.

[Gir71] J.-Y. Girard. Une extension de l'interpretation fonctionelle de gödel à l'analyse et son application à l'élimination des coupures dans et la thèorie des types'. *Proc. 2nd Scandinavian Logic Symposium*. North-Holland, 1971.

[Gir72] J.-Y. Girard. *Interprétation fonctionelle et élimination des coupures de l'arithmétique d'ordre supérieur.* PhD thesis, Université Paris VII, 1972.

[Gir73] J.-Y. Girard. Quelques résultats sur les interprétations fonctionells. *Lecture Notes in Mathematics 337.* Springer, 1973.

[Gir86] J.-Y. Girard. The system F of variable types, fifteen years later. *Theoretical Computer Science*, 45, 1986.

[GL93] H. Goguen and Z. Luo. Inductive data types: Well-ordering types revisited. In G. Huet and G. Plotkin, editors, *Logical Environmentss.*Cambridge University Press, 1993. Also as LFCS Report Series ECS-LFCS-92-209, Dept of Computer Science, University of Edinburgh.

[GLT90] J.-Y. Girard, Y. Lafont, and P. Taylor. *Proofs and Types.* Cambridge University Press, 1990.

[GTW78] J.A. Goguen, J.W. Thatcher, and E.G. Wagner. Abstract data types as initial algebras and the correctness of data representation. In R. Yeh, editor, *Current Trends in Programming Methodology, Vol. 4.* Prentice Hall, 1978.

[Hay91] S. Hayashi. Singleton, union and intersection types in program extraction. *Lecture Notes in Computer Science*, 526, 1991. Revised version to appear in Information and Computation.

[Hey71] A. Heyting. *Intuitionism: An Introduction.* North-Holland, 1971.

[HH86] J. Hook and D. Howe. Impredicative strong existential equivalent to Type:Type. Technical Report TR86-760, Cornell University, 1986.

[HHP87] R. Harper, F. Honsell, and G. Plotkin. A framework for defining logics. *Proc. 2nd Ann. Symp. on Logic in Computer Science.* IEEE,1987.

[Hoa72] C.A.R. Hoare. Proofs of correctness of data representation. *Acta Informatica*, 1(1), 1972.

[How80] W. A. Howard. The formulae-as-types notion of construction. In J. Hindley and J. Seldin, editors, *To H. B. Curry: Essays on Combinatory Logic.* Academic Press, 1980.

[HP91] R. Harper and R. Pollack. Type checking, universe polymorphism, and typical ambiguity in the calculus of constructions. *Theoretical Computer Science*, 89(1), 1991.

[HS87] J.R. Hindley and J.P. Seldin. *Introduction to Combinators and λ-calculus.* Cambridge University Press, 1987.

[Hue87] G. Huet. A calculus with type:type. unpublished manuscript, 1987.

[Hyl82] M. Hyland. The effective topos. In A.S. Troelstra and van Dalen, editors, *The Brouwer Symposium.* North-Holland, 1982.

[Hyl88] M. Hyland. A small complete category. *Annals of Pure and Applied Logic*, 40, 1988.

[Jon86] C.B. Jones. *Systematic Software Development using VDM.* Prentice-Hall, 1986.

[Klo80] J. W. Klop. Combinatory reduction systems. *Mathematical Center Tracts 127*, 1980.

[Kol32] A.N. Kolmogorov. Zur deutung der intuitionistischen logik. *Math. Z.*, 35, 1932.

[Kre68] G. Kreisel. Functions, ordinals, species. In B. van Rootselaar and J. Staal, editors, *Logic, Methodology and Philosophy of Science III.* North-Holland, 1968.

[LB92] Z. Luo and R. Burstall. A set-theoretic setting for structuring theories in proof development. LFCS Report Series ECS-LFCS-92-206, Department of Computer Science, University of Edinburgh, 1992.

[Lev79] A. Levy. *Basic Set Theory.* Springer-Verlag, 1979.

[LM88a] G. Longo and E. Moggi. Constructive natural deduction and its 'modest' interpretation. Technical Report CMU-CS-88-131, Computer Science Dept., Carnegie Mellon Univ., 1988.

[LM88b] G. Longo and E. Moggi. Constructive natural deduction and its 'modest' interpretation. Report CMU-CS-88-131, Computer Science Dept., Carnegie Mellon Univ., 1988.

[LP92] Z. Luo and R. Pollack. LEGO Proof Development System: User's Manual. LFCS Report ECS-LFCS-92-211, Department of Computer Science, University of Edinburgh, 1992.

[LPT89] Z. Luo, R. Pollack, and P. Taylor. *How to Use LEGO: a preliminary user's manual.* LFCS Technical Notes LFCS-TN-27, Dept. of Computer Science, Edinburgh University, 1989.

[Luo88a] Z. Luo. $CC^{\infty}_{\subset}$ and its meta theory. LFCS report ECS-LFCS-88-58, Dept. of Computer Science, Edinburgh University, 1988.

[Luo88b] Z. Luo. A higher-order calculus and theory abstraction. LFCS Report ECS-LFCS-88-57, Dept. of Computer Science, Edinburgh University, 1988.

[Luo89] Z. Luo. **ECC**, an Extended Calculus of Constructions. In *Proc. of the Fourth Ann. Symp. on Logic in Computer Science*, Asilomar, California, U.S.A. IEEE, 1989.

[Luo90a] Z. Luo. *An Extended Calculus of Constructions.* PhD thesis, University of Edinburgh, 1990. Also as Report CST-65-90/ECS-LFCS-90-118, Department of Computer Science, University of Edinburgh.

[Luo90b] Z. Luo. A problem of adequacy: conservativity of calculus of constructions over higher-order logic. Technical report, LFCS report series ECS-LFCS-90-121, Department of Computer Science, University of Edinburgh, 1990.

[Luo91a] Z. Luo. A higher-order calculus and theory abstraction. *Information and Computation*, 90(1):107–137, 1991.

[Luo91b] Z. Luo. Program specification and data refinement in type theory. *Proc. of the Fourth Inter. Joint Conf. on the Theory and Practice of Software Development (TAPSOFT), LNCS 493*, 1991. Also as LFCS report ECS-LFCS-91-131, Dept. of Computer Science, Edinburgh University.

[Luo92] Z. Luo. A unifying theory of dependent types: the schematic approach. *Proc. of Symp. on Logical Foundations of Computer Science (Logic at Tver'92), LNCS 620*, 1992. Also as LFCS Report ECS-LFCS-92-202, Dept. of Computer Science, University of Edinburgh.

[Luo93] Z. Luo. Program specification and data refinement in type theory. *Mathematical Structures in Computer Science*, 3, 1993. An earlier version appears as [Luo91b].

[LZ75] B. Liskov and S. Zilles. Specification techniques for data abstraction. *IEEE Trans. on Software Engineering*, SE-1(1), 1975.

[Mac81] D.D. MacQueen. Structures and parameterization in a typed functional language. *Proc. Symp. on Functional Programming and Computer Architecture*, 1981.

[Mac86] D. MacQueen. Using dependent types to express modular structure. *Proc. 13th Principles of Programming Languages.* IEEE, 1986.

[McK92] J. McKinna. *Deliverables: a categorical approach to program development in type theory.* PhD thesis, Department of Computer Science, University of Edinburgh, 1992.

[Mes88] J. Meseguer. Relating models of polymorphism. Technical Report SRI-CSL-88-13, Computer Science Lab, SRI International, 1988.

[Mit86] J.C. Mitchell. A type inference approach to reduction properties and semantics of polymorphic expressions. *Proc. 1986 ACM Symp. on Lisp and Functional Programming*, 1986.

[ML71] P. Martin-Löf. An intuitionistic theory of types. manuscript, 1971.

[ML72] P. Martin-Löf. An intuitionistic theory of types. manuscript, 1972.

[ML75] P. Martin-Löf. An intuitionistic theory of types: predicative part. In H.Rose and J.C.Shepherdson, editors, *Logic Colloquium'73.* North-Holland, 1975.

[ML82] P. Martin-Löf. Constructive mathematics and computer programming. In L.J. Cohen *et al.*, editor, *Logic, Methodology and Philosophy of Science VI.* North-Holland, 1982.

[ML84] P. Martin-Löf. *Intuitionistic Type Theory.* Bibliopolis, 1984.

[ML85] P. Martin-Löf. Truth of a proposition, evidence of a judgement, validity of a proof. Talk given at Workshop of Theories of Meaning, Florence, June 1985.

[Mog85] E. Moggi. The PER-model as internal category with all small products. manuscript, 1985.

[MP85] J. Mitchell and G. Plotkin. Abstract types have existential type. *Proc. 12th Principles of Programming Languages.* ACM, 1985.

[MTH90] R. Milner, M. Tofte, and R. Harper. *The Definition of Standard ML.* MIT, 1990.

[NPS90] B. Nordström, K. Petersson, and J. Smith. *Programming in Martin-Löf's Type Theory: An Introduction.* Oxford University Press, 1990.

[Ore92] C.-E. Ore. The Extended Calculus of Constructions (**ECC**) with inductive types. *Information and Computation*, 99(2):231–264, 1992.

[Pau87] L. Paulson. *Logic and Computation: Interactive Proof with Cambridge LCF.* Cambridge University Press, 1987.

[Pit87] A. Pitts. Polymorphism is set theoretic, constructively. *Proc. of the Summer Conf. on Category Theory and Computer Science, Edinburgh.* 1987.

[PM89] Ch. Paulin-Mohring. Extracting F^{ω} programs from proofs in the calculus of constructions. *Proc. Principles of Programming Languages.* ACM, 1989.

[Pol89] R. Pollack. The theory of LEGO. manuscript, 1989.

[Pol90a] R. Pollack. Implicit syntax. In the preliminary Proceedings of the 1st Workshop on Logical Frameworks, 1990.

[Pol90b] R. Pollack. The Tarski fixpoint theorem. communication on TYPES e-mail network, 1990.

[Pot87] G. Pottinger. Strong normalization for terms of the theory of constructions. Technical Report TR 11-7, Odyssey Research Associates, 1987.

[Pra65] D. Prawitz. *Natural Deduction, a Proof-Theoretic Study.* Lmqvist and Wiksell, 1965.

[Pra73] D. Prawitz. Towards a foundation of a general proof theory. In P. Suppes *et al.*, editor, *Logic, Methodology, and Phylosophy of Science IV.* North-Holland, 1973.

[Pra74] D. Prawitz. On the idea of a general proof theory. *Synthese*, 27, 1974.

[Qui62] W.V. Quine. Carnap and logical truth. In B. Kazemier and D. Vuysje, editors, *Logic and Language: Studies Dedicated to Professor Rudolf Carnap on the Occasion of His Seventieth Birthday.* Dordrecht: Reidel, 1962.

[Qui86] W.V. Quine. *Philosophy of Logic.* Harvard University Press, second edition, 1986.

[Ram25] F.P. Ramsey. The foundations of mathematics. *Proceedings of the London Mathematical Society*, 25:338–384, 1925.

[Rey74] J.C. Reynolds. Towards a theory of type structure. *Lecture Notes in Computer Science*, 19, 1974.

[Rey84] J. C. Reynolds. Polymorphism is not set-theoretic. *Lecture Notes in Computer Science*, 173, 1984.

[RP88] J. C. Reynolds and G. D. Plotkin. On functors expressible in the polymorphic typed lambda calculus. LFCS report ECS-LFCS-88-53, Dept. of Computer Science, Univ. of Edinburgh, 1988.

[RS93] B. Reus and Th. Streicher. Verifying properties of module construction in type theory. *Proc. of Mathematical Foundations in Computer Science, LNCS* 711, 1993.

[Rus03] B.A.W. Russell. *The Principles of Mathematics.* Routledge, 1903. Paperback edition, 1992.

[SB83] D. Sannella and R. Burstall. Structured theories in LCF. *Proc. of the 8th Colloquium on Trees in Algebra and Programming*, 1983.

[See86] R.A.G. Seely. Categorical semantics for higher-order polymorphic lambda calculus. *J. of Symbolic Logic*, 52(4), 1986.

[SST92] D. Sannella, S. Sokolowski, and A. Tarlecki. Toward formal development of programs from algebraic specifications: Parameterization revisited. LFCS Report Series ECS-LFCS-92-222, Dept. of Computer Science, University of Edinburgh, 1992.

[ST87] D. Sannella and A. Tarlecki. Extended ML: an institution-independent framework for formal program development. *Proc. Workshop on Category Theory and Computer Programming, LNCS 240*, pages 364–389. Springer, 1987.

[ST88a] D. Sannella and A. Tarlecki. Specifications in arbitrary institutions. *Information and Computation*, 76, 1988.

[ST88b] D. Sannella and A. Tarlecki. Toward formal development of programs from algebraic specifications: implementation revisited. *Acta Informatica*, 25, 1988.

[Str88] T. Streicher. *Correctness and Completeness of a Categorical Semantics of the Calculus of Constructions.* PhD thesis, Passau, 1988.

[Str93] T. Streicher. Investigations into intensional type theory. Hablitation Thesis, Ludwig Maximilian Universität, 1993.

[SW83] D.T. Sannella and M. Wirsing. A kernal language for algebraic specification and implementation. Technical Report CSR-155-83, Dept of Computer Science, University of Edinburgh, 1983.

[Tai67] W.W. Tait. Intensional interpretation of functionals of finite type i. *J. of Symbolic Logic*, 32, 1967.

[Tai75] W. W. Tait. A realizability interpretation of the theory of species. In R. Parikh, editor, *Logic Colloquium, Lecture Notes in Mathematics,* 453, 1975.

[Tho91] S. Thompson. *Type Theory and Functional Programming.* Addison-Wesley, 1991.

[Tro73] A. S. Troelstra. Notes on intuitionistic second-order arithmetic. *Lecture Notes in Mathematics,* 337, 1973.

[vD80] D. T. van Daalen. *The Language Theory of Automath.* PhD thesis, Technological University, Eindhoven, 1980.

[Wan92] P. Wand. Functional programming and verification with Lego. Master's thesis, Department of Computer Science, University of Edinburgh, 1992.

[WB89] M. Wirsing and M. Broy. A modular framework for specification and implementation. *TAPSOFT'89, LNCS*, 351, 1989.

[Wir86] M. Wirsing. Structured algebraic specifications: a kernel language. *Theoretical Computer Science*, 42:123–249, 1986.

[WL93] D. Wang and J. R. Lee. Pictorial concepts and a concept supporting system. *Journal of Visual Languages and Computing,* 4:177–199, 1993.

[WR25] A.N. White and B.A.W. Russell. *Principia Mathematica.* Cambridge University Press, 2nd edition, 1925.

[Zuc75] J. Zucker. Formalization of classical mathematics in AUTOMATH. *Colloque Internationaux du CNRS,* 249, 1975.

Notation and symbols

Terms and judgements

Symbol	Meaning	Pages
$Prop$	impredicative universe of propositions	21, 175
$Type_i$	predicative universes	21, 182
$\Pi x{:}A.B$, $\Pi(A,B)$	dependent product type	22, 180
$A \rightarrow B$	function space	22, 180
$\Sigma x{:}A.B$, $\Sigma(A,B)$	dependent strong sum type	22, 180
$A \times B$	product type	22, 180
$\lambda x{:}A.b$, $\lambda(A,B,f)$	Lambda abstraction	22, 181
MN, $\mathbf{app}(A,B,F,a)$	functional application	22, 181
$\langle a,b\rangle_A$, $\mathbf{pair}(A,B,a,b)$	pair	22, 181
$\pi_i(c)$, $\pi_i(A,B,c)$	projections of a pair	22, 181
$\sum[x_1{:}A_1,\ ...,\ x_n{:}A_n]$	special notation for Σ-type	133
$\langle a_1,...,a_n\rangle$	tuple notation	134
$x_i[a]$	projection notation	134
$\exists_U(A,B)$	existential type	43
$T_\Gamma(M)$, $T_\mathcal{E}(M)$	the principal type of M	63, 70
$[a/x]b$, $b[a]$	substitution of a (for x) in b	22
$[a_1,...,a_m/x_1,...,x_m]b$	simultaneous substitution	90
$\mathrm{red}_\mathbf{k}(M)$	the key-reduct of M	71
$\langle\rangle$	empty context	24
$\mathbf{Type}$	kind of types	166, 169
$El(A)$	kind of objects of type A	166, 169
$(x{:}K)K'$, $(K)K'$	dependent product kind	166, 168
$[x{:}K]k'$	functional operation	166, 168
$f(k)$	application of functional operation	166, 168
$\mathcal{M}[\bar{\Theta}]$	inductive data type	178
$\iota_i[\bar{\Theta}]$	introduction operator for $\mathcal{M}[\bar{\Theta}]$	178
$\mathbf{E}[\bar{\Theta}]$	elimination operator for $\mathcal{M}[\bar{\Theta}]$	178
$\Gamma \vdash a : A$	judgement form in ECC	24
$\mathcal{E} \vdash a : A$	'judgement form' in environment	70
Γ **valid**	judgement in LF	166
$\Gamma \vdash K$ **kind**	judgement in LF	166
$\Gamma \vdash k : K$	judgement in LF	166
$\Gamma \vdash k = k' : K$	judgement in LF	166
$\Gamma \vdash K = K'$	judgement in LF	166

Internal logic

true, false	propositions true/false	35, 104, 176
$\supset$, &, $\vee$, $\neg$	implication, conjunction, disjunction, negation	35, 104, 176
$\forall$	universal quantification	35, 104, 175
$\exists$	existential quantification	35, 104, 176
$a =_A b$	the Leibniz equality over type A	35, 109, 182
$\mathbf{Prf}(P)$	proof type of proposition P	5, 175
$\Lambda(A, P, f)$	canonical proof	175
$\mathbf{E}_\forall$	elimination operator for proof type	175

Sets

ω	set of natural numbers	21
$\mathcal{U}$	set of universes	112
$\mathcal{T}$	set of terms	22
$FV(\_)$	set of free variables in _	22, 24
V_α	cumulative hierarchy of sets	122
$CR(A)$	set of A-candidates of reducibility	73
$Sat(A)$	set of A-saturated sets	72
$SN(A)$	set of strongly normalisable terms of type A	72
$V(M)$	set of possible denotations of M	89
$\|A\|$	carrier set of ω-set A	118
$\mathsf{Obj}(\_)$	object set of category _	123
$\text{TYPES}_\Gamma(\bar{\Theta})$	set of types occurring in schemata $\bar{\Theta}$	183

Relations

$\equiv$	syntactical identity	22
$=_{\text{df}}$	notational definition	30
$\triangleright$	reduction (computation) in ECC	22
$\triangleright_1$	one-step reduction in ECC	22
$\simeq$	conversion (computational equality) in ECC	22
$\leadsto_\beta$	β-contraction	22
$\leadsto_\eta$	η-contraction	50
$\leadsto_\sigma$	σ-contraction	22
$\leadsto_\pi$	contraction of surjective pairing	50
$\preceq$	the cumulativity relation	23
$\prec$	the strict cumulativity relation	23
$\preceq_i$	the 'level-i' cumulativity relation	51
$\prec_i$	the strict 'level-i' cumulativity relation	51
$\approx$	cumulativity equivalence	51
$\Vdash_A$	the realisability relation of ω-set A	118

Environment and measures

$\mathcal{E}$	environment	70
$\mathcal{E}^i$	the first i components of environment $\mathcal{E}$	70
$\mathcal{E}_i$	the ith component of environment $\mathcal{E}$	70
e_i	the ith variable of environment $\mathcal{E}$	70
$\mathcal{L}(\_)$	level of type _	74, 75
$\mathcal{D}_j(\_)$	j-degree of type _	77, 79, 83
$\beta(\_)$	complexity measure of type _	79
$\delta_{\mathbf{j}} R$, $\gamma_{\mathbf{j}} M$	complexity measures	84

Categories and functors

ω-**Set**	category of ω-sets	118
ω-**Set**(j)	category of ω-sets within V_{κ_j}	122
M	category of modest sets	118
PROP	category of 'propositions'	123
Set	category of sets	123
back	category equivalence from **M** to **PROP**	124
inc	inclusion functor from **PROP** to **M**	124
Δ	embedding functor from **Set** to ω-**Set**	123

Specification and data refinement

SPEC, **Spec**(S)	type of specifications	142
Str$[SP]$	structure type of specification SP	142
Ax$[SP]$	axiomatic requirement of specification SP	142
$\Longrightarrow_\rho$	refinement relation	146, 160
Sat(ρ)	satisfaction condition	146
$\otimes$, $\sum$	specification operations	150, 151
Extend, **Join**$_S$	specification operations	153
Con$_\rho$, **Sel**$_\rho$	specification operations	154

Miscellaneous

κ_j	the jth inaccessible cardinal	122
$dom(f)$	domain of function f	89
$A \rightarrow_{FPP} B$	FPP-morphisms from A to B	120
$Eval_\rho$	the evaluation function	92
v_M	the canonical denotation of M	90
$\mathcal{C}(\_;\ \_)$	the algorithm of type inference	112
σ, σ_Γ, π_Γ	ω-set constructors	120, 121
$[\![\_]\!]$	the interpretation of judgement _	120

Index

α-convertible, 22
η-equality, 170, 198
λ-cube, 11
ω-set, 118
  carrier set of an _, 118
  category of _s, 118
  realisability relation of an _, 118

abstract axiom, 135
abstract data type, 144
abstract implementation, 146
abstract proof, 135
abstract reasoning, 133, 136
abstract theorem, 135
abstract theory, 133, 134
adequacy of specification, 143
admissible rule, 54
ALF, 47
algebraic specification, 162
array, 148
asserting computation rule, 171
assignment, 90
  $\mathcal{E}$-_, 91
Automath, 47
axiom of choice, 10

base term, 71

calculus of constructions, 11
candidate of reducibility, 66, 73
canonical object, 4
canonical proof, 6
Church-Rosser property, 27
Church-Rosser theorem, 49
Church-style representation of data types, 12
complexity measure, 67, 79
  _ of types, 79
compositional understanding, 204
computation, 4, 26
computation rule, 7, 27, 129, 170
computational equality, 4, 27, 173
computational theory, 127
conceptual universe, 4
  _ of objects, 4
  _ of types, 4, 8, 15
concrete data type, 143
concrete implementation, 143
congruence relation, 144
consistency theorem, 105
constant, 21, 170
  _ declaration, 170
constant expression, 174
  declaring _, 175
constant letter, 174
construction, 3
constructive mathematics, 10
constructor (spec operation), 153
constructor implementation, 156
context, 24
  consistent _, 105
  empty _, 24
  valid _, 26, 28, 166
context replacement, 55
contraction, 22,
  β-_, 22
  σ-_, 22
  η-_, 50

_ of surjective pairing, 50
contractum, 22
conversion, 22
Coq, 47
cumulativity relation, 23
inductive definition of _, 51
cumulativity rule, 25, 36
cut, 56

data refinement, 141, 146
data types vs. logical propositions, 12
decidability, 46, 112
_ of conversion and cumulativity, 112
_ of type checking, 114
_ of type inference, 112
definitional equality, 169
degree of types, 76, 77, 83
deliverable, 140
denotation, 88
set of possible _s, 89
dependent product kind, 168
dependent product type, 9, 30, 180
derivation, 24
direct proof, 6
divide and conquer, 150

ECC, 16, 21
elimination operator, 179
elimination rule, 7
environment, 69
equality reflection theorem, 110
evaluation, 92
excluded middle, 203
existential type, 41
Extended Calculus of Constructions, 16, 21
extensionality, 43
_ of type equality, 45, 64

family of inductive data types, 181
filling-up rule, 201
formula, 103
provable _, 103
FPP-morphism, 120
functional operation, 168

Heyting/Kolmogorov's interpretation, 5
hierarchical understanding, 202
horizontal composition, 161

identification of propositions and types, 9
implementation of parameterised specifications, 159
implementation relation, 146
impredicative type theory, 11
impredicativity, 9
inaccessible cardinal, 122
indirect proof, 6
inductive data type, 128, 177
inductive family of types, 184, 204
inductive schema, 173
inference rule, 24
inhabited term, 26
insert sorting, 132
intensionality, 43
_ of the Leibniz equality, 111
internal logic, 6, 34, 103, 175
interpretation (or evaluation), 92
introduction operator, 179
introduction rule, 7

judgement, 4, 24, 28, 166, 172
derivable _, 24, 172
hypothetical _, 24
non-hypothetical _, 24

key redex, 71
key variable of base term, 71
kind, 166
small _, 169

large Σ-type, 14, 15
large impredicative Σ-type, 14, 41

Lego, 47
Leibniz equality, 35, 109, 182
Leibniz principle, 35
level of types, 74
LF, 166
    _ as meta-language, 172
LF_θ, 174
logical η-rule, 199, 201
logical framework (see also LF), 47, 166
    _ with inductive schemata, 174
    Edinburgh _, 166
    Martin-Löf's _, 166
logical operator, 35, 104, 176
logical theory, 127

major term, 22
Martin-Löf's type theory, 10
meaning, 6, 28, 29,
minimum type, 62
modest set, 118
    category of _s, 118
monotonicity of specification operations, 150

non-propositional type, 26, 29, 70, 176
normal form, 23
    uniqueness of _, 50
NuPRL, 47

object, 3, 26, 169
    Γ-_, 26
    $\mathcal{E}$-_, 70
    canonical _, 4, 179
    quasi-normal _, 76, 82
openness, 8
operational meaning theory, 6
operational semantics, 2, 5
operational understanding, 202

paradox, 9
    Girard's _, 9

parameterised specification, 156
partial equivalence relation, 123
    category of _s, 119
partial order w.r.t. conversion, 23
Peano's axioms, 128
polymorphic type, 11
predicate, 35
    Γ-_, 104
    internal _, 35, 104, 182
    meta-level _, 176
predicativity, 66
principal type, 61, 63, 70
program development, 139
program specification, 139, 142
projection operator, 181
proof, 26, 103, 176
    Γ-_, 26
    $\mathcal{E}$-_, 70
proof inheritance, 136
proposition, 5, 26, 34, 176
    Γ-_, 26
    $\mathcal{E}$-_, 70
    provable _, 34, 103, 176
propositional type, 176
propositions-as-types, 5
pure logical truth, 13, 187

quasi-normal form, 76
quasi-normalisation, 65, 74
quasi-normalisation theorem, 77

realisation (of specification), 143
redex
    β-_, 22
    σ-_, 22
    key _, 71
reducibility method, 66
reduction, 22
    one-step _, 22
refinement map, 146, 160
reflection principle, 32
relation, 35
    internal _, 35, 104, 182

satisfaction condition, 146, 160
saturated set, 66, 72
second-order logic, 176
selector (spec operation), 153
selector implementation, 156
set universe, 122
setoid, 145
simple type theory, 9
simultaneous substitution, 90
small Σ-type, 15, 42
SOL, 175
soundness theorem, 98
specification, 142
    realisable _, 143
stack, 145
strengthening, 60
strictly positive operator, 173
strong equality type, 10
strong normalisation, 27, 65, 88
strong normalisation theorem, 100
strong sum type, 14, 15, 26, 31, 180
strongly normalisable, 23
structure, 142
structure sharing, 150
structure type, 142
subject reduction, 27
subject reduction theorem, 58
substitution, 22
substitution property, 96
subtyping, 208
syntactical identity, 22

T-context, 172
term, 21
theory morphism, 136, 137
truth schema, 187
type, 4, 26, 29, 169
    Γ-_, 26
    $\mathcal{E}$-_, 70
    Π-_, 15, 30, 180
    Σ-_, 14, 15, 31, 180
type cumulativity, 36
type equality, 36
type inference, 112
    algorithm of _, 112
    correctness of _, 114
type of all types, 9
type of natural numbers, 128, 171
type of proofs, 5, 175
type reflection, 57

unifying theory of dependent types, 15, 165
universe, 21
    impredicative _, 34, 175
    predicative _, 32, 182
    type _, 8
universe polymorphism, 48
use, 6, 201
UTT, 175, 185

value, 4, 27
valuation, 90
    $\mathcal{E}$-_, 91
verification, 6
verificationistic meaning theory, 5
vertical composition, 147, 160

weak equality type, 10
weakening, 55
weakly extensional, 182
well-foundedness of cumulativity relation, 53
well-typed term, 26

The manufacturer's authorised representative in the EU for product safety is Oxford University Press España S.A. of el Parque Empresarial San Fernando de Henares, Avenida de Castilla, 2 – 28830 Madrid (www.oup.es/en or product.safety@oup.com). OUP España S.A. also acts as importer into Spain of products made by the manufacturer.

www.ingramcontent.com/pod-product-compliance
Ingram Content Group UK Ltd.
Pitfield, Milton Keynes, MK11 3LW, UK
UKHW021533300726
14060UKWH00011B/388
9780198538356